Trade Secrets

Trade
Secrets:

Intellectual Piracy

and the Origins of

American Industrial Power

Doron S. Ben-Atar

Yale University Press   *New Haven & London*

Published with assistance from
the Annie Burr Lewis Fund.

Set in Minion types by Keystone Typesetting, Inc.
Printed in the United States of America.

Library of Congress Cataloging-in-Publication Data

Ben-Atar, Doron S.
Trade secrets : intellectual piracy and the origins of American industrial power /
Doron S. Ben-Atar.
p. cm.
Includes bibliographical references and index.
ISBN 0-300-10006-x (alk. paper)

1. Business intelligence—United States—History. 2. Trade secrets—United States—
History. 3. Technological innovations—United States—History. 4. Piracy (Copyright)—
United States—History. 5. Industrial property—United States—History. I. Title.
HD38.7.B455 2004
338.0973–dc22   2003062506

A catalogue record for this book is available from the British Library.

10   9   8   7   6   5   4   3   2   1

TO THE MEMORY OF

Aryeh Yehuda Ben-Atar

Istanbul 1919–Kfar Shmaryahu 1998

Contents

Acknowledgments

Milan Kundera wrote that modern times make it easy "to betray friends in the name of what are called convictions. And to do so with moral righteousness. . . . Unlike pretentious fidelity to convictions, fidelity to a friend is a virtue, perhaps the only virtue, perhaps the only one left." I have, in the process of writing this book, relied on others to point me in the right direction, correct my errors, and give me personal and professional support. I take great pleasure not only in acknowledging their help on this particular project, but in thanking them for the loyalty and friendship that made the completion of this project possible. I have been fortunate to know many virtuous people.

Peter Gay is a wonderfully loyal friend who has been a phenomenal intellectual model and mentor for over a decade. He went over the manuscript and asked questions that made me reconsider and rewrite. John Demos was the first professor I met when I came to do my undergraduate studies at Brandeis in 1979. Over the years he tolerated my professional wanderings and did not lose faith in my abilities. John was there for me during the lowest points of this project, when I wanted to drop it altogether and quit the profession. John's personal encouragement and commitment to finding the human story pushed me to incorporate human narratives in this study. David Bell, who has been the most dependable friend and confidant for the past twelve years, has helped me sort out some of the theoretical issues and gave wonderful advice on things big and small. Connie Gersick took time off from working on her own manuscript and gave this book a critical read from the perspective of economics and organizational behavior. Finally, Barbara Oberg, who migrated from the Franklin to the Jefferson papers midway through this project, has generously given of her scholarly knowledge and has been a co-author and a reliable friend.

I am not a technology buff. In fact, my eyes glaze over when I read the simplest instruction booklet. I therefore had to learn a great deal to be able to do this work. David Jeremy, whose work I admire, was instrumental in helping me get my feet wet, providing insight and direction when he was the outside reader for my first foray into the history of technology—an essay I published in the *William and Mary Quarterly* in 1995. Darwin Stapleton, who left academia to run the Rockefeller archives, gave me wonderful advice when this project was just in its infancy. And most importantly, this work could not have been written without the help, kindness, and hard work of Carolyn Cooper. Carolyn has been my tech mentor from the outset. While I am a notorious klutz, Caroline is a whiz at the inner workings of eighteenth-century technology. She patiently explained to me, sometime drawing on a napkin at lunch, the way these machines really worked. She diligently went over the manuscript, helping me sort out the various stages of innovation and patenting.

Because intellectual property is a legal concept, I had to master important and subtle legal issues. Bruce Mann introduced me to legal history in 1989 and has been a friend and supporter since. Anne Dailey invited me to present a portion of this work at the University of Connecticut School of Law faculty seminar where I received many helpful suggestions. John Witt, a former student turned scholar, invited me to present another chapter at the Yale Law School history seminar where I learned a great deal. I have never met Edward Walterscheid, but over the last few years we have engaged in a series of academic exchanges that taught me a great deal about the history and mechanics of the American patent law.

I am grateful to Yale and Fordham for providing me financial support in the form of academic leaves and research grants so that I could complete the project. This book was much improved from discussions I had when I presented portions of the work at the McNeil Center for Early American Studies, the Library Company of Philadelphia's inaugural conference on early American economic history, and faculty seminars at Tel Aviv University and the Hebrew University. Special thanks to Roy Goodman of the American Philosophical Society; Ene Sirvet of the Jay Papers; Ellen Cohen, Kate Ono, and Jonathan Dull of the Franklin Papers; the late Eugene Sheridan of the Jefferson Papers; David Mattern of the Madison Papers; Ryan Shepard of the Historical Society of Washington, D.C.; Charlene Peacock of the Library Company of Philadelphia; Kristen Froehlich of the Historical Society of Pennsylvania Collection Atwater Kent Museum; and Susan Newton of the Winterthur Museum. The following scholars have made invaluable suggestions when commenting on various portions of the book: James M. Banner, Jacob Cooke, Elaine Crane, J. Robert Glen, Arnon Gutfeld, Michael McGiffert, Peter Onuf, Eric Papenfuse, and Herb Sloan. I also wish to acknowledge the help of Yehoshua Arieli, Greg Flynn, Tim Gilfoyle, Glenda Gilmore and Rebecca Keith.

The staff of Yale University Press, particularly Keith Condon, helped me sort out all the details involved in turning the manuscript into a book. Gavin Lewis's careful copyediting corrected many errors, large and small. Most of all, I am very fortunate to have worked with my editor, Lara Heimert. Lara was in my corner from the outset and supported the project with the board of the press. She went over the manuscript with great care and made insightful suggestions. She brought news of the changes she desired with great tact and care, sometimes over lunch, and did not complain when we had to skip dessert. She was a responsive sounding board, promptly answering my e-mails at various hours of the day and from various locations on the earth.

Pinchus Cohen, Yaacov Kazes, Leon Segal, and Ron Zuckerman have been my closest friends since I was four. They have been at my side to celebrate victories and to nurse me through defeats. Our occasional retreats in Israel, Egypt, Italy, and Turkey provided a much-needed break from the ordinary grind. As witnesses of my past and present they have been both my mirror and my memory.

I owe a great deal to my family. My children, Assaf, Heddy, and Daniel, could not care less about technology piracy and intellectual property in the early republic. For them, this book symbolizes my wasted earning potential. Jo has been a wonderful and supportive companion who has thus far tolerated academia quite well. One day she may indeed feel at home at dinner parties where the punch line to a joke is in German. I am also fortunate to have had the love and support of my family in Israel, my mother Roma Ben-Atar and my sister's family, Irit, Oded, Michal, and Yonathan Barr.

I am dedicating this book to the memory of my father, Aryeh Yehuda Ben-Atar. Born in Istanbul in April 1919 to a poor mercantile family, he did not enjoy the privileges of education and economic security he provided his children. While he never graduated from high school, he mastered many European tongues and helped me to translate some of the foreign language texts I used in researching the book. He did not live to see it to its completion. He died on July 15, 1998. I think of him daily.

Introduction

Who hasn't heard of Eli Whitney and his cotton gin? Every schoolchild, from New England to the Middle East, learns of the mechanical whiz who went down south in the early 1790s and developed a contraption that separated the cottonseed from its surrounding fiber. Whitney's machine removed the most daunting obstacle to the production of cotton—the labor-intensive process of separation—and made the growing of short-staple cotton economically profitable. It revived southern agriculture, boosted western expansion, generated capital for northern industrialization, and entrenched the American addiction to chattel slavery. The man who left his mark on every major aspect of the nineteenth-century United States has been immortalized as towns, neighborhoods, streets, museums, and websites took his name. Visitors to New Haven stop by the Grove Street cemetery to have their pictures taken by Whitney's pretentious gravestone, modeled after that of the Roman general Scipio who defeated Carthage.

The machine that secured Whitney's place in the pantheon of great Americans, however, drained his financial resources. Whitney did not rush to secure a patent for his invention, and a few local planters in Georgia, upon hearing of the machine, broke into his workshop, stole a model, and before long duplicates appeared all over the south. Whitney returned to Connecticut in hopes of perfecting his invention, getting a patent, and returning to the south with the exclusive right of selling the machine. He secured capital by partnering with lawyer Phineas Miller. On June 20, 1793, Whitney presented his petition for a patent to Secretary of State Thomas Jefferson and the following October took an oath in New Haven in front of a notary to the effect that he was the original inventor of the cotton gin.

Whitney and Miller, however, could neither monopolize nor control the manufacturing of cotton gins. They filed suits against infringers of their patent and turned to state legislatures in search of legal remedies and monetary compensation. Yet their legal maneuvers and lobbying efforts proved frustrating. Southern manufacturers disputed Whitney's claim to originality. In Georgia, a legislative committee declined to pay him a licensing fee, citing the testimony of a Columbia county doctor who claimed he had seen a similar machine in use forty years earlier in Switzerland. In the numerous court cases that Whitney and Miller filed, southern defendants brought forth witnesses who claimed to have seen the cotton gin in action decades earlier in England and Ireland. This argument proved so effective that Whitney contemplated traveling to Europe in 1799 to file for a patent for his cotton gin in all nations that had cotton-producing colonies.

Whitney stayed in America and his legal fortunes improved. He won a few cases in southern courts and persuaded the state legislatures of North and South Carolina to pay him some licensing fees. Yet, the fees he collected and the damages he won did not cover his legal costs—he initiated over sixty lawsuits for patent infringements in Georgia alone. Moreover, only in 1807, some fifteen years after his famous trip, did the courts validate his exclusive claim to the cotton gin. The legal wrangling embittered him. Shortly before his death he confided to an intimate friend that "all he had received for the invention of the cotton gin, had not more than compensated him for the enormous expenses which he had incurred, and for the time which he had devoted during the best years of his life in the prosecution of this subject."[1]

The challenge to Whitney's claim of originality rested on supposedly preexisting devices already in use outside the borders of the United States. Southern juries and state legislatures believed that the cotton gin was brought over from Europe rather than invented by Whitney because just about everywhere they turned they encountered imported technology. Whitney's failure to cash in on the fruits of his invention highlights the central paradox of the emerging American understanding of intellectual property. The United States enacted a patent law in 1790 that restricted patent protection exclusively to original inventors and ruled that prior use anywhere automatically invalidated a patent. Alas, this principled commitment to absolute intellectual property had little to do with reality. Smuggling technology from Europe and claiming the privileges of invention was quite common and most of the political and intellectual elite of the revolutionary and early national generation were directly or indirectly involved in technology piracy. And they were following in the footsteps of their ancestors. Americans had welcomed such practices since the early days of European colonization. The American nickname "Yankee" originated in the Dutch word for "smuggler," and suggests that violation of European economic restrictions had been second nature to the colonists from the early days of settlement.

The gap between law and practice is still with us. Presently, the battle over intellectual property has risen to the forefront of contemporary international contests in which developed and developing nations often find themselves in opposing camps. As developed nations moved to high-tech industries and services in the last few decades of the twentieth century, they came to rely on knowledge as the central component of their economies. The movement of manufacturing to the developing world where raw materials are readily available and labor costs are low has rendered intellectual capital the most important asset of developed nations. International organizations have adopted Western standards of intellectual property and have erected an international agency—the World Intellectual Property Organization (WIPO)—"dedicated to helping to ensure that the rights of creators and owners of intellectual property are protected worldwide and that inventors and authors are, thus, recognized and rewarded for their ingenuity." For all their economic and diplomatic might, however, developed nations have thus far failed to enforce their intellectual property regime. In 1999 the European Union issued a study of the gargantuan cost of counterfeiting and piracy to the West. The infringements range from computer software to spare automobile parts, from musical recordings to medical instruments. Hundreds of billions of dollars are lost annually—the software industry alone loses almost $12 billion a year, and 80 percent of the software used in the Third World is pirated. The missing revenue and trade in pharmaceuticals alone are responsible for the loss of some 200,000 jobs in the United States.

Developing nations, on the other hand, resist Western standards of intellectual property, charging that they are economically self-serving and that the developed world, led by the United States, applies these standards in an inconsistent manner. Societies struggling to lift their people out of abject poverty and to provide them with minimal health care cannot afford the luxury of protecting the intellectual property of the rich and powerful. Many consumers in the developing world who live on a dollar a day cannot afford to pay for an officially sanctioned popular music CD or computer software program. In the name of protecting intellectual property, Western-based companies have marshaled international agencies to enforce their claims with mind-boggling cruelty. Drug patents, in particular, are used to block access to anti-HIV/AIDS drugs in Asia and Africa. And the Western mania for ownership of ideas reached new heights in the 1990s as private companies and academic institutions took out patents on their "discoveries" of the human genome, thereby staking an ownership claim over the genetic makeup of the human race.[2]

The paradoxes of the age of Whitney are still with us. The United States champions worldwide originality and innovation as objective criteria that establish a claim to intellectual property. It is a home for thousands of tinkerers and innovators who develop mechanical solutions to practical problems. And just like two centuries ago, it draws on the education and initiative of foreign nationals. Immigrants form the rank and file of teaching and research at departments of natural sciences in American universities. Engineers from all corners of the globe have turned Silicon Valley into the leading center of innovation and creativity of our time. And as America prospers, those left behind in the immigrants' homelands wonder how to stop the brain drain and how to persuade their brightest not to opt for research and business opportunities in North America. The same questions that plagued Whitney's generation are still with us. Does intellectual property transcend political borders? Can states claim part ownership over the inventions and innovations of their citizens? Should states respect each others' patent and intellectual property laws even at great cost to the welfare of their own citizens?

As individuals and nations struggle to define the limits and attributes of modern intellectual property, we should recognize that the concept is a unique recent abstraction and that unlike physical property, is hardly ever self-evident. Technology defined as intellectual property assumes that knowledge of techniques, processes, and machines has an intrinsic commercial value that is separate from the goods produced by this knowledge. Unlike physical property, intellectual property has no "natural" manifestation. It is a perceptual fiction that depends exclusively on the authority of the state. It privileges those who can afford to shut down their competitors through litigation. Microsoft, the most powerful owner of ideas in our time, just like the most successful patentee of the eighteenth century, Richard Arkwright, owes its standing less to creative genius and more to deep pockets that allows it to dominate competitors through the courts. Finally, without international agreements extending local arrangements across borders, intellectual property does not exist outside the jurisdictional boundaries of the coercive central authority that sanctions it.

I came to the study of the problem of technology smuggling in a rather roundabout way. While conducting research for a book on Jeffersonian commercial policy and diplomacy I encountered much evidence showing that technology piracy was often undertaken not only with the full knowledge, but often with the aggressive encouragement of officials of the federal and state governments. What struck me the most was the absence of ambivalence. I expected political leaders of the early republic (circa 1770–1820) to have the same mixed feelings about smuggled technology as they had about all other aspects of emerging market capitalism. After all, they had rebelled against the mother country in order to preserve the simple and virtuous social order of the New World. The ideal vision of the founders supposedly excluded a priori the industrialization they associated with the Old World's social and economic polarization. The embrace of smuggled technology, however, transcended political and diplomatic distinctions. Americans of different classes and opposing political persuasions embraced the technology of the Industrial Revolution as if the machinery and the social consequences of the Industrial Revolution were unrelated to each other.

The triumph of industrialization in Europe and North America depended on the diffusion of manufacturing technology, and historians of the Industrial Revolution have written at some length about the phenomenon. I have learned a great deal from their work. They study the routes of technology diffusion. They ponder how and why particular cultures and societies were more or less hospitable to particular innovations. Their work demonstrates that technology, while hardly an autonomous force outside human ideas and institutions, did not conform to political boundaries.[3] My questions, however, are different. I study the problem from the perspective of the relations between states in the context of the emergence of national consciousness in the Age of Revolutions. Political entities became embroiled in the struggle over technology diffusion from the outset. In the context of sanctioning the importation of smuggled technology by sponsoring efforts to acquire mechanical innovations of others while preventing others from learning their industrial secrets, states defined the relationship between intellectual property and political borders.

The phenomena I document in this book fall under the modern understanding of "piracy."[4] Applying such terminology to illegal acquisition of protected technology in the eighteenth and early nineteenth centuries, however, is problematic because at that time, piracy connoted a very specific criminal practice. Moreover, there was no international legal regime of intellectual property during the period under study. Individuals who illegally exported technology across national borders did not violate international law because there was none to violate until the 1880s. They were, however, engaged in an activity that was illegal within the jurisdictional boundaries of states. Their crime did not fall under the legal definition of smuggling because the transgression involved illegal exporting of knowledge rather than evading tariffs or importing contraband. I have thus opted for the terminology of technology piracy because it is the most precise way to describe in contemporary language the illegal appropriation of technology protected in one jurisdiction by another. Yet, readers should remember that none of the people engaged in technology piracy during the period under study referred to their actions as piracy; even though the term evoked associations of criminal behavior, I attach no normative value to the practice of technology piracy then and now.

Modern distinctions between intellectual property embodied in literature (i.e., copyright) and in machines (i.e., patents) do a disservice to our understanding of the historical development of the concept. The categorization of ideas as property belonging to their author or inventor originates in the same philosophical orientation and in the same historical era. While my focus is, for the most part, on physical expressions of intellectual property, my discussion is never divorced entirely from authorship. The crystallization of ownership of ideas belongs to an era, from the seventeenth to the nineteenth centuries, that ordered society according to the principles of private property.[5] Initially, ideological identification of ownership of ideas with their originator was confined to the internal operations of the emerging nation states. Alas, bourgeois notions of intellectual property followed the realization that ideas cannot be confined to a physical space. Without an international intellectual property regime, abiding by these notions was left to the voluntary actions of states. The United States merely paid lip service to the principle of international intellectual property. Ignoring intellectual property entitlements across national lines enabled Americans to build an industrial powerhouse founded upon the intellectual labor of Europeans.

In the following pages I offer an interpretive study of the American appropriation of forbidden European know-how from the perspective of a diplomatic historian of the early republic. The technology and the manner in which Americans acquired it came in three forms that were never quite independent of one another. First there was the knowledge itself—the mechanical and scientific discoveries that made innovations possible. Second, there were the innovations that improved existing production processes and allowed for the creation of new products that were smuggled across the Atlantic

Ocean. Third, and most important, were the workers who immigrated to North America bringing with them the professional training they had acquired in Europe's factories. These three distinct historical phenomena constitute a unified problem from the perspective of the relations among states—namely the rules and boundaries of national ownership of intellectual property in the international scene. A comprehensive account of the transfer of technology between Europe and the United States during the early republic is beyond the scope of this study. My concern here is with the origins of the American understanding of international intellectual property during the crucial time of national formation.

This book focuses, then, on the role policies relating to intellectual property played in promoting the appropriation of smuggled technology which led to the emergence of the United States as the premier industrial power in the world. I study the evolution of the American approach to the problem of the relations between international boundaries and intellectual property from the colonial period to the age of Jackson. I examine the role of federal and state governments in that transformation and study the contradictory (some would even call it hypocritical) American policy. Officially, the young republic pioneered a new criterion of intellectual property that set the highest possible standards for such claims—worldwide originality and novelty. At the same time, through a variety of measures, the government endorsed and supported the violation of intellectual property of European states and individuals. The United States emerged as the world's industrial leader by illicitly appropriating mechanical and scientific innovations from Europe.

CHAPTER 1

Knowledge as Property in the International State System

Intellectual property is a historical development of the last five hundred years. In the ancient world, once a machine was developed and gained acceptance, its fate was beyond the inventors' control. Inventions were distinct forms of nonmaterial commodities that did not have a specific value in the marketplace. Neither Greek nor Roman law protected intellectual property, though accusations of theft of knowledge and plagiarism were not uncommon. The value of technical knowledge was embodied in the product. Ancient artisans did not distinguish between the processes and technical skills they used and the goods they made.

Notions of knowledge as a distinct concept representing an economic value emerged in the late medieval period and the early Renaissance. Artisans' guilds played a crucial role in this development. In an attempt to protect their members' power in the emerging market economy, guilds regulated access to knowledge of processes and operation of machinery. By assigning a value to the skill itself, as distinct from the product, the guilds fostered the abstraction of intellectual property. It was not in the interests of guilds, however, to encourage the use of new machinery. The main feature of technical development, after all, is the transfer of functions in the process of

production from man to machinery. Guilds, then, opposed measures that could undermine job security and render some of their
protected knowledge obsolete. Thus, when rulers wanted to adopt
new technologies they often had to overcome the resistance of their
local guilds.

The emergence of a protocapitalist commercial economy and the
consolidation of some nations into distinct geographical and political units in parts of early modern Europe forced a reconfiguration of
the boundaries between individuals and their communities. This
period of continued economic expansion saw the consolidation of
political power into dynastic-centered states. The ideal of a united
Christendom gave way to competing dynasties unified by religious
particularism (Catholic, Protestant, Anglican, etc.) and seeking to
best rivals in all spheres. At the same time, Renaissance celebration
of genius placed individuals at the center of the creative process and
granted them ownership over the fruits of their minds. Marketplace
notions associated innovations with the individuals who supposedly
originated them and thus entitled them to enjoy their rewards. States
increasingly adopted the practice of securing rights and royalties to
authors and inventors in an effort to encourage innovation from
within and attract innovators from abroad. Strategies to accomplish
this goal varied. In prerevolutionary France, for example, an inventor or introducer who successfully persuaded a certain group of
judges that his innovation was useful was awarded a payment in cash
by the state.[1] Other states, like England, at times followed the continental practice of giving cash rewards and at other times took a less
direct route of encouraging mechanization. Men in possession of
useful mechanical knowledge were granted a temporary monopoly
on the use or sale of the device in return for a detailed description of
it. The British Empire of the eighteenth century opted for awarding
patent monopolies for a specified number of years as the strategy of
choice for promoting innovation and industrialization.[2]

Modern discussion of intellectual property often assumes that an invention has a something-out-of-nothing quality to it—an assumption that fades as soon as one takes a closer look at most so-called "inventions," for close scrutiny often reveals marginal originality and great dependency on previous knowledge. The gap between what is original and what is merely derivative is rather narrow. An innovation that is deemed an invention worth protecting is wholly a political and legal construct. An invention that is not followed by practical application funded by investors is of little value. James Watt's 1769 development of a separate condenser for steam engines, for example, was a technological breakthrough of the first order. Its market potential, however, was undermined by Watt's failure to perceive other possible applications besides pumping water out of mines. It took Matthew Boulton's investment of time and capital and Watt's application of "double action" of steam on both sides of the piston in 1781, thereby making rotary motion possible, to turn the engine into a source of power for mill machinery. Boulton and Watt formed a powerful partnership of ingenuity and business acumen and got along famously. They were, however, the exception, as tensions between investors and inventors over the ownership of ideas were frequently difficult to resolve. Finally, it is impossible to protect intellectual property in organizational and procedural changes that often account for leaps in production far more than improved machinery.[3]

Natural rights and utilitarian arguments combined in the seventeenth and eighteenth centuries to justify a patent monopoly system as a just reward for socially useful inventiveness. Natural rights philosophers argued that man's right to property is inalienable and that he is entitled to the wealth created by his labor. In the words of the great prophet of liberalism and individualism, John Locke: "every Man has a Property in his own *Person*. This no Body has any Right to but himself. The *Labour* of his Body, and the *Work* of his Hands, we may say, are properly his. Whatsoever then he removes out of the State that Nature hath provided, and left it in, he hath mixed his *Labour* with, and joyned to it something that is his own, and thereby makes it his *Property*."[4] From the natural rights perspective inventions are a form of property and all individuals are entitled to benefit from the fruits of their labors. An inventor has a right to his invention just as an artisan does to a tool he makes. Society has to recognize that it has to protect intellectual property in the same way that it is obligated to protect physical property. In other words, it should treat unlicensed imitation as if it were an actual theft of physical property. Granting authors and inventors an intellectual property right over their creations is a just extension of their natural rights, for it was their labor alone that gave their creations their value.

Natural rights arguments bridge the tension that is inherent in a patent system between capitalism's commitment to a free market and the countercompetitive nature of monopolies. Accordingly, society is obligated to reward inventors for their labor only in proportion to its value. The most appropriate rewards that take into account the social usefulness of inventions are limited monopolies. The National Assembly of revolutionary France declared in 1790 that benefiting from intellectual discoveries and innovations was the natural right of authors and inventors. The preamble to the French patent law of 1791 employed similar reasoning. Nineteenth-century international agreements on patents and copyrights sounded similar notes. Both the International Conference on Intellectual Property Rights held in Paris in 1878 and the International Convention for the Protection of Industrial Property ratified by the U.S. Senate in 1887 used natural rights reasoning to explain their commitment to the protection of intellectual property.[5]

But natural rights association of intellectual and physical property is problematic. First, physical property is inherently a zero-sum game while knowledge is not. An owner of an ax loses his ability to use it when it is stolen. An inventor, however, can still use his invention even when others duplicate it. The impact of technology piracy on the inventor is the loss of exclusivity that undermines his potential profit margin. The public at large, on the other hand, benefits from the dissemination of superior technologies among producers because lower prices for consumers are generally the by-product of such competition. Second, physical property does not cease to exist in law through time while intellectual property, in the form of either a patent or copyright, is always confined to a specific number of years. Finally, the natural rights perspective runs counter to the interests of the state, for it locates the value of an innovation in the creative individual and concludes that intellectual property is not confined by international boundaries. On the one hand it stipulates that each country is obligated to respect intellectual properties of all others within its own borders and must consider imitation as theft. On the other hand, since the property is embodied in the individual himself, he may carry the patent monopoly with him as he moves between locations. In the context of the persistent rivalry among European states, it is not surprising that rulers in Renaissance and early modern Europe privileged their own economic interests over abstract commitment to the principles of natural rights philosophy.

Utilitarian considerations proved a more powerful impetus to the codification of ideas as a form of property. Granting special benefits to authors and inventors supposedly encouraged innovation that ultimately benefited society as a whole. By assuring inventors and/or their assignees and licensees a time-specific monopoly in their respective field and hence offering the possibility of great financial rewards, states hoped to generate growth that would trickle down to all sectors of the economy. Governments granted patents in exchange for disclosure of the secrets of trade. The act of registration amounted to depositing the desired knowledge in the public vault to be shared with all members of society after the term of the patent expired. Often, individual patentees and bureaucratic agencies fought over the degree of specificity that was needed in patent applications, with the patentees trying to disclose as little as possible. The dramatic rise in literacy following the invention of movable type printing by Gutenberg made the content of patents application more accessible, though seventeenth- and eighteenth-century verbal descriptions were often vague and general. Nonverbal communication, primarily drawings, also proved an extremely useful agent of technology diffusion. In order to limit the monopolistic powers of patents to their specific fields, courts demanded exact specification of all the applications of an invention. Inventors, on the other hand, feared that listing such details in their patent applications would allow competitors to emulate inventions and destroy inventors' competitive advantage of exclusivity. It was none other than Matthew Bolton and James Watt who used their reputation and resources to combat the general hostility of late eighteenth-century judges to patents, and established the requirement of precise specifications as a quid pro quo for the privilege of monopoly.[6]

States had to define who was entitled to such lucrative monopolies. Modern distinctions between invention, discovery, and the acquisition of knowledge by other than mental effort did not exist in the language of the sixteenth and seventeenth centuries. The terms "invention," "discovery," and "first finding out" were used indiscriminately in the patent registration rolls and in the legal literature of the period. Often it was not the inventor per se who benefited from a monopoly. Protecting one's patent was technically and financially burdensome. Success depended on the ability to litigate, not on inventive merit. Many inventors who did not have the budget for financing lengthy court battles did not register their patents, opting for nondisclosure over patent exposure. Secrecy was effective less in hiding mechanical innovation than in hiding the cost and profit margins involved in adopting new machinery. Without these economic data investors had a harder time deciding whether or not it was beneficial to alter the production process.[7]

Success in obtaining state-sanctioned monopoly depended on the ability of would-be patentees to persuade governmental bodies with coercive powers that the innovations they championed were in their exclusive possession and of great value to society and its rulers. Such campaigning required resources that were not at the disposal of all inventors, and many turned to selling and leasing their rights over their patents to others. Keeping innovations secret by not patenting them was a viable alternative only for inventors of processes who could use their monopolized knowledge to increase production and decrease costs without divulging their methods to competitors. Inventors of machines, however, usually had to sell them in order to make a profit, and buyers could analyze the innovations and build their own copies. Even within small communities restrictions on the diffusion of technical knowledge depended on the ability of first users to persuade society to coerce others to respect their monopoly. As critics of capitalism were quick to point out, control of the mode of production was a development of utmost significance in the distribution of political and economic power in the early modern age. In the precapitalist system of production the master owed his dominant role in the production process to his knowledge of the secrets of the craft rather than his ownership of the means of production. Modern industry, however, wrote Karl Marx, "sweeps away by technical means the manufacturing division of labor, under which each man is bound hand and foot for life to a single detail operation. At the same time, the capitalistic form of that industry reproduces this same division of labour in a still more monstrous shape; in the factory proper, by converting the workman into a living appendage of the machine." Owners of patent monopolies sought to restrict the spread of knowledge by defining it as property, thus controlling the pace of industrialization and keeping all the economic benefits of innovations to themselves.[8]

Early modern patent law did not distinguish between inventors on the one hand, and introducers of skills, devices, or processes from abroad on the other. In fact, in the precapitalist world, introducers enjoyed greater privileges than inventors. Rewarding local inventors was at the complete discretion of rulers. Princely control of movement between localities meant that inventors had no other choice except to try and use their invention in their home countries and be exposed to technological piracy. Foreign know-how, however, was beyond the control of rulers, who had to find ways to attract it. Countries offered inducements to immigrants who would dare to violate restrictions on the dissemination of knowledge and transplant themselves and their skills. Rulers believed that imported technologies could convert their nations' natural resources into valuable international assets and swing the import-export ratio in their favor. The battle over the diffusion of technology, then, became an integral component of European nations' economic and political competition.

England led the way in adopting the practice of awarding patent monopolies to foreigners to entice them to introduce skills or processes without checking whether they were the inventors in their countries of origin. English patents, in fact, were originally granted to introducers rather than inventors. During the reign of Edward III, in the fourteenth century, letters of protection from competition were given to foreign artisans, in order to entice them to settle in England and teach their English apprentices their trades. Two hundred years later, during the reign of Elizabeth I, the exclusive right to the use of a particular imported innovation for a period of years was added to the patent grant. Patents of importation preceded patents of inventions because of the widespread belief in the superiority of continental technology and the desire to replace imports and correct the balance of trade—the premier barometer of the strength of nations in the mind of mercantilists.

The English state did not grant patents to inventors until 1623, when James I issued the first patent for an invention that secured the patentee a fourteen years' production monopoly. The following year Parliament passed a statute regulating the practice of rewarding invention, though royal cash rewards and patents of importation to introducers of new technologies persisted.[9] Even though the direction of industrial espionage was reversed by the second half of the eighteenth century, the English policy of encouraging the appropriation of smuggled technology persisted. As late as 1778 the British courts upheld the legality of patents of importation. The Swiss inventor John Liardet and the English assignee of his patented stucco sued John Johnson for violation of the patent and for pirating the knowledge through inducement of workers to switch employers. The case of *Liardet v. Johnson* was tried twice, and both times the English judge and jury sided with a foreigners' patent of importation over an English claim. The British policy remained by and large unchanged until 1852 and was highly successful. England attracted skilled European artisans in sufficient numbers to turn it from a technological debtor nation into the world's center of industry and innovation.[10]

English support of technology piracy was not unique. Continental governments realized the value of technology and set out to promote technical improvements by attracting new industrial skills and modernizing machinery. Departments of state in most continental governments acted as ministries of industrial development. Official emissaries acted as undercover labor recruiting agents in their host countries, endeavoring to induce craftsmen to emigrate illegally to the countries they represented. By the same token, they tried to preserve their technological advantage by preventing competitors from acquiring their protected know-how, and by reporting to their superiors at home about upcoming efforts to lure artisans. Nearly every early modern European government labored to prevent outflow of skill and technique through a variety of measures that were sometimes even draconian. Venice, for example, settled its glass workers on the island of Murano and threatened to put to death anyone caught trying to leave the island with a view to emigrating. British sulfuric acid producers conceived of a different strategy to keep competitors in the dark. They recruited for their factories only Welsh operatives who spoke Welsh exclusively.[11]

The Industrial Revolution raised the stakes in the international battle over technology. The application of theoretical knowledge to industry and agriculture yielded successive incremental technological breakthroughs. Organizational changes in the mode of production and the cultural and legal embrace of the absolute right of property transformed the economy and society of Europe and its satellites. The structure of local economies and patterns of interregional trade underwent a dramatic change. The rise of commercial and industrial capitalism in the eighteenth century reverberated from New France to India, and affected everyone from local spinners and weavers to merchants and champions of industry. The massive irreversible application of machines to materials in the production process ushered in the modern technological-industrial system and raised Western Europe to the status of the world's dominant region. Technological development established the pattern of exchange of raw materials, exotic foodstuffs, and slaves from Asia, Africa, and America for European manufactured goods.[12]

Industrialization coincided with the emergence of Great Britain as the most powerful nation on the globe. Successive victories in a series of eighteenth-century colonial wars, climaxing in decisive triumph in the Seven Years War (known in America as the French and Indian War), left Britain in control of territories from India to North

America. The accumulation of skilled laborers who manufactured goods for export in the British Isles set the nation apart from its European competitors. To be sure, English and American manufacturing in the seventeenth and eighteenth centuries must not be confused with nineteenth-century machine-centered factories. It began as hand production at home organized in putting-out systems and gathered into centralized manufactories where, in time, machine production assumed center stage. Still, as early as the late seventeenth century, home-manufactured goods, primarily woolen textiles, dominated English exports. The trend accelerated in the eighteenth century as English manufactured leather goods, hardware, and tools reached markets all over the globe. The development of coal fuel technology allowed manufacturers to replace human and some animal energy with coal, providing a tremendous production boost. In the 1770s, with the beginning of modernization in the textile industry, the development of deep mines and large-scale metal fabrication, British engineers and artisans emerged as Europe's technological leaders not only in finished goods, but also in the crucial branch of machine making. Exports of manufactured goods accounted for 10 to 15 percent of the British gross domestic product in the eighteenth century. The wave of innovations enabled English manufacturers to meet the growing demand for English finished goods around the world and even the loss of the North American colonies in the 1770s did not affect Britain's industrial dominance.[13]

Rivals looked upon the rise of English economic might with a mixture of envy and trepidation. Mercantilist politicians of the eighteenth century who measured the power of nations by their balance of trade realized that "the plough-share is as essential as the sword to the strength of a state." They believed that the boom in English industrial exports accounted for the dramatic rise in English military and political power. Curtailing the import of foreign articles by manufacturing them at home meant reducing the outflow of gold from the state, thus enhancing its position in the international balance of power. States turned to developing their own manufacturing by setting up and running government-owned factories, subsidizing specific sectors, and purchasing from local manufacturers. Champions of industry and mercantilists, however, recognized that these efforts were doomed unless local industries could close the technological gap with foreign competitors. And they were not the only ones who believed that acquiring new technologies was the key to national prosperity. No less than the great prophet of liberalism, Adam Smith, argued that every society could clearly see the advantages in acquiring improved machinery from abroad. Intense competition among the European states made for a high degree of receptivity to new technologies and encouraged assimilating them quickly regardless of their origins. The extent of espionage efforts by foreign countries in Britain demonstrates their conviction that technology was the key to England's industrial and political power and that acquiring this protected know-how would allow them to catch up. For all their efforts, only in the second half of the nineteenth century did European nations manage to free themselves from their dependence on English skill.[14]

Recognizing the importance of technology to its political and economic power, England intensified its commitment to protecting its industrial secrets. The British government did not orchestrate all these efforts. British industrialists themselves barred strangers from entering their factories. The private voluntary blocking of access by individuals, however, was not as effective as direct governmental involvement. Sometime this policy took a semiprivate form. Successful enticing of papermakers by French agents, for example, propelled the British government to take the Company of White Paper Makers into royal protection and to prohibit recruiting of artisans and exporting of papermaking materials. Such individual intervention aside, legislation held the most promise for denying rivals access to technology. In fact, England criminalized the diffusion of technology in the eighteenth century. All in all ten major laws were passed between 1695 and 1799 against the emigration of artisans and the export of machinery. They covered the metal, clock, glass, pottery, harness, mining, and certain machine-making trades as well as textiles. From 1749 on, enticement of immigrants from Britain and Ireland to the colonies was also pronounced "a criminal act."[15]

Paradoxically, the battery of regulations against the export of machinery and migration of skilled workers stimulated rather than suppressed efforts to recruit artisans and get hold of protected machinery. Industrial espionage and technology piracy were common practice for practically every European country with any ambitions to industrialize. The tsarist government heavily sponsored the import of iron technologies by offering great benefits to skilled foreign workers willing to resettle in Russia. This effort was highly successful as German master craftsmen heavily outnumbered Russians in the St. Petersburg ironworkers' craft guild by the mid 1760s. Sweden sent scientists and experienced workers to spy on the English iron and copper industries and provided them with cash to purchase production secrets. The highest echelons of the royal French government orchestrated industrial espionage in England, regardless of the state of Anglo-French relations. Even in 1777, when France was taking special care not to antagonize its rival so as not to be drawn into the War of the American Revolution, foreign secretary Vergennes sent an industrial spy to Boulton's works. The engineer managed to enter the factory and make a few drawings before exposure forced him to flee back across the English Channel. Indeed, the effort to acquire British technology was a constant in French diplomacy for much of the eighteenth century and beyond. The royal policy of pirating English technology and enticing English workers to migrate to France persisted in the revolutionary and Napoleonic periods.[16]

England emerged as the technological leader of the Industrial Revolution and as the target of most efforts at industrial espionage. Strides in industrial technology, however, were not confined to the British Isles. All European states were in some ways involved in the production and transfer of technological and scientific information, and the British government supported appropriation of protected technologies of its rivals while at the same time it erected legal barriers against the outflow of technology. As continental observers marveled at the British innovations, British firms continued to seek various continental industrial techniques and to attract skilled laborers. It was quite common for English professionals to go abroad, learn a trade, and upon their return file for patent monopoly in England. For example, the Smithfield chemist Humphrey Jackson went in the 1750s to Russia to study a new method of brewing, and in March 1760 obtained a patent for the process. When England coveted other nations' industrial techniques, it did not hesitate to employ all the methods it prohibited at home. In an attempt to acquire the French technique of cast plate glass, high-level British officials tried to tempt senior French managers as well as regular workers to come and build an imitative factory in England. Though plagued by economic upheaval and unemployment, the most advanced center of manufacturing in the world continued its policy of attracting footloose skilled workers. In fact, throughout the Industrial Revolution Britain continued to draw heavily on Continental technology.[17]

Industrial espionage by states and individuals only partly accounts for the failure of states to confine the fruits of innovations to their national borders. As early as 1699 the great German mathematician and philosopher, Gottfried Wilhelm Leibniz, argued in his *Memorandum on the Founding of a Learned Society in Germany* that the growth of European scientific enterprise depended on free communication among scientists of different nations. Growing communication among academics, scientists, and intellectuals further undermined official efforts to control the diffusion of knowledge. Modern distinctions between theoretical knowledge and practical applications do not apply to the eighteenth century. Men of science often dabbled in inventions. The advance in scientific knowledge taught men of letters all over Europe why certain innovations worked. Technological breakthroughs and scientific discoveries were reported in the same journals, making them widely accessible and allowing innovators to build on the discoveries of colleagues all over the continent. Measurements and calculations that underlay the Scientific Revolution of the seventeenth century had frequently an immediate practical application. The popularization of the scientific enterprise in the eighteenth century coincided with increased specialization in production and accelerated the links between utility and science. [18]

In this highly competitive atmosphere, governments, not to be outdone by rivals, invested in the development of scientific and intellectual institutions. Many academies were founded in eighteenth-century England, France, Germany, and Italy. The British government patronized the arts and sciences. In France alone more that a hundred academies were established from 1700 to 1776. Knowledge gained in these endeavors was not kept from rivals and competitors. On the contrary, most European academies published proceedings that were devoted to summarizing and popularizing advances in knowledge. Victory in this competitive culture involved advertising accomplishments—a practice that ran counter to efforts to keep knowledge exclusive to one nation. The London Royal Society of Arts displayed in its public gallery models that had been entered in its periodic contests for the best solutions to particular technological problems. The most important example of the internationalization of knowledge in the eighteenth century was the Encyclopedia. An impressive display of the state of knowledge around the middle of the eighteenth century, this collective accomplishment of the French

Enlightenment included entries on arts and crafts, philosophy, politics, theology, and language. Articles displaying cross-references manifested the view that all knowledge is related and dependent on other knowledge. The state of war that characterized Anglo-French relations for much of the eighteenth century did not affect the flow of scientific information between the two nations. These wars, for the most part, took place in the colonies, and in contrast to the bloody seventeenth century, most European nations in the eighteenth century, with the exception of Prussia, were spared the horrors and devastation of wars from the end of the War of the Spanish Succession in 1713 to the beginning of the wars of the French Revolution in 1792. Peace made restrictions on the diffusion of technology difficult to enforce.[19]

Eighteenth-century Europe saw a dramatic acceleration in geographic mobility. Rapid demographic growth, from eighty-one million people in 1700 to one hundred twenty-three million in 1800, placed additional demands on the diminishing supply of agricultural land. The creation of substantial employment outside agriculture and the absence of bloody conflicts allowed an increasing number of people to move into urban areas. Industrialization was not confined to the growing commercial urban centers. In search of lowering the costs of production, capitalists invested in rural areas, creating vibrant rural industries. The productive process connected distant economies. Goods produced in villages were finished in towns and marketed across national and continental borders. The emerging market capitalism and the Industrial Revolution tied workers, in urban centers and remote rural areas alike, into the web of Europe's growing economy. Naturally, those who did not own land and who consequently made a living off the emerging cottage industries were the most mobile. For the first time in Europe's history hundreds of thousands of individuals literally packed up and left their homes and cultures in search of livelihoods in other countries. Confining workers to a particular locality became all the more difficult in this context of rising mobility and massive displacements.[20]

What stood in the way of technology diffusion in the eighteenth century, above all, was the centrality of the artisan to the new methods. Many of the important innovations that were so instrumental in quickening the pace and lowering the costs of production were adjustments by individual artisans. Technical knowledge was organized like a pyramid with steeply pitched sides. In every industry there were a few knowledgeable artisans. The level of technical skill beyond this select few was markedly inferior. The empirical origins and craft basis of the new technology meant that little of it was put into writing, less into print, and even what was published was difficult to copy. The most efficient and direct way of acquiring new technology was to entice artisans with the right skills to migrate.[21]

The growing geographical mobility of the era combined with promises of patent monopolies and cash rewards undermined states' efforts to control the diffusion of technology. The American republic was born into a world that could not resolve the tension between national economic development and international intellectual property. The following pages chronicle the particular American manner of living with and resolving the tension. They analyze the manner in which underdeveloped former British colonies on the Atlantic North American coast that cared little about the rights of foreign inventors emerged as the primary agents of state-bounded intellectual property.

CHAPTER 2

The Battle over Technology within the Empire

When England began colonizing the North American continent early in the seventeenth century, no imperial statesman envisioned that these struggling outposts could become actual economic rivals. With the country torn by dynastic and civil wars, and hardly the center of industry and innovation, early imperial policy did not regulate the transfer of technology between the metropolis and the peripheries, assuming that at best the colonies would become sources of raw materials and potential markets. The nature of the economic and technological relationship between England and its North American continental colonies was transformed over the one hundred and seventy years of colonial rule. Whereas in the initial stages of colonization the metropolis allowed, and at times even encouraged, skilled artisans to migrate to the New World, in the second half of the eighteenth centuries, as some branches of the colonial economies began to compete with British counterparts, the Board of Trade tried to put the brakes on industrial development in North America by restricting the transfer of technology across the Atlantic. Indeed, the evolution in attitudes in Great Britain and America toward technology transfer foretold the deteriorating relations leading to the breakup of the Empire. American

embrace of clandestine and illegal appropriation of English industrial technology was at the heart of the revolutionary project.

Dependent Colonies

The joint stock companies that sponsored the early colonization efforts understood that if they hoped to profit from their
ventures they had to entice workers to leave the homes they knew for
a risky adventure in the wilderness. To make life in North America
attractive to potential immigrants, expeditions had to include skilled
artisans who could create in the New World some of the comforts of
the old. As early as 1629, before John Winthrop and his famous
entourage set foot in North America, the Massachusetts Bay Company hired Thomas Grove, a jack-of-all-trades, to move to America
and help found the colony even though "[h]is salarie costs this
Companie a great some of mony."[1]

The New England and Mid-Atlantic colonies attracted a sufficient number of immigrants and in the latter part of the seventeenth
century generated enough homegrown artisans to make the shortage less acute. The colonies of the south, however, failed to attract a
significant number of skilled immigrants and their slave economies
were inhospitable to the growth of an indigenous independent free
class of artisans. Early in the eighteenth century three Virginians
anxiously reported that the absence of towns, markets, and capital
left "but little Encouragement for Tradesmen and Artificers," and
thus the colony was plagued by "the Dearth of all Tradesmen's Labour and likewise the Discouragement, Scarcity, and Insufficiency of
Tradesmen." Nearly all of the capable master builders in the southern colonies before the Revolution were brought over to complete
specific jobs. As late as 1746 South Carolinian recruiting agents traveled to London in search of printers, watchmakers, carpenters, sail
and rope makers, and blacksmiths.[2]

In the initial stages of settlement the governments of Britain's North American colonies followed their European counterparts in trying to encourage the development of local manufacturing by a variety of legislative means. For the leaders of the Massachusetts Bay Colony the need for increased self-sufficiency became evident within the first two decades of its existence. The outbreak of a civil war in England in the 1640s consumed the metropolis and reduced interest in colonization. Some artisans who came over in the 1630s for ideological reasons returned to England to take part in the struggle. Alarmed by the seemingly bleak economic prospects of New England, the General Court undertook to develop the natural resources of the region, enacting measures to promote local industries. In 1640 it passed a program to encourage the manufacture of linen because it was an "absolute necessity" for the colony's welfare. The program called on those "skillful in that manifacture [to determine] what course may bee taken to raise the materials & pduce the manifacture, & what course may be taken for teaching the boyes and girls in all townes the spinning of the yarne." The General Court concluded by requesting that localities report on the impact of the program during the court's following year's session. In 1641 the colony's "Bodies of Liberties" outlawed all monopolies with the exception of those aimed at encouraging "such new inventions that are profitable to the Country, and that for a short time." Other colonies enacted similar legal provisions. William Penn's original plan of government for the colony of Pennsylvania, for example, called on the colony's governor to "encourage and reward the authors of useful sciences and laudable Inventions."[3]

In emulation of Old World practices, colonial governments began to issue patents. In 1641 the General Court of Massachusetts issued the first patent of invention in English America to Samuel Winslow, who received a ten-year monopoly for manufacturing salt by a new method that was supposed to make salt cheaper and more plentiful in the colony. The monopoly was restricted to the production process exclusively as other salt makers were not precluded from continuing to make salt in the old way. In 1645 the General Court gave an exclusive production monopoly for twenty-one years to a company sponsored by John Winthrop Jr., who brought over English workers and Scots prisoners of war to launch the ironworks venture at Saugus (near present day Lynn), Massachusetts, because it was for "the good of the country." [4] Two years later the General Court gave Joseph Jenks, who worked at Saugus, a patent monopoly over a process of production, explaining that, moved by the "necessity of raising such manufactures," it had decided that a fourteen-year monopoly would conduce to the public good. Jenks's patent petition echoed the language of the English patent law, and the General Court's allocation of a monopoly for fourteen years was also in line with the British practice.

Colonial authorities did not distinguish between patents awarded on account of originality and those on account of introduction. While Jenks claimed he was an inventor, he was actually an immigrant who had learned the iron trade in England from a German immigrant who specialized in making swords and was brought to develop the Massachusetts works. Similarly, in 1652 the Virginia House of Burgesses awarded George Fletcher and his heirs a fourteen-year monopoly of distilling and brewing in wooden vessels and threatened potential violators of this monopoly with a hundred-pound fine, even though Fletcher did not prove he was the original inventor and was most likely the introducer of the technology to the commonwealth.

Even if there had been a desire to make effective distinctions between emulation and invention, the minimal size of governmental bureaucracies in the seventeenth-century colonies rendered effective regulation impossible. Given the overwhelming need for the importation of skills, colonial authorities were disinclined to explore in depth the question of originality.

Patent monopolies, however, were quite rare in seventeenth-century America. Colonial legislatures were torn between their desire to promote economic development through the granting of patents on the one hand, and principled hostility to monopolies on the other. Moreover, the economic effectiveness of such patents was minimal. Because colonial authorities exercised very limited control over their own territories and none over neighboring jurisdictions, patentees could not and did not expect effective enforcement of monopolies. Thus, colonial inventors preferred applying for awards for their efforts rather than trying to secure manufacturing monopolies. English patentees could not expect the automatic extension of their privileges across the Atlantic. In 1717, for example, Thomas Masters took the trip from Pennsylvania to England in order to establish his ownership of his wife's inventions of a maize-stamping mill and devices for working and staining straw and palmetto leaves for making women's bonnets. Masters protected his and his wife's interests by getting patents in "Several Plantations in America." His actions demonstrate the limits of the crown's ability to protect intellectual property in the colonies. The state of the colonial economies called for improvisation and adaptation of existing techniques to new circumstances, not industrial innovation. And as England began to formulate a consistent colonial policy around the turn of the eighteenth century, the question of governmental support for technological innovation in North America became part of the tangled web of imperial politics. [5]

Imperial policy regarding the diffusion of industrial technology to North America mirrored British confusion as to the nature of the exact relationship between the metropolis and its overseas outposts. The Board of Trade, established in 1696 to devise and enforce a coherent colonial policy, shifted back and forth between viewing the colonies as an integral element in the organic economy of the Empire and as competitors with the domestic economy of the British Isles. Considering the colonies as part of the British nation meant that the same rules and regulations that applied to the movement of technology between York and London should apply to the diffusion of knowledge from Liverpool to Philadelphia. If the colonies and mother country were economic competitors, however, then the restrictions on the outflow of technology to Europe applied. When the colonies were in their economic infancy, during the seventeenth and the early part of the eighteenth century, the metropolis favored the development of the colonies because continued dependence on the mother country for essentials undermined their ability to become profitable cash crop economies. Imperial policy allowed and even encouraged the recruitment of skilled workers and the transfer of technology to the New World. Recruiting agents and imperial companies openly tried to entice workers to come and help found the colonial economies. Thomas Bray, for example, wrote a passionate essay in 1697 in favor of establishing libraries throughout the British Empire to encourage the dissemination of religious and technical knowledge and thereby raise the productiveness and moral fiber of His Majesty's subjects.[6]

The Board of Trade also promoted colonial appropriation of technologies from England's rivals in Europe. Mills were central to the colonial economies as they were used for a variety of functions, from grinding grain to sawing logs into planks. Practically every colonial village built at least one water-powered mill. The art of building waterwheels for mills was highly developed in Denmark and Holland. Individual localities turned to offering material inducements for artisans to migrate. A mill site in Europe was very expensive and owning one was a mark of wealth. Some Massachusetts towns advertised mill sites for free and threw in free use of common land and wood for anyone who would build and operate a local mill. Colonial investors thus enticed builders to come and settle in the colonies and introduce that technology. In this context London encouraged colonial technological development.

Competitors within the Empire

When the colonies began to produce finished goods that competed with English and Scottish industries, the imperial mood swung against allowing free flow of machine and skilled workers across the Atlantic. As early as 1666 London began to check westward transfer of technology by prohibiting the export of frames for knitting to the colonies. The growing concern in London over technology diffusion found its way into official policy in the fundamental rules of the Empire—the Navigation Acts. The Wool Act of 1699 openly stated the crown's aim "to prevent the setting up of the woolen manufactures" in the colonies, and prohibited the migration of wool artisans to New World.[7] This restrictive policy was strengthened in the eighteenth century with the Hat Act of 1732 and the Iron Act of 1750. As the Board of Trade declared: "More trades [are] carried on and more manufacturers set up in the province on the continent of America to the northward of Virginia, prejudicial to the trade and manufactures of Great Britain, particularly in New England, than in any of the British colonies."[8]

By the middle of the eighteenth century, imperial ambivalence disappeared as the Board of Trade determined to privilege British manufacturers over colonial ones. The logic of mercantilism taught that attracting skilled artisans to the metropolis and keeping them there would improve its balance of trade with its European rivals—that all-important criterion of power and wealth in mercantilist political economy—while creating employment at home. By the same token, it was important to prevent the emigration of valuable artisans to the New World because in the mind of British mercantilists this terminated their contribution to the production of exports. Imperial immigration restrictions, however, were difficult to enforce. Prospective migrants could be stopped only at the port of exit. Once the ship carrying a skilled immigrant departed from England to the New World the game was over. No immigrant was ever sent back on account of transferring restricted skills and no enforcement agents were sent to look for illegal immigrants and return them to England. Indeed, less than two years after the passage of the Wool Act a committee set up to examine its effectiveness reported that the colonies had ignored imperial restrictions on the development of local wool manufacturing and urged stricter enforcement of the measures.[9]

London prescribed specifically what industries could be established and what stages of the industrial production process could take place in America. It encouraged colonial shipbuilding, for this branch did not endanger a thriving British one. It looked favorably on American attempts to manufacture partly finished raw materials because increased production of these items supplemented shortages in the Empire's economy. It insisted, however, that most finished products be made in the British Isles. The Iron Act epitomized this approach. On the one hand Parliament abolished the duty on American-made pig iron and bar iron. On the other hand, it prohibited establishing factories in America for making finished iron products. Similarly, the production of potash (potassium carbonate), a forest-based industrial chemical made from wood ashes that was used in manufacturing glass and soap and in bleaching and dyeing, was greatly encouraged by London. During the first half of the eighteenth century England imported potash from Europe's forest regions. In 1751, however, Parliament removed the duty on American potash and British technical tracts were circulated to teach Americans how to produce it.[10]

The efforts of the Board of Trade to confine the colonial economy to the production of raw material and small-scale manufacturing were somewhat successful. The colonies remained primarily agricultural and their people and governments directed most of their energies to the concerns of farmers, husbandmen, and planters. Imperial restrictions on the dissemination of certain industrial information held back the issuing of patent monopolies, which remained quite rare throughout the colonial period.[11] Restrictions on the diffusion of technology retarded the development of some American industries. In textiles, in particular, late eighteenth-century England bustled with innovation, yet in the North American colonies spinning wheels and looms were hardly changed from the seventeenth century. Americans were slow to adopt new technologies, however, even in industries where no restrictive imperial policy existed. Printing presses were heavy and complex and until the middle of the eighteenth century all colonial printers had to import them from England because no local carpenters could build them. Even the fonts had to be imported from England before 1768 when Abel Buell established a type foundry in Killingworth, Connecticut.

In general, American industrial backwardness had less to do with the British restrictions than with the specific conditions and business practices in the colonies. The continental colonies of North America were supposed to provide raw materials—wool, cotton, and flax—but the cloth had to be made in England; otherwise, according to mercantilist reasoning, the metropolis would lose its dominance in trade. The crown allowed Americans to spin and weave for local home consumption, but prohibited them from exporting the finished products. These restrictions however, failed to check the growth of colonial spinning and weaving because there was another economy in which notions of sharing technology were privileged over secrecy. Women from all classes and in a variety of regions engaged in domestic manufacturing of clothing. Wives, widows, and daughters taught one another how to operate newer looms and spinning wheels and wove for their families and the local market. The impact of these women on the American economy was so great that colonial officials complained that household manufactures came at the expense of British imports. Ultimately, the colonial textile industry might have lagged behind that in the metropolis because of the preeminent market position of homespun cloth.[12]

While shortages of natural resources in Europe fueled searches for technological improvements, abundance in the New World made the adoption of new technologies less necessary. The forests of the northeastern and Mid-Atlantic colonies provided wood for constructing homes, ships, and furniture, as well as providing the colonial economy's main source of energy. Traditional European energy conservation practices were replaced by reckless colonial overuse, ultimately leading to the radical deforestation of the region. European commentators were appalled by the "incredible amount of wood" that was "squandered" in the colonies.[13] Differing attitudes toward the use of energy slowed down the transfer of some technologies across the Atlantic. The burning of coal powered England's industrial revolution well into the nineteenth century. In North America, however, wood and charcoal were cheaper and readily available. Moreover, the colonies were rich in waterpower sites that rendered steam engines unnecessary except at geographically flat locations. Consequently, the economy of colonial America all but ignored most industrial innovations regarding fuel in England. For all their technological deficiencies and industrial dependency on the metropolis, however, the economy of the colonies grew at a rapid pace and generated widespread prosperity.[14]

The spectacular growth of the American colonial economy in the eighteenth century generated greater purchasing power for women and men who increasingly acquired manufactured goods. The American colonies earned the reputation of being the best poor men's country as by the third quarter of the century white Americans enjoyed the highest standard of living in the world. This prosperity ushered in a revolutionary transformation in consumption habits. Common folk, whose ancestors' lives had been shaped by a constant struggle for subsistence, turned to purchasing what had been hitherto considered luxuries reserved for the rich. The availability and affordability of furniture, tools, and clothing to the vast majority of white residents of New England and Mid-Atlantic colonies dramatically altered their daily lives and raised their economic expectations. Initially, local artisans and handcraft industries met the demand, but they could not keep pace with the growing appetite of consumers who quickly turned to imports. Manufactured goods accounted for more than 80 percent of imports to the colonies in the third quarter of the century.[15]

The colonists' appetite for European culture and goods seemed insatiable. American architects copied models from English books. American magazines devoted their pages to informing their readers of the most recent mechanical developments in Europe. The practice of getting education in Europe was a prominent feature of late eighteenth-century America. More than half of the founders of the College of Physicians of Philadelphia were educated in Europe, primarily in Edinburgh and London, including future physicians of the Continental Army John Morgan and Benjamin Rush. The men who returned with this knowledge became the founding fathers of the American medical profession and turned Philadelphia into the medical capital of North America.[16]

Americans increasingly recognized their intellectual and technological deficit and looked to emulate Europe. Foreign origins became synonymous with superior quality. Advertisements in newspapers boasted of products made by English-trained artisans. Immigrants capitalized on the perception that superior products were made in Europe and by Europeans and demanded higher wages than natives. Upon their arrival many European artisans used their places of origin in their advertisements to distinguish themselves from local craftsmen. English migrants to Philadelphia, for example, looked for local investors to put up the necessary capital for erecting textile factories and promised that they were acquainted with the most recent European developments.[17] Peter Hasenclever, a German ironmaster, established in northern New Jersey the largest and most successful industrial enterprise in the colonies, which employed hundreds of skilled ironworkers he imported from Germany. Hasenclever resented his continued dependence on foreign workers. "They made bad work; I complained and reprimanded them; they told me they could not make better work at such low wages and, if they did not please me, I might dismiss them. I was, therefore, obligated to submit, for it had cost me a prodigious expense to transport them from Germany; and, had I dismissed them, I must have lost these disbursements, and could get no good workmen in their stead."[18]

Some investors decided to capitalize on the growing consumption of industrial goods in America and establish local manufacturing. Hindered by chronic labor shortages, entrepreneurs who sought to produce industrial goods in a competitive market environment scrambled for artisans who knew the most advanced and labor-saving production methods. Recruiting skilled industrial immigrants, however, was problematic. While European farm laborers came to the New World with a realistic expectation of improving their lot by becoming independent landowners, skilled workers were in high demand in industrializing Europe. A European craftsman who moved to the New World was, in effect, cutting himself off the professional network that had taught him his trade and sustained his status in the Old World. And since most masters in Europe were well compensated, few took the physical and economic risk of crossing the Atlantic and setting up shop in the colonies. Even those who came found duplicating European production processes next to impossible. The cost and risk of smuggling machinery hampered their ability to transport to America the equipment they had used in Europe. The raw materials in North America were sufficiently different to make exact duplication of seventeenth- and eighteenth-century technology very difficult. Since both chemistry and botany were in their infancy, materials were identified for the most part by where they came from. English ironmakers, for example, had little available charcoal and relied on Abraham Darby's discovery that coking coal could make it suitable to replace the needed charcoal. In the colonies, by contrast, there was plenty of wood for making charcoal. Since charcoal was far more fragile than coke, however, it would be difficult if not impossible for an immigrant to use English iron-making technology in New England. Every artisan depended on others who made the machinery he was familiar with, and since these supporting artisans hardly ever came along, migrants who wanted to continue as artisans in the colonies had to abandon their European specializations and become jacks-of-all-trades. Finally, unlike in Europe, land in the New World was readily available which tempted many to exchange their trades for farming.[19]

The most efficient carriers of innovative technology were the artisans who used such technology in Europe. Labor shortages, however, have been America's economic Achilles heel since the first settlers disembarked on its shores. Those eager to establish manufacturing in the colonies and looking for immigrant artisans to bring the most recent industrial European innovations to the New World had to come up with creative ways to stimulate artisans' interest in emigrating. Some relied on the duplicitous activities of unsavory characters. William Cunningham confessed just prior to his execution in London that in the 1770s he had worked at enticing English mechanics "to ship themselves for America, on promises of great advantage, and then, artfully getting an indenture upon them; in consequence of which, on their arrival in America they are sold or obliged to serve a term of years for the passage."[20] Most artisans, however, were not easily fooled and had to be persuaded to give up their middle-class life and status in Europe and endure the physical and emotional difficulties involved in migrating to the New World. Thus, colonial agents had to offer powerful inducements to offset the comforts and security of staying in Europe. American entrepreneurs and communities openly dangled handsome rewards in front of immigrants, placing advertisements in English newspapers to attract artisans willing to move to the colonies. The *New York Journal* reported in 1767 on the successful recruiting of thirteen "of the best" ironworkers from Sheffield, who came after they were offered a guaranteed salary for two years, a cash award for migrating, and day-to-day support for those whose families did not make the Atlantic crossing. English restrictions on the development of colonial glass manufacturing did not prevent colonial businessmen from placing want ads in English newspapers offering inducements to prospective skilled migrants. Thousands of artisans from the British Isles and northern Europe, sensing they could receive higher wages than in their native lands, migrated to the colonies in response to these advertisements. English workers, in particular, proved an adventurous lot, willing to trade their homes for better opportunities in the New World.[21]

The change from a symbiotic technological relationship between the metropolis and the peripheries in the seventeenth century to an antagonistic one in the eighteenth pitted the Board of Trade against colonial governments. Colonial legislatures refused to kowtow to dictates from London and openly challenged imperial industrial policy. Cognizant of America's industrial infancy, they promoted manufacturing not by protecting inventors, but by violating the rights of inventors in other countries, primarily England, and encouraging the introduction of European machinery and processes. Thomas Bernard, pastor of the First Church of Salem, told the

Boston Society for Encouraging Industry and Employing the Poor in 1758 that establishing manufacturing was the best way of providing alternative employment for the colony's growing class of landless poor. Alas, in order to develop such employment know-how was needed that was scarce on this side of the Atlantic. Bernard pointed out that it had "been found advantageous, to invite in industrious strangers" and called on the colony's leaders to encourage the immigration of skilled "*foreign Protestants.*"[22]

The most effective strategy available to colonial authorities was awarding patents of importation to introducers of new technologies. The colonies never adopted the practice of issuing patents exclusively to inventors and innovators. Pennsylvania, the center of colonial manufacturing in the eighteenth century, did not award patents to inventors before the Revolution. It did, however, award a £150 prize to two Englishmen who introduced a new secret method of manufacturing lead glass to the colony. There is little evidence that the colonists assigned the qualities of property to any kind of knowledge. Massachusetts was the only American province that gave some recognition to the principle of copyright. Colonial monopolies were generally designed to protect newly emerging industries and technologies, showing little regard to the intellectual property of inventors. Legislatures granted patents to men who introduced rather than invented technologies that could help struggling local industries. Connecticut, for example, ruled in 1715 that anyone who introduced previously unknown technology should be treated as an inventor. In 1728 the colony issued a ten-year patent grant to Samuel Higley and Joseph Dewey for introducing a process to "convert, change, or transmute common iron into good steel" because Higley was "the first that ever performed such an operation in America," and for "having obtained the perfect knowledge" and bringing it over. In 1753 the state awarded a fifteen-year patent monopoly to Jabez Hamelin and Elihu Chauncey for introducing a water-powered flax-dressing machine from Scotland and Ireland. The General Court of Massachusetts did not check into the validity of patentees' claim for originality, but rather formed committees that examined the usefulness of machines and processes to the colony. In 1750, for example, Benjamin Crabb received a ten-year patent monopoly for the production of candles out of crude spermaceti oil. Crabb, who imported the technique, promised to teach it to five local artisans, though he successfully concealed the process for over twenty years even from the center of North American whaling, the neighboring Nantucket. Rhode Island awarded its only colonial patent not to an inventor, but to James Lucena of Portugal for importing the technique of making Castile soap. [23]

The British colonies of North America underwent a profound transformation in the eighteenth century. In 1700 they were small outposts totaling about 250,000 people; half a century later there were 1,170,000 residents in the territory that was going to become the United States. And yet, while the economic and demographic boom generated optimism and confidence among the colonists, labor shortages continued to plague the economy of British North America. Colonial reliance on manufactured imports from England grew in spite of a concerted effort by private entrepreneurs and public agencies to develop American industries. Imperial authorities, for their part, feared that the economic boom in the colonies would undermine British industries' exclusive control of colonial markets. In 1756 the Board of Trade, in an effort to stem the rise of colonial manufacturing, banned the export of machines to the colonies. In the second half of the eighteenth century prominent Imperial officials grew alarmed by the "Numbers of our manufacturers [who] are shipping themselves off for the regions of America." February 1767 alone saw over a hundred skilled weavers emigrate to Boston and New York. From 1760 to 1775, 125,000 new immigrants came to North America from the British Isles. Finally, in 1774, a year before the outbreak of hostilities, the crown prohibited the emigration of mechanics to the colonies.[24]

Growing tensions between the metropolis and the peripheries fired up the competition between England and its North American colonies. In 1767 the governor of colonial New York tried to calm anxious members of the Board of Trade who feared the rise of local industry, informing them that "the price of Labour is so great in this part of the World, that it will always prove the greatest obstacle to any Manufactures attempted to be set up here, and the genius of the People in a Country where every one can have Land to work upon leads them so naturally into Agriculture, that it prevails over every other occupation." Far from accepting such assurances, imperial agents grew increasingly alarmed by rising American industry. General Thomas Gage, commander in chief of the British forces in North American from 1763 to 1775, worried that colonial manufacturing was getting too competitive and urged the British government to keep "the Settlers within reach of the Sea-Coast as long as we can; and to cramp their Trade as far as it can be done prudentially." American cities "flourish and increase by extensive Trade, Artisans and Mechanicks of all sorts are drawn thither, who Teach all sorts of Handicraft work before unknown in the Country, and they soon come to make for themselves what they used to import." Such enterprises, Gage warned, "must create Jealousy in an Englishman."[25]

The Battle over Technology and the American Revolution

As the imperial struggle approached, Americans increased their efforts to uncover the techniques and processes of English industry in order to compete successfully with the metropolis. Parliament's punitive measures in the years leading to the Revolution only encouraged the colonists to persist in their efforts to build local industries. Debates over the importation of technology took place in the context of the general discourse of the imperial crisis. Talk of republican simplicity, with its emphasis on separation from Europe and rejection of luxuries, that dominated revolutionary pamphlets did not stand in the way of pirating machinery and luring artisans. Efforts to raise the level of American technology were justified in terms of attaining economic independence, undermining the British hold on the American economy, and guaranteeing the maintenance of a high standard of living in the new nation. Political self-determination, economic independence, and technology piracy seemed to go hand in hand.

Restrictions on American manufacturing were embodied in the Navigation Acts which assigned the colonies the role of raw material producers in the imperial order. Adam Smith had warned in the *Wealth of Nations* that these measures are "impertinent badges of slavery imposed" upon the American colonists by "the groundless jealousy of the merchants and manufacturers of the mother country." Smith was certainly on the mark as far as the Americans were concerned. The colonists challenged the legitimacy of these acts from their early opposition to the Stamp Act onward. Daniel Dulany's attack on the Stamp Act, for example, charged that the mercantile restrictions made British industrial imports "dearer and not so good in quality," and declared the rising American manufacturing to be the "Symbol of Dignity, the badge of Virtue" of the new self-sufficient colonies. Such rhetoric was the standard staple of colonists' complaints in the coming decade of imperial discord.[26]

During the colonial era advocates of American manufacturing avoided openly challenging the Empire's restrictive industrial colonial policy. When a Society for the Promotion of Arts, Agriculture, and Economy was established in 1764 in New York, it announced that it would "encourage such Manufactures as will not interfere with those of England, and to promote such Growths and

Productions as may best Answer for Returns to Great Britain." Thus the society offered premiums to encourage agricultural and textile technologies. It operated a putting-out linen factory that survived for some eighteen months employing some three hundred workers. (Linen was considered nonprovocative because it challenged continental, rather than British, production.) Nevertheless, the colony's governor had to explain to the Board of Trade that the American linen production did not endanger British mercantile domination. He stated that "No more than fourteen Looms are employed in it, and it was established in order to give Bread to several poor families which were a considerable charge to the city." The society disbanded in the aftermath of the Stamp Act crisis. Meanwhile, in the early stages of the imperial crisis, the colonists distanced themselves from open challenges to British manufactures. "One of the principal arguments made into use by the enemies of our Colonies," wrote an anonymous pamphleteer in 1765, was "that the inhabitants of these settlements have already set up a number of Manufactures, which must not only render the alliance of the mother country still less and less necessary, but materially affect its interest to boot." The colonists, however, "never attempted to set up any Manufactories which could possibly obstruct the Interest of this Kingdom."[27]

As tensions between the metropolis and the colonies intensified, the British ministry reevaluated its industrial policy. Colonial borrowing and emulating of British technology challenged the basic principles of imperial mercantile policy. The Board of Trade requested in 1766 and 1768 that colonial governors prepare reports on all American manufacturing established since 1734. In 1774, in recognition that the colonies had become an economic adversary, Parliament prohibited the export of all textile machinery and tools to North America. A similar attitude emerged on the American side. The very same year the House of Burgesses directed Elisha and Robert White who set out to establish a woolen factory in Virginia to import skilled workers from England. Before the first shots of the Revolution were fired, as far as technology was concerned, Britain and the colonists considered each other a rival.[28]

The colonies rebelled just as the pace of industrialization and technological improvements picked up. Criticism of Britain's polarized society was a standard staple of revolutionary rhetoric. Propagandists often referred to the connection between the emerging industrial political economy and the social and economic inequality that accompanied it, pointing to English urban centers as a prime example of social inequality and human misery. At the same time these very critics could not help noticing the improved productivity of English manufacturing. Reports of English mechanical inventions greatly excited American projectors. Private correspondence and the public press were full of accounts of various new enterprises, from the famous steam-powered grist mill at Blackfriars Bridge in London to innovations in the textile industry. American newspapers and magazines often copied from English and French sources the latest news of technological innovations. Thus, just as they were trying to protect the New World from the corruption of the Old, many became enthusiastic supporters of the mechanization of American industry. Paradoxically, the very same revolutionaries who rejected British society and politics focused from the outset on importing Britain's technology and industry to the United States.[29]

The parliamentary legislation of the imperial crisis, from the Sugar Act to the Coercive Acts, stimulated efforts to develop local American manufactures. The revolutionaries rejected the efforts to restrict immigration, believing that, as Jefferson declared in 1774, "nature has given a right to all men" to leave "the country in which chance, not choice has placed them" for "new habitations." Nonimportation, the colonists' favorite anti-British measure prior to Lexington, and the successive British restrictions on American economic activities, brought about a spate of attempts to replace British with American goods. Societies were founded to encourage consumption of American products and rebellious governments encouraged the development of local industries. The Massachusetts Provincial Council declared in 1774 that it was necessary to develop local manufacturing in order "to render this state as independent of every other state as the nature of our country will admit." The economic difficulties of the period further stimulated efforts to encourage American manufacturing, the most prominent measure being the campaign to buy and wear American-made clothes. David Rittenhouse, whose standing in the American scientific community was second only to Franklin's, declared in 1775 that the importation of English manufactured goods hindered the development of American science. "Luxury and tyranny," he argued, "pretend at first to be the patrons of science and philosophy, but at length fail not effectually to destroy them." Intoxicated with the revolutionary rhetoric that portrayed the conflict as one between a corrupting Old World and the virtuous colonies, Rittenhouse called for severing all ties with Europe.[30]

The boycotts and nonimportation of British goods during the years of struggle brought with them the realization that the United States ought to become self-sufficient. As early as 1768, America's best-known physician, Benjamin Rush of Philadelphia, associated "encouraging American manufactures" with revenge on the "mother country." A year later he wrote from London in a letter published in the *Philadelphia Journal* on April 6, 1769: "There is but one expedient left whereby we can save our sinking country, and that is by encouraging American manufactures. Unless we do this, we shall be undone forever. There is scarce a necessary article or even a luxury of life but what might be raised and brought to perfection in some of our provinces." Rush recommended inviting "hundred of artificers of every kind . . . to come over from England and settle among us." In 1775 Rush was the honorary speaker at the founding of the United

Company of Philadelphia for Promoting American Manufactures, the first large-scale attempt at cotton manufacturing in America, which within a year of its launching already employed hundreds of workers. The company was founded on illegally appropriated British technology. Christopher Tully and Joseph Hague, immigrant artisans who illicitly made their way to Philadelphia and built the machinery for the company, each received fifteen pounds from the Pennsylvania legislature as a reward for introducing the hitherto restricted English technology. Such enterprises, Rush told his listeners, were necessary to achieve independence because "A People who are entirely dependant upon the foreigners for food or clothes, must always be subject to them."[31]

The end of British rule meant that the economic order that had dominated the North American colonies for over a century was no longer enforced. Independence engendered cultural nationalism with its demand that overthrowing the chains of the British Empire be extended to the spheres of science and technology. One of the benefits of independence, argued activist and future historian of the Revolution David Ramsay in 1778, was that without the restrictions of the metropolis, technology and the arts would "raise their drooping heads" and transform the New World into a technological paradise. Another writer complained that during the colonial period "we were dependent on Great Britain, her policy and laws restrain us as much as possible from manufacturing.—Even the great mr. Pitt, in one of his famous speeches, was against permitting so much as a hob-nail to be made in the colonies." Philadelphia patriot Timothy Matlack, speaking in 1780 before the American Philosophical Society, declared: "*British* Tyranny restrained us from making of Steel, to enrich her Merchants and Manufacturers." The meaning of independence, Matlack continued, was that "we can now make it ourselves as good as theirs." And Hugh Williamson of North Carolina implored his countrymen: "Let us turn our attention to manufactures. . . . instead

FIGURE 1. Benjamin Rush (1745–1813). Portrait by Charles Willson
Peale, 1783. Rush was a physician, a professor of chemistry at the College of Philadelphia, a spokesman for the revolutionary cause, and an
activist for various humanitarian causes, from antislavery to education
and prison reform. In the second half of the eighteenth century even
Americans of Rush's standing, reputation and virtue openly advocated
technology piracy. Courtesy of the Winterthur Museum, Winterthur,
Delaware.

of toiling in the field, and becoming poor, that we may enrich the manufacturers of other countries, we shall prosper by our own labour, and enrich our own citizens."[32]

In the early days of the Revolution, proponents of manufactures had hoped that the self-evident advantages of life in the New World would attract many skilled immigrants. Robert Styrettel Jones believed that immigrants would flock to America because "Empire and the arts have been long taking their western tour, and in all their progress have yet found no shore so suitable as this, upon which to fix their lasting residence." Thomas Paine declared in *Common Sense* that "our knowledge is hourly improving." Travelers' accounts of the high standard of living and economic possibilities in the New World encouraged European migration. One of the most widely read texts of this genre was Hector St. John de Crèvecoeur's *Letters from an American Farmer*. Crèvecoeur came to North America in 1765 and after the Revolution became the French consul in New York. The New World, he declared in 1782, "has so many charms, and presents to Europeans so many temptations to remain in it." An immigrant never felt like a foreigner because he could find in the United States all the varieties of European climate and culture. A skilled artisan who chose to immigrate could "expect to be immediately hired, well fed at the table of his employer, and paid four or five times more than he can get in Europe."[33]

During the war, revolutionary leaders naturally recognized that acquiring technology could speed up the attainment of economic independence. Many of the states subsidized iron factories and urged a speed-up in the production of linens and woolens. Fortunately for the war effort, women in New England and the Mid-Atlantic states had by the 1770s mastered homespun techniques to prevent severe shortages. The British seemed equally aware of this dimension of the conflict. When John Hewson, America's first calico printer, escaped from English custody after he was taken prisoner in the battle of Monmouth, the British offered fifty guineas for information leading to his recapture because they knew of his value to American manufacturing.[34]

Leaders of the war effort recognized the need to privilege industrialization. Workers engaged in the production of iron were exempted from army service. John Jay, for example, believed that taxes should be collected in the form of "salt petre, wool or yarn" so as to "encourage manufactures." The Privy Council's 1774 prohibition on the exportation of gunpowder created severe munitions shortages. Congress launched an aggressive campaign to produce saltpeter, gunpowder's key constituent. Jay, for one, was pleased with the "encouragement given . . . to the manufacture of arms, powder, salt petre and sea-salt." The patriotic effort was echoed by the various states that through a variety of subsidies tried to promote the creation of an American munitions industry. Alas, efforts during the Revolutionary war to build up American iron and munitions manufacturing were frustrated by persistent labor shortages. The Continental Congress resolved in November 1777 to instruct U.S. representatives in Europe to entice "two or three persons, well acquainted with the making of gun-flints" to migrate to America so that they could "instruct persons in that business, and introduce into these states so useful a manufacture." Patriotic intellectuals also tried to help. Benjamin Rush published an essay on the making of saltpeter, reporting on manufacturing processes in Europe and calling for their emulation. Newspapers and magazines published detailed instructions, written by leading American scientific and technological authorities, on how to make saltpeter and gunpowder. In all these official measures and private initiatives, the theme of American technological difficulties and the need to emulate European technology was constant.[35]

The outbreak of hostilities sealed the transformation in the industrial relationship between Britain and its North American colonies. The symbiosis of the early years gave way to a hostile competition over skilled workers and industrial know-how. By the time the shots heard around the world were fired in Concord and Lexington in April 1775, improving the level of American technology through the "illegal" appropriation of England's protected industrial technology became a prominent feature of the struggle for political and economic independence.

CHAPTER 3

Benjamin Franklin and America's Technology Deficit

I n 1784, shortly after concluding the peace treaty with England, Benjamin Franklin published in France a short pamphlet entitled *Information to Those Who Would Remove to America*, advising those planning to immigrate that opportunities in the New World were limited. Why did the man who celebrated America's demographic boom for much of his life, and who had a very high opinion of economic opportunities in the New World, write such a discouraging pamphlet? Franklin explained that numerous prospective emigrants had approached him with questions and requests that attested to their "mistaken ideas and expectations of what is to be obtained there." These men imagined that Americans were "rich, capable of rewarding, and disposed to reward, all sorts of ingenuity; that they [Americans] are . . . ignorant of all the sciences; and consequently, that strangers, possessing talents in the belles-lettres, fine arts, &c. must be highly esteemed, and so well paid, as to become easily rich themselves." The pamphlet set out to correct once and for all these "wild Imaginations."

Franklin directed his discouraging remarks at one particular group: European manufacturers. The United States, he explained, did not follow the practice of European princes who offered high salaries and privileges to manufacturers to induce them to migrate and introduce hitherto unknown advanced industrial technology. Many artisans had approached Franklin believing that America's industrial underdevelopment would allow them to condition their migration on receiving various advantages from Congress and the states. They demanded transportation subsidies, land grants, and salaried government positions in exchange for their industrial skills. But "Congress have no power committed to them, or money put into their hands for such purposes." All in all, the pamphlet encouraged hardworking Europeans willing to engage in agriculture and home manufacturing to emigrate, and discouraged those with dreams of English-like industrialization.[1]

For artisans expecting that the separation of the agricultural colonies from the industrializing mother country would open up great opportunities to migrate and accumulate wealth, the words of America's most prominent spokesman must have sounded very disappointing. The new country, he declared, was not about to follow the European practice of offering inducements to entice skilled artisans.

Benjamin Franklin was the preeminent intellectual of the American Enlightenment. He had been an outspoken champion of American science and technology since the middle of the eighteenth century. As early as 1751 he wrote in "Observations Concerning the Increase of Mankind" that those who "invent new Trades, Arts or Manufactures . . . may be properly called Fathers of their Nation."[2] He recognized the infant state of American manufactures and their technological deficiencies, and neither ruled out technology piracy nor urged his countrymen to respect European prohibitions on the diffusion of technology. Yet, while aware of the degree of American technological dependence on England, first as a loyal subject and later as a patriotic American, Franklin did not succumb to the nationalist view of knowledge and never became a technology protectionist. Franklin thus stands for the path not taken by the young republic, in which science and technology were constructed in the universalist tradition as the shared property of mankind.

The Pro-Development Colonist

The organizing principle of the economy of the British Empire in the eighteenth century centered on the accumulation of skilled laborers in England capable of producing manufactured goods that could profitably be traded in the world market. To maintain the status quo the colonies had to remain producers of raw materials rather than of finished goods. And for much of the colonial era the system worked. Franklin's earliest experience as an adult taught him the extent of American dependence on English knowhow. His brother James, in whose shop Franklin learned the secrets of the printing trade, had to go to England to purchase printing presses and fonts of type, since none were manufactured in the colonies. Later on, when Franklin traveled through Europe in his various official capacities, he wrote to his American correspondents detailed descriptions of the technologies he came across and urged their adoption in America.[3]

As tensions between the colonists and the mother country came to the forefront in the 1760s Franklin recognized that news of American industrialization would only play into the hands of those in Britain favoring a stronger crackdown in the colonies. He was thus displeased with triumphant declarations of the type that appeared in the London *Complete Magazine* in August 1764: "Some beautiful samples of the cotton manufactures, now carried on at Philadelphia, have been lately imported and greatly admired." He sought to assure British manufacturers that the development of home manufacturing in the colonies would not decrease colonial consumption of English clothing. The colonists "wear the manufactures of Britain," he wrote to the *London Chronicle,* "and follow its fashions perhaps too closely, every remarkable change in the mode making its appearance there within a few months after its invention here." He urged his son, New Jersey governor William Franklin, to downplay the quality of clothing produced in the colony so that the ire of those in Parliament bent on restricting American manufactures would not be aroused. "You have only to report a glass-house for coarse window glass and bottles and some domestic manufactures of linen and woolen for family use, that do not half clothe the inhabitants." Assure Parliament, he recommended, that "all finer goods" were still being imported from Britain.[4]

In 1751, just as he entered the Pennsylvania Assembly to begin his glorious public career, Franklin wrote a brief pamphlet entitled "Observations Concerning the Increase of Mankind." The piece has since attracted a good deal of scholarly attention. Some analysts have marveled at Franklin's sophisticated demographic analysis—he observed that the population of the British colonies of North America doubled every twenty years whereas that of England remained stable, and he predicted, quite accurately as it turned out, the future demographic growth of British North America. Others have focused on the last passage of the pamphlet in which Franklin complained that immigrants were contaminating the Englishness of the colonies and made a rather astonishing declaration of his strong personal preference for white people. However, Franklin wrote his controversial pamphlet neither as a theoretical treatise on colonial demography nor as an exclusionary ethnic manifesto, but as a specific political argument against the Iron Act of 1750 which restricted the construction of new rolling and slitting mills in America. The act did not seek to destroy the manufacturing of iron in America, but to steer colonial pig and bar iron to British mills. The crux of Franklin's essay was not its xenophobic concluding paragraph but its advocacy of the free movement of technology across the Atlantic. Franklin sought to ease English fears that the development of industry in America would result in colonial industrial self-sufficiency and loss of market share for English manufacturers. Britain had no reason to fear that its colonies would become its industrial competitors because manufacturing depended on cheap labor. Men turned to such grueling and low-paying jobs only when agricultural opportunities were exhausted. Restricting the development of industry in North America was unnecessary because "Labour will never be cheap here," as no land shortage could be anticipated in the foreseeable future. In 1764, shortly after the conclusion of the French and Indian War, Franklin turned to mockery to protest the British restriction of American industrial development. Writing to the Englishman Peter Collinson, a close scientific associate, he reported the "discovery" of a beach in which all the pebbles were "in the form of buttons, whence it is called Button Mould Bay." Alas, Franklin would not disclose the location of this magic beach "lest some Englishman get a Patent for this Button-mine as one did for the Coal mine at Louisburgh, and by neither suffering others to work it, not working it himself, deprive us of the Advantage God and Nature seem to have intended us. As we have now got Buttons, 'tis something towards our Clothing; and who knows but in time we may find out where to get Cloth?" Turning serious, Franklin argued that it was "Folly to expect" that "your little Island" would continue to be the sole supplier of the rapidly growing North American colonial consumer market. "Nature has put Bounds to your Abilities, tho' none to your Desires. Britain would, if she could, manufacture and trade for all the World; England for all Britain; London for all England; and every Londoner for all London. So selfish is the human Mind!"[5] A few years later, while representing the colonies in London, Franklin warned that attempts of the metropolis to restrict colonial economic growth might backfire. The regulations would undermine the colonies' meteoric demographic boom, thereby checking American demand for

British manufactures. It was in the interest of the Empire to allow its colonies to import the industrial technology of the mother country. Rather than rejecting European political economy on account of the tyranny and social polarization it generated, Franklin believed that the future development of North America depended on its ability to acquire and apply European industrial know-how. He was wholly committed to the ethos of technological emulation.[6]

Franklin distinguished between the piracy of innovations by individuals belonging to the same jurisdictions and the diffusion of technology across jurisdictional boundaries. In taking over the *Pennsylvania Gazette* in 1729 he set out to communicate and advertise innovations that "may contribute either to the Improvement of our present Manufactures, or towards the Invention of new Ones." In 1743, in arguing for the establishment of an Association for the Promotion of Knowledge in Philadelphia, he wrote that "many useful Particulars remain uncommunicated, die with the Discoverers, and are lost to Mankind." The proposed association set out to facilitate communication about, among other things, "New Mechanical Inventions for saving Labour." Franklin's past as a printer conditioned him to think of information in such a manner. American newspapers, including his *Pennsylvania Gazette,* routinely reprinted news stories from European papers without acknowledging the sources. The need to circulate information in the colonial setting superseded all notions of intellectual property.[7]

Franklin backed up his rhetoric with action in favor of free dissemination of technology. In 1740 Franklin designed a wood-burning stove that was supposed to fit inside a fireplace. The new design consumed far less wood and generated more heat than existing stoves. The governor of Pennsylvania offered Franklin exclusive rights to sell the stove he developed provided he registered it as a patent. For ideological reasons Franklin declined to capitalize on his invention. "*As we enjoy great Advantages from the Inventions of others,"* he explained, *"we should be glad of an Opportunity to serve others by any Invention of ours, and this we should do freely and generously."* He went on to publish a detailed sketch of his invention in 1744. Franklin, who dedicated his retirement years to appearing as a generous-minded gentleman, could afford such largess, but a London artisan who, as Franklin later learned, patented the stove and made "a little Fortune by it" abused his generosity. This episode, he concluded in his autobiography, was "not the only Instance of Patents taken out for my Inventions by others . . . which I never contested, as having no Desire of profiting by Patents my self, and hating Disputes."[8]

Like many eighteenth-century intellectuals, Franklin did not draw a clear distinction between science and technology. Proud of the practical applications of his discoveries, he saw technology as a derivative of science. Just as the international exchange among scientists advanced science everywhere, so would the dissemination of technological know-how encourage mechanical improvements in every nation. "The rapid progress true Science now makes," he wrote in 1780, "occasions my regretting sometimes that I was born so soon." He fantasized about a future when technological advances would free man from gravity and cure all illnesses, and when agriculture would demand less labor and double its productivity. National and geographical boundaries played no role in this vision. Science through technology was the medium through which Franklin expected universal social and moral improvement.[9]

Franklin could afford to declare: "I have no private Interest in the Reception of my Inventions by the World, having never made nor proposed to make the least Profit by any of them." After all, by the time he was forty-two years old he was rich enough to retire and devote himself to political and intellectual pursuits. Yet Franklin recognized that most inventors were not in his position and that in order to encourage innovation, societies ought to reward individual

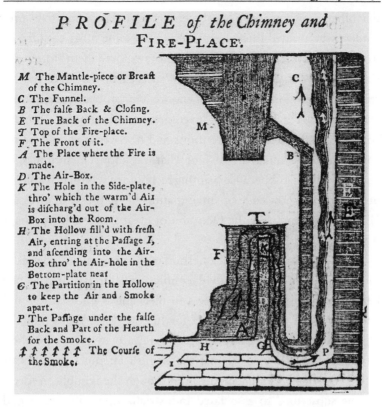

PROFILE of the Chimney and FIRE-PLACE.

M The Mantle-piece or Breaſt of the Chimney.
C The Funnel.
B The falſe Back & Cloſing.
E True Back of the Chimney.
T Top of the Fire-place.
F The Front of it.
A The Place where the Fire is made.
D The Air-Box.
K The Hole in the Side-plate, thro' which the warm'd Air is diſcharg'd out of the Air-Box into the Room.
H The Hollow fill'd with freſh Air, entring at the Paſſage I, and aſcending into the Air-Box thro' the Air-hole in the Bottom-plate near
G The Partition in the Hollow to keep the Air and Smoke apart.
P The Paſſage under the falſe Back and Part of the Hearth for the Smoke.
↑ ↑ ↑ ↑ ↑ The Courſe of the Smoke.

FIGURE 2. Franklin's stove diagram, 1744. The publication of the diagram manifested Franklin's commitment to sharing his inventions with the public rather than profiting from establishing an ownership claim over them. Reproduced from Benjamin Franklin, *An Account of the new-invented Pennsylvania fire-places* (Philadelphia 1744). Courtesy of the Library Company of Philadelphia.

inventors. Widespread access to mechanical improvements, then, must not come at the expense of appropriate compensation for the inventor. He bemoaned the plight of inventors who met much scorn and doubt when they published the products of their genius. "There are everywhere a number of people," he explained, "who being totally destitute of inventive faculty themselves, do not readily conceive that others may possess it." Most men considered inventors to be pretenders who pirated their inventions "from some other country or from some book." The failures of inventors exposed them "to general ridicule and contempt." When they succeeded, they received no reward and recognition, but must endure "envy, robbery, and abuse." His sympathy for the plight of inventors notwithstanding, Franklin continued to believe that inventions and discoveries should be recorded and disseminated. Much of what was known in antiquity, he wrote, had been lost because printing technology was unavailable. In our time "the knowledge of small matters being presrv'd, gives the Hint that is sometimes the Occasion of great Discoveries, perhaps Ages after."[10]

Franklin's approach to the question of the physical boundaries of intellectual property embodied conflicting strands. On the one hand, he favored universal access to mechanical information and had renounced possible rewards for his own inventions. On the other hand he recognized the need to reward inventors for their efforts. He campaigned against the English attempts to suffocate infant American manufacturing even though the republican ideology he subscribed to associated industrialization with social and moral degeneracy. He feared that the technological backwardness of the United States was undermining the peace and prosperity of the young nation, and championed the development of local industry. At the same time, he criticized the social consequences of English industrialization and believed that an agricultural economy could protect North America from following in the footsteps of the corrupt and unjust Hanoverian monarchy. These conflicting approaches came to a head in the debate over immigration.

For most of the colonial period, official British policy encouraged raiding continental Europe for migrants to North America. Parliament and the crown allocated substantial sums to assist Protestant refugees. Alarmed by the outflow of people, every eighteenth-century European government enacted anti-emigration laws. Unfavorable travelers' accounts were published to discourage those who might consider moving to North America. One such tract warned prospective migrants that economic distress often forced German immigrants to "give away their minor children" who "never see or meet their fathers, mothers, brothers, or sisters again." Those who "suffer themselves to be persuaded and enticed away by the man-thieves," it cried, would join the miserable and wretched life of other German immigrants. In Germany, rulers required that emigrants get permission to leave and demanded payment for the right to be free of feudal lords. These efforts failed to stem the tide, as some 125,000 German immigrants came to North America in the eighteenth century.[11]

From the British perspective, the restrictions on the migration of skilled artisans which had been on the books since the late seventeenth century applied only to artisans moving to foreign countries. Since the colonies were considered an integral part of the Empire, there were no constitutional grounds to prevent English artisans from settling in America. Yet, the crown and Parliament realized that allowing the colonies to develop their industrial technology could undermine the foundations of the mercantile arrangement. Parliament began in 1718 to pass legislation to curb the migration of artisans to the colonies. The centrality of workers to technology diffusion meant that unless the migration of skilled artisans was halted, British efforts to check colonial industrial development were doomed.[12]

Technological breakthroughs in Britain coincided with the rising tensions between the colonies and the metropolis. James Hargreaves's spinning jenny and Richard Arkwright's water frame, developed and patented in the late 1760s, signaled the new age of industrial innovation just after the 1763 Peace of Paris, which concluded the French and Indian War, cemented England's position as the dominant European power and simultaneously marked the beginning of the conflict between Parliament and the North American colonies.[13] And as the metropolis and peripheries evolved from complementary parts of a single whole into political adversaries, British writers and politicians began to question the wisdom of allowing emigration. English writers recognized that England had reached its dominant industrial position largely because it had managed to entice foreign workers to immigrate. Robert Wallace, for example, writing in 1764, attributed Britain's powerful international standing to its absorption of skilled French immigrants. The Protestant artisans expelled by Louis XIV "made a prodigious addition to the trade and manufactures of England, and was to France such an error in politicks, that it will probably never recover." He urged the crown not to allow this pattern to repeat itself in its relations with its North American colonies. Some unfavorable travelers' accounts were published to discourage migration. A reverend who had sojourned in the middle colonies in 1759–60 announced that while he had found a certain degree of happiness, the idea that the heart of the British Empire was moving westward "was illusory and fallacious."[14]

On the political front, the earl of Hillsborough, who in 1763 became the president of the Board of Trade and in 1768 the secretary of state for the colonies, set out to stop emigration to America. Hillsborough was obsessed with depopulation of the countryside. The owner of nearly 100,000 acres of agricultural land in Ireland, Hillsborough worried about losing cheap labor to America. Others in London were less concerned with the departure of farm workers and more with maintaining the division of economic roles between the colonies and the metropolis. One English writer, for example, opposed the Stamp Act because it was a general tax on the North American colonies rather than a specific measure that assured continued employment and prosperity in the British Isles. He warned that "we daily see many of our Manufacturers and useful People getting on that side of the Water." Thus the most prudent policy was not taxing the colonists, but "to favor their Industry in every Way but manufacturing, and securing to ourselves the Fruits thereof, by furnishing them with our Manufactures on cheaper Terms than they can procure them elsewhere." By the early 1770s, some Englishmen feared, as one Yorkshire writer warned, that unless something was done "England will really be drained of multitudes of mechanics of all sorts."[15]

As the debate over the imperial crisis intensified, discussion in Parliament in November 1773 centered on the problem of emigration. Fears that emigrants from continental Europe fueled separatist tendencies in the colonies led the ministry to issue an order in council forbidding all naturalization of such emigrants. As to emigration from the British Isles, instead of passing an act to restrict it, Parliament undertook to examine the phenomenon. The resulting study concluded that England was rapidly losing men of skill to the colonies.[16] Restrictionist sentiment intensified. Josiah Child wrote in 1775 that because wool is the foundation of the English riches, all possible means ought to be used to keep it "within our own kingdom," and he hoped Parliament will enact "severe laws to prevent" the exportation of skilled wool artisans and their machinery. After fighting between the colonies and Britain erupted, the lord advocate of Scotland, Henry Dundas, ordered his port authorities not to give clearance to vessels suspected of carrying emigrants to the rebellious colonies.[17]

Franklin participated in the debates over emigration even before they reached the forefront of British politics. In his "Observations Concerning the Increase of Mankind" he argued that the Imperial government ought not to interfere with emigration because those leaving were being naturally replaced. "A Nation well regulated is like a Polypus; take away a Limb, its Place is soon supply'd." In London, representing the North American colonies, Franklin's

successful campaign against Hillsborough's anti-emigration initiatives forced the latter to resign from his post as secretary of state for
the colonies. When it seemed as if Parliament was ready to enact
restrictions, Franklin mocked it in the pages of the *Public Advertiser,*
suggesting that the surest way to "put a stop to the emigrations from
this country now grown so very fashionable" was to castrate all
American men so that potential male immigrants would realize that
moving to America would cost them their manhood.[18]

But Franklin did not take the new initiative lightly. He prepared a
public response to those calling for a check on emigration to North
America and planned to submit it to the London's *Public Advertiser,*
which had published an account of the proposed bill on November 16, 1773. In his rebuttal Franklin explained that restricting the
flow of immigrants across the Atlantic was as practical as "calling for
a Law to stop the Thames, lest its Waters, by what leave it daily at
Gravesend, should be quite exhausted." The real cause of migration
was the widespread misery in England and Scotland. The solution
should be improving the lot of the people, not turning the British
Isles into jails. "God has given to the Beasts of the Forest and to the
Beasts of the Air a Right when their subsistence fails in one Country,
to migrate into another, where they can get a more comfortable
Living; and shall Man be denied a Privilege enjoyed by Brutes,
merely to gratify a few avaricious Landlords?" Franklin, thus, considered the free choice of where to live and work a natural right.[19]

Occasionally Franklin got involved in the direct recruiting of
artisans. In 1765, for example, he complained of the "Difficulty here
to meet with good Workmen and sober that [are] willing to go
abroad." He often complied with requests for introductory letters
for industrial immigrants. He asked the prominent Philadelphian
Richard Bache to assist a migrating tanner to establish himself in the
New World.[20] In the 1770s he reported to American associates on
English and Dutch canal technologies and recommended the re-

cruitment of an experienced engineer to plan and supervise the construction of a canal in Philadelphia. Franklin's most important venture in this field involved the migration of John Hewson, who introduced the British technology of calico printing and bleaching to the colonies. Rumors of Hewson's upcoming move excited the American press. The *Pennsylvania Gazette* reported on January 30, 1772, that "a person who has for many Years been a master in several large manufactories for linen, cotton and Calico printing . . . intends some Time this month to leave England for America with six Journeymen and all Materials for carrying on the said Business." The paper added that "unknown to English manufacturers," Hewson had shipped prohibited machinery to America, and concluded: "A manufactory of this kind will doubtless be encouraged by wellwishers to America." Two and a half years later Hewson announced in the same paper that he had opened a shop in Philadelphia, which was technologically on a par with the latest British calico printing and bleaching technologies. Franklin actively encouraged Hewson to move to the colonies and after the latter made up his mind, Franklin recommended him to leading men in Philadelphia and New York.[21]

Nationalist Republican

To conceive of American national intellectual property in the eighteenth century one had to think first in terms of a collective American identity. More than any other man of his generation, Franklin stands for the best in the burgeoning new nation and its culture. Author of the 1754 Albany plan for intercolonial cooperation during the French and Indian War and supposed originator of the revolutionary call "we all must hang together or we will hang separately," Franklin searched persistently for continental North American unity throughout his public service career. After the outbreak of

Dr. Benjamin Franklin, in the month of July, 1773, who was then in the city of London, present-ing to Captain John Hewson letters of address to General Roberdeau and several other gentlemen of the cities of Philadelphia and New York.

FIGURE 3. Contemporary illustration of Benjamin Franklin giving let-ters of introduction to John Hewson. Technology smugglers like Hewson approached American representatives in Europe and asked for financial support and for letters of introduction to potential American investors. Hewson gained much credibility from advertising that he had the backing of Benjamin Franklin. Reproduced from *A Brief History of the Revolution: with a Sketch of the Life of Captain John Hewson, Including the Constitution of the United States, a Statistical View of the Grand Federal Procession, Mr. Wilson's Oration: Washington's Farewell Address, &c. &c.* (Philadelphia, 1843). Courtesy of the Franklin Collection, Yale University Library, New Haven, Conn.

the Revolutionary War, Franklin assumed the role of the nation's preeminent statesman in Europe, the only arena where the United States truly behaved as a collectivity until 1789. He was, in short, the standard bearer of protonationalist consciousness in America.[22]

Franklin's nationalism, however, evolved in a rather dramatic way. Before he went to London for the second time in 1764 he was an enthusiastic British patriot who followed the ethnically exclusive linguistic-based English nationalist model.[23] His "Observations Concerning the Increase of Mankind" is one of the earliest conceptualizations of the North American colonies as a coherent unit. Yet Franklin concluded this short and brilliant social and demographic analysis of the colonies with an ethnic exclusionary outburst: "The Number of purely white People in the World is proportionally very small. All Africa is black or tawny. Asia chiefly tawny. America (exclusive of the new Comers) wholly so. And in Europe, the Spaniards, Italians, French, Russians, and Swedes, are generally of what we call a swarthy complexion; as are the Germans also, the Saxons only excepted who with the English make the principle Body of White People on the Face of the Earth. . . . Perhaps I am partial to the complexion of my Country," he conceded, yet "such partiality is natural to Mankind."[24] In the next decade and a half the number of German immigrants who flocked to Pennsylvania alarmed Franklin. When he was a young printer he had supported German-language newspapers, and even had his own *Pennsylvania Gazette* translated into German. In the 1760s, however, he joined the Anti-Propriety party, which sought to control German immigration. The 1764 Pennsylvania elections pitted Franklin and his party against the original Quaker proprietors of the colony. Franklin's party stood for English homogeneity while his opponents symbolized the civic inclusiveness of the emerging America by running on its eight-man slate two Germans and one Scots-Irishman.[25]

Thereafter Franklin traveled to London, where his opposition to imperial measures slowly eroded both his English patriotism and his ethnic conceptualization of American identity. His presentation to the House of Commons of the American arguments against the Stamp Act established him as the voice of the American colonies. Snubbed by the British elite who could not accept the self-made man from the colonies as their equal, Franklin found his social niche among Scots and Quaker radicals and dissenters. He was embittered by the descriptions of the colonists in London's newspapers as a "mixed rabble of Scotch, Irish and foreign vagabonds, descendants of convicts, ungrateful rebels &c."[26] By 1770, Franklin represented a cross-section of the North American colonies, from Georgia to Massachusetts, and had come to view the colonies as having an identity and interest that differed from those of the mother country. Imperial measures, from the Stamp Act to the closing of the port of Boston, encountered little opposition in Parliament because they expressed a newly developed British nationalist consensus that transcended domestic rivalries. Indeed, the reign of George III saw an unusual display of British political unity as the ministry was formed of both Whigs and Tories and the monarch projected himself as the embodiment of the new patriotism. The colonies were defined out of the new nationalist consensus. In the eyes of British patriots, the colonists became, as Franklin put it, not "fellow subjects, but subjects of subjects."[27]

The man who returned to Philadelphia had come to conceive American identity in a civic and inclusive manner. He who in the 1750s and 1760s feared the declining Englishness of Pennsylvania was calmly projecting in 1783 "great Emigrations from England, Ireland, and Germany." Franklin also reread his 1751 pamphlet on population as a celebration of immigration, for "every Man who comes among us and takes up a piece of Land" adds to the nation's strength. Franklin's tenure in Europe transformed him from an ethnic to a civic nationalist.[28]

Nations, however, are not made of mere civic abstractions. A collective identity is but a fiction without a cohesive, integrated state and economy marked by effective internal communication. When writing for foreign consumption revolutionary Americans declared that "Our union is perfect." Below the surface, however, the founders worried about the disintegration of the confederation, which lacked political, cultural, and economic bonds. As Franklin wrote in 1760, the colonies "are not only under different governors, but have different forms of government, different laws, different interests, and some of them different religious persuasions and different manners. Their jealousy of each other is so great that however necessary an union of the colonies has long been . . . they have never been able to effect such an union among themselves, nor even to agree in requesting the mother country to establish it for them."[29] Anxious that factious and divided colonial society were incompatible with political stability and nationhood, Franklin believed that economic growth and transregional interdependence were the surest route to unification. But what kind of growth and interdependence? Agriculture heightened regional competitive tensions within the confederation. Commercial activity was accompanied by a high degree of dependence on British mercantile houses. Turning his back on traditional mercantilism, Franklin favored liberalizing trade and encouraging the growth of domestic manufactures. Properly managed industrial development promised to glue the different regions and interests of North America together while launching the young nation toward independence and self-sufficiency.[30]

The sharp rise in colonial consumption of English manufactured goods in the second half of the eighteenth century redefined imperial relations. Consumption allowed women and men of the common people to assert their equality with the gentry. Standardized goods themselves created a common colonial vocabulary. Yet, many were alarmed by the acquisitiveness, selfishness, and cruelty of the new order. Parliamentary measures which targeted consumption politicized the American public and reinvigorated the movement to establish home manufacturing. News of the Townshend Revenue Act of June 29, 1767, for example, revived the faltering American Society for Promoting and Propagating Useful Knowledge.

The colonists' weapon of choice in their battle with England—the boycott of British manufactured goods—tied independence and prosperity to industrial self-sufficiency.[31] When nonimportation and nonconsumption of British manufactured goods were adopted in the late 1760s, the development of home industries became part of the patriotic struggle for freedom. A Massachusetts poet put this new attitude into verse:

> Boston, behold the pretty Spinners here
> And see how gay the pretty Sparks appear:
> See Rich and Poor all turn the Spinning Wheel,
> All who Compassion for their Country feel,
> All who do love to see Industry live,
> And see Frugality in Boston thrive.[32]

As Edinburgh-educated physician and scientist Cadwalader Evans wrote from Philadelphia, "no country . . . can subsist without some manufactures. I am very confident [we] cannot in Pennsylvania, and till we manufacture more than we do, we shall never be able to pay [our] debts."[33]

Franklin, however, did not wholly share these sentiments. He recognized the superior know-how of English workers and urged Americans to develop their own industry. At the conclusion of the French and Indian War, for example, he praised England's superior "sensible, virtuous and elegant minds," that made victory possible and predicted that following peace British know-how would "travel westwards. You have effectually defended us in this glorious war," he declared, "and in time you will improve us." In 1771 Franklin predicted that English clothing production would not be able to keep up with America's demographic boom and therefore America must develop its own textile industry. A few months later he rejected the anxieties of agriculturalists who feared the development of American manufactures might come at their expense, explaining that industrial enterprises raised the value of adjacent land, and it was "therefore the Interest of all our Farmers and Owners of lands, to encourage our young Manufacturers in preference to foreign ones imported among us from distant countries."[34]

It was precisely because Franklin recognized the frailty of both union and independence that he understood the need to create an integrated North American economy. To be sure, Franklin was prone, like many of his revolutionary compatriots, to make statements about the ethical superiority of farming and about the need to preserve the virtuous colonial agricultural political economy. England, he explained to a Philadelphia friend, "is fond of Manufactures beyond their real value," and he insisted that only "Agriculture is truly *productive* of *new wealth*" while "Riches are not *increased* by Manufacturing." In 1771 Franklin toured the mill towns of England and Scotland, saw much misery and poverty, and concluded that England's industrial production was "pinch'd off the Backs and out of the Bellies of the miserable Inhabitants." Franklin's 1784 pamphlet against migration similarly echoed republican clichés about the relationship between morality and agriculture. He declared: "Great establishments of manufactures, require great numbers of poor to work for small wages; these poor are to be found in Europe, but will not be found in America, till the lands are all taken up and cultivated, and the excess of people, who cannot get land, want employment."[35]

Yet, Franklin's republicanism was tempered by his recognition that the construction of an integrative, self-sufficient North American economy depended on industrial development. True, Franklin attacked England's political economy as the imperial conflict intensified, but his rejection of urban and industrial political economy did not transcend the context of the struggle between the metropolis and its colonies. As the conflict between the colonies and London intensified he confidently told members of Parliament: "I do not know a single article imported into the northern colonies, but what they can either do without or make themselves." Shortly after peace with England was signed he asked from Paris: "Is not the Hope of one day being able to purchase and enjoy Luxuries a great Spur to Labour and Industry? . . . without such a Spur People would be, as they are naturally enough inclined to be, lazy and indolent." Franklin's lead essay in the first issue of Mathew Carey's *American Museum* assaulted the thesis that the United States must remain wholly agricultural and dependent for its manufactures on imports. He was, in other words, hardly an agrarian idealist.[36]

Franklin's inconsistent statements on the future of manufacturing in republican America, which were quite typical of the revolutionary generation, betray his inner conflict over the question of encouraging the forbidden transfer of industrial technology. The moralist who associated industrial production with oppressive exploitation of England's poor inhabitants was an unlikely advocate of introducing a similar order to the New World. The patriot who believed American economic and political independence was contingent upon weaning itself from its dependence on British industrial production, however, opposed emigration restrictions and favored the introduction of technologies that were likely to make the young nation self-sufficient.[37] The abundance of land in America mediated between these conflicting approaches. Americans would not be forced to pile on top of one another in inhumane urban conditions because men could always opt for the life of independent yeomen. The transfer of manufacturing technology could thus ensure the country's economic independence without the risk of emulating the horrible conditions in England's industrial towns.

Without prosperity the confederation that defeated the British Empire could disintegrate. Imaginary bucolic fantasies aside, Franklin realized that the republican model was inherently counterdevelopmental. He understood that the civic construction of American identity depended on a political economy balanced between agriculture, commerce, and industry. Since the newly independent nation did not have the know-how and machinery to compete with British industry, America had to import them from Europe. Franklin's next great national assignment as the preeminent representative of the independent United States in Europe placed him at the axis of the politics and diplomacy of technology diffusion.

The Besieged Diplomat

Franklin's American stay between his missions to London and Paris was brief. On September 26, 1776, he was appointed to a three-man delegation headed for Europe to negotiate commercial agreements with European powers. Shortly thereafter, with the war going poorly for the American rebels, Franklin was put in charge of securing the diplomatic and military alliance of France. The Revolution transformed his work on behalf of American technology from a private concern into an important element in the colonies' struggle for independence. Indeed, one of the first things Franklin did in his new capacity was to request engineering assistance for the American war effort.[38]

Independence heightened the importance of closing the technology gap. Patriots warned that "if America is to be wholly indebted to any foreign loom, we may be allowed to exclaim—adieu to the religion! farewell the liberties of our country."[39] One of the richest men in America, Charles Carroll of Maryland, asked Franklin in 1777 to devote his energy to promoting artisanal migration. Military and economic hardship called for skilled migrants who could strengthen the colonies' economy and help them sever their dependence on the Empire. Franklin replied that Carroll "can have no Conception of the Numbers that apply to me with that View; and who would go over if I could assist them." Franklin explained that if a national consensus about the usefulness of such a measure was reached, "and

Congress could afford the charge and could confide in my judgment of the Persons and knowledge of the Arts wanted among us, I am persuaded I could send you over many People who would be valuable acquisitions to our Country." However, since Congress endowed him with neither funding nor authority, his effectiveness as a recruiter of forbidden technologies was obviously limited.[40]

During his tenure in France Franklin was besieged by artisans and inventors who claimed their skills and invention were of great potential value to the young nation and offered to migrate. In his diary he noted that the "number of wild Schemes propos'd to me is so great, and they have heretofore taken so much of my time, that I begin to reject all, tho' possibly *some* of them may be worth Notice." Men from various walks of life told of their plans to move to North America. They were leaving Europe for reasons ranging from ill success in love, marriage fatigue, religious persecution, and ideological conversion to the republican promise. Most of the applicants were men who believed that they had something special to offer the colonies—their industrial know-how.[41]

European artisans approached Franklin in his official capacity, expecting that he would recognize the tremendous contributions they could make to the fledgling republic, and use his position, resources, and reputation to assist them. They told of plans to start Old World–modeled enterprises in North America and claimed to have knowledge and access to secret skills hitherto unknown in the New World. Richard White, for example, wrote that he had made a unique discovery "of what has been the Attempt of Europe for Century's but has Never Succeeded with any person myself excluded." A couple of months later White boasted that he could "Color Cotton Wool yarn of manufactur'd goods of the Cotton Kind from a pink to a Scarlet or Crimson." Two Frenchmen claimed that their unique knowledge of modern silk technology was in such demand that the Dutch East India Company wanted to subsidize their operation. They nevertheless preferred the United States and planned to emigrate to America accompanied by their skilled family members, and promised that other skilled workers would soon follow them. Another Frenchman claimed to have invented a dyeing and bleaching machine and proposed to build a factory for the process in America.[42]

European artisans assumed that America's industrial infancy would propel its politicians to offer a variety of inducements to introducers of new technologies. Some expected official positions. A printer looked to run the government-sponsored press; a pharmacist demanded a position with the military; a physician asked Franklin to find him a job. Others conditioned their migration on some form of assistance. White wrote that he preferred America, but had other options: "England, France [and] Spain has offer'd Ten Thousand pound Each." White threatened that unless Franklin came through with a travel subsidy he would take his know-how back to England. A tapestry manufacturer and dyer wrote: "We are determined to emigrate to the colonies, either as a teacher or director of dyeing or as a master dyer, provided that we can find support on arrival." A master glassmaker offered to migrate if the United States government or private citizens helped him build a glass factory. A playing card maker conditioned his migration on a Congressional subsidy for establishing a factory. An engineer/miner requested a travel subsidy and Franklin's recommendation to Congress. And a German printer demanded a travel subsidy so he could open a press in America, which would serve the large number of German settlers.[43]

In both London and Paris, Franklin consistently turned down requests for direct financial subsidy. "[O]btaining Money from our poor Treasury to forward such Schemes," he wrote in 1772, "is out of all expectation."[44] But Franklin was not averse to helping industrial immigrants in other ways. He had heard of massive Irish immigration to America from Sir Edward Newenham, a prominent Irish politician who was highly sympathetic to the American cause. In response, he declared: "I shall always be ready to afford every assistance and security in my power to such undertakings, when they are really meant and are not merely schemes of trade with views of introducing English manufactures into America, under pretense of their being the substance of persons going there to settle."[45] When Jesse Taylor of Belfast asked Franklin to help a group of Irish artisans to migrate to America, the American minister asked for the names, sexes, and ages, and the names of the vessels they plan to take, in order to "procure them all the security desired" to make the trip. Passports were used to identify them, should an American or French ship stop them on the high seas, and to introduce them as friends rather than spies in American ports. Taylor sent the list by messenger because the regular channels would have led to trouble, "should such a paper be Intercepted, & fall unto Improper hands." Franklin, in turn, instructed his close associate in London, Edward Bancroft, to assist the group.[46]

One surprisingly full account of Franklin's dealings with a prospective group of industrial immigrants has survived to give modern historians a complete insight into Franklin's evolving attitude towards the problem of technology piracy during the Revolutionary War. In 1778, while Englishmen and colonists were fighting each other in North America, a group of textile workers from the Stockport area near Manchester formed an association called the "Emigrant Club." The Stockport district was a hotbed of industrial espionage in the 1770s and 1780s, and even during the War of Independence local newspapers warned of the many industrial spies roaming the region. In the fall of 1781, Henry Royle, a skilled calico printer, approached Franklin on behalf of the group and proposed a deal. The potential emigrants, he explained, would bring their know-how to the underdeveloped United States in exchange for "the following Conditions." (1) The emigrants requested that the government of the United States support them while they waited for their

Atlantic journey and subsidize their transportation to the New World; (2) they demanded immediate naturalization upon arrival and exemption from military service; (3) they expected the government of the United States to grant them a seven-year monopoly on the manufacturing of the cotton and silk goods that they promised to produce with the machinery and knowledge they planned to smuggle out of Britain.[47]

On January 2, 1782, one of the group's leaders, Henry Wyld, gained an audience with Franklin in Paris.[48] Franklin was initially warm. He saw no problems with the second and third demands, but resisted the passage subsidy. "Having therefore no Orders or Authority either from Congress or the State of Pennsylvania to procure Settlers or Manufacturers, by engaging to defray them, I cannot enter in the Contract proposed. The other articles would meet with no difficulty." He suggested that the emigrants wait until the peace treaty was signed and then go via Ireland to avoid the "Law to restrain the Emigration of Manufacturers." While Franklin did not back up his support with cash he openly attacked the British restrictions on artisanal migration and called on the Stockport group to violate them. He called these laws "weak," "wicked," and "tyrannical" and charged that that they "make a Prison of England, to confine Men for no other Crime but that of being useful and Industrious." For Franklin, the anti-emigration laws were symbolic of the capricious hypocrisy of the British ministry and of the social injustice of English society. They restricted the movement of hardworking artisans "while they suffer their idle and extravagant Gentry to travel and reside abroad at their Pleasure, spending the Incomes of their Estates, rack'd from their laborious honest Tenants in foreign Follies, and among French and Italian Whores and Fidlers." Franklin concluded his reply urging the group to ignore the British law because it was "too glaringly unjust to be borne with."[49]

In a show of support Franklin lent Wyld ten guineas to be repaid upon his return to England. Franklin also gave Wyld a passport to go to Ostend in the Low Countries on January 5, 1782, and apparently promised to issue passports to the entire group. Disappointed by Franklin's refusal to lay out any cash beyond the small personal loan to cover travel expenses, Wyld asked him to inform the Pennsylvania legislature of the group's pending arrival and arrange for a subsidy to cover transportation and initial operating costs. Again, he clearly stated that they expected an inventor's monopoly of pirated technology: "give us an only Right in such Machinery as we may introduce."[50]

Franklin's encouragement of the Stockport immigrants was short-lived. A delay in the repayment of the ten guineas soured his feelings for the group. He ignored their letters and used a technicality to refuse their requests for individual passports. The Stockport leaders nevertheless kept him abreast of their project and of their anticipation of great rewards from the introduction of pirated technology to North America. Edmund Clegg informed Franklin that they were "amply provided with kinds of Models for the perfecting of our Purpose." A silk specialist, Clegg inquired what silk machinery was available in the United States, explaining that while he would try to bring some over from England, "the laws make it very dangerous to attempt such a thing." Wyld, sounding somewhat bitter over Franklin's sudden change of heart, wrote that "in any Country where manufactures are wanted, we should meet with more indulgences than we wished to ask for, [than] from the States you so honorably represent." In spite of the "distress and confusion" caused by the American diplomat's coolness toward the group, Wyld reported that he had assembled "some of the ablest Artists in the Country, who . . . earnestly desire, to be the first persons who may arrive there in the Capacity of Manufacturers in our Branches."[51]

Franklin finally yielded and issued a passport for the group as a whole with a general recommendation to the Pennsylvania legislature to assist them. Responding to the specific questions about silk machinery, Franklin suggested that Clegg ignore the prohibitions and bring some machinery over with him upon his migration. Finally, the group departed from Liverpool to Londonderry in the summer of 1782. British authorities, however, were forewarned, and the emigrants were arrested. After a short stay in an Irish jail they were released and enlisted to help industrialize Ireland.[52]

The American representative to the court of Louis XVI had neither the funds nor the authority to promise state subsidies for technology transfer and consequently, save for the symbolic small loan to Wyld, he gave no material support to the Stockport group. Yet, Franklin encouraged the group to defy Britain's restrictions on the emigration of artisans and their machines. He promised safe passage to America and was willing to put the group in touch with men of means in Pennsylvania who could help them get things started. He advised that they leave for Ulster and from there go to America, an advice they followed. All the while, British authorities believed that Franklin was heavily involved in the Stockport scheme of industrial espionage. The letters in Wyld's possession and the passport signed by Franklin were the evidence used by John Swindell, an engineer who infiltrated the group to learn of its intentions, to conclude that Franklin "promised to establish them, as the united Company, supported by Congress."[53]

During the war technology diffusion took a back seat to the pressing issues of forming international alliances and negotiating peace with Great Britain. With independence secured, the dependence of the young republic on imported manufactured goods, and the seemingly mad rush of Americans to purchase English products, underscored the importance of developing an independent economy. One of the central issues of the 1780s was, after all, British monopoly of American trade. The shortage of industrial know-how in the United States meant that industrial development depended on the importation of technology from Europe. The widespread prohibitions on technology diffusion at the end of the eighteenth century made the project a delicate maneuver in the affairs of states. Franklin's reputation as a scientist and mechanical innovator on the one hand, and a prophet of American nationalism on the other, made him a particularly effective spokesman for promoting scientific and mechanical development as a revolutionary measure aimed at ridding the young republic of its colonial economic dependence on Britain.[54]

Even before the official signing of the peace on September 3, 1783, the emigration of skilled artisans from England to the United States came to occupy an increasing share of Franklin's busy schedule. His correspondents in Europe and America reported about mass migration to North America. Richard Bache wrote from Philadelphia that "our numbers have increased in a most astonishing degree; such an influx of foreigners from every Country in Europe, exceeds every expectation." Thomas Pownall, former royal governor of Massachusetts, then living in England, asked Franklin to reply to a list of questions about migration to the new republic so that he could "state to my Countrymen *the real facts* of the Good and the Bad which must arise to those who seek New settlements." Pownall reported that a great number of British citizens planned to emigrate and that no action by the crown could prevent them. The Earl of Buchan reported from Edinburgh in February 1783 of "a spirit of Emigration" of which he was a part, and asked Franklin's advice. The many letters and petitions showed that artisans were crossing the Atlantic of their own accord and at their own expense. It was unnecessary to devote any resources to encouraging emigration. Thus, when Franklin was asked for material assistance he repeatedly replied that while immigrants were welcome, success in the New World depended "on a Man's own Industry and Virtue. . . . the Publick contributes nothing but Defence and Justice."[55]

News of the Anglo-American accord of 1783 stimulated further interest in migration. During the war Franklin offered prospective immigrants information about America, letters of introduction, and, most importantly, passports to assure safe passage. Peace made the passports unnecessary. And while Franklin responded with encouraging platitudes and occasional letters of introduction but failed to deliver more concrete assistance, the stream of applications grew. Men continued to expect assistance in exchange for enriching America with their technical knowledge.[56] Better-informed immigrants knew that Franklin did not distribute any subsidies. Some simply asked for the customary letter of introduction, hoping that Franklin's reputation might open doors hitherto closed to foreigners. Others asked for support in getting other official agencies to cover the transportation of skilled immigrants.[57]

A prominent application was filed by James Milne, described by George Washington as "an English Gentleman, who has been many years introducing those [cotton] manufactures into France." In 1780 Milne approached Franklin to discuss "objects which concern America." Three years later Milne submitted three memoirs in which he claimed to have invented cotton machinery. He offered to establish textile manufacturing in North America and asked for transportation assistance and a patent monopoly for introducing his innovations to the republic. He campaigned simultaneously for an introducer monopoly in France and in America, and though Franklin was of no help, the French government capitalized on the offer and the Milne brothers became the leading textile industrialists in France.[58]

Some requests reached unprecedented heights of impudence. A man proposed to import black slaves to operate a textile factory in America and asked Franklin, who by then had come out strongly against slavery, to introduce him to wealthy men and congressmen who in turn would finance the initial costs of the operation. Most audaciously, Charles Grossett of Brunswick proposed in January

1784 to remedy America's industrial and scientific retardation all on his own. He planned to open a textile factory in America and had "100 Protestant emigrants ready to embark." These men, however, would emigrate for economic reasons and "As such they expect encouragement." They were confident of their ability to make a decent living in the New World, but expected to have their transportation costs covered plus some living money for the first six months "before their respective labours can be brought to a Marketable State." All in all, the enterprise would cost the United States eight thousand pounds, "an advance exceedingly moderate When Compared to the Sums invested by Many private individuals in the Manufactures in England." Grossett, who claimed to have acquired over the last quarter century "a thorough knowledge of Manufactures in General," explained that if Franklin were willing to pay the transportation costs he would come to Paris with his "Chief manufacturer" to discuss the venture in greater detail.[59]

The stream of applications and the demanding expectations of the prospective immigrants exasperated Franklin. "I am pestered continually with Numbers of Letters from People in different Parts of Europe," he explained to Secretary of Congress Charles Thomson, "who would go to settle in America, but who manifest very extravagant Expectations, such as I can by no means encourage; and who appear otherwise improper Persons." To save himself the trouble of explaining American policy to each and every correspondent, in 1784 Franklin penned a pamphlet to discourage immigration, intending to send it as his reply to such inquiries. Thomson shared Franklin's sentiments. "The ports of the United States," he wrote, "are open to all foreigners and the several states are ready to receive any men of science or abilities who may be willing to settle among them, but the sovereign body of the Union do not seem to think it necessary to give any particular encouragement to any nation or to any individuals."[60]

At home for the final stretch of his monumental political, intellectual and scientific career, Franklin continued to be appealed to by European artisans who looked for advice, encouragement, and support. Joseph Guillotin asked him to support the immigration of twelve families of men possessing the most up-to-date knowledge of architecture, agriculture, mechanics, physics, chemistry, and medicine who were headed for Ohio. James Hughes of Manchester proposed that the government set aside a region in the United States for manufacturing, give prospective immigrants land grants small enough to "prevent their turning to Agriculture," and exempt the region from taxes and military service for half a century. Franklin offered no material assistance to those applicants. To his last day, however, he continued to speak against British emigration restrictions, and promote the introduction of European technology to the United States.[61]

Franklin's responses certainly disappointed those who turned to him. I have found no case in which Franklin provided significant material reward to the potential carriers of forbidden industrial know-how. All the same, Franklin supported the dissemination of European technology in America and opposed European restrictions on the emigration of technology and skill. He believed that the very existence of the United States was contingent upon its ability to wean itself from its dependence on British industrial production. To accomplish this goal even he, "the most traditionalist of the diplomats of the American Revolution," who was known for "his scrupulosity about working in proper channels,"[62] subversively supported technology piracy.

Yet, Franklin never became an intellectual property nationalist or tried to prevent the diffusion of American know-how back to Europe. During his Paris stay he developed a new method of typefounding. But he did not contemplate using the innovation for his own private use or reserving it for his newly arisen country. On the contrary, he showed his innovation together with his newly designed fonts to the king's printer. Franklin imported the first copying machines to France and gave them to French carpenters so that they could duplicate them. He is also credited with giving the abbé Rochon the ideas for inventing an engraving machine.

Even at the height of the Revolutionary War, Franklin sought to shield the pursuit of knowledge from the conflict. On March 10, 1779, he ordered "all Captains and Commanders of armed Ships acting by Commission from the Congress of the United States of America, now in war with Great Britain" to spare Captain James Cook's expedition because his men were not America's enemies, but the "common friends of mankind." For all the bitterness he felt toward Britain, he did not contemplate preventing American innovations from being emulated there. Almost as soon as the peace accord was signed, he informed British printers of the method of type-founding he had developed in Paris during the war. Occasionally he introduced American artisans to his London colleagues and asked that the Americans help the Londoners make use of their inventions. In 1788 Franklin was a member of the Rumseyan Society, which raised funds to send James Rumsey to London in search of the capital needed for further development of his steamboat. The notion that Rumsey's innovations should be kept in the United States to give the country an economic edge did not cross his mind.[63]

Franklin, who around the middle of the eighteenth century had joined a vibrant international circle devoted to the cultivation of knowledge, remained faithful to that circle's disregard of borders as far as science and technology were concerned. This did not mean that he thought invention should not be rewarded, or that he took a principled stand against all monopolies. He did not. It was prudent for nations to encourage innovation and development by promising local exclusionary monopolies, and Franklin was willing to secure such an arrangement for the Stockport group. Such arrangements, however, had to be limited in time and place. They could not be extended across national boundaries. Franklin never respected European restrictions on international diffusion of know-how, and kept to the idea that knowledge was unlike physical property. Humanity, regardless of national boundaries, was entitled to enjoy the fruits of innovation. His principled support for the free exchange of science and technology, like his embrace of a civic ethnically inclusive national model, had few followers among his countrymen, who embraced a protectionist and exclusive national construction of intellectual property. His was the path not taken.

CHAPTER 4

After the Revolution
"The American Seduction of
Machines and Artisans"

In the second week of November 1787, Phineas Bond, British consul in Philadelphia, received a visit from two English nationals. Thomas Edemsor, a cotton merchant from Manchester, and Henry Royle, a calico printer from Chadkirk in Cheshire, were greatly distressed. They feared lynching at the hands of a mob led by the city's leading merchants and they looked to the envoy of His Britannic Majesty's government for shelter. Their story went as follows.

In 1783, concurrent with British recognition of American independence, an Englishman named Benjamin H. Phillips determined to establish a cotton manufactory in America. In spite of severe restrictions on the exportation of textile machinery and the emigration of skilled artisans, Phillips purchased a carding machine and three spinning machines in England, packed them disassembled into crates declared to British customs to contain Wedgwood china, and boarded the U.S. ship *Liberty* at Liverpool bound for Philadelphia. He had earlier sent his son to Philadelphia in anticipation of the machinery's arrival. The elder Phillips died before reaching America and his son received the crates, but lacking his father's knowledge of the machinery he could not reassemble the equipment. He then sold it to another Englishmen, Joseph Hague, who managed to assemble it but found he was unable to make it work properly. Having no capital and despairing of covering the operating expenses, in the spring of 1787 Hague sold the equipment to Royle, who in turn sold it to Edemsor. Edemsor once again disassembled the four machines and shipped them back to England. According to his testimony, he patriotically purchased and repatriated the equipment "to Check the Advancement of the Cotton Manufactory in America."

In the meantime, a group of Philadelphia merchants, concerned with advancing the cause of U.S. economic independence from Britain to complement the nation's newly found political independence, had formed the Pennsylvania Society for the Encouragement of Manufactures and the Useful Arts. The group had instigated a search for Hague's cotton machinery and became infuriated upon learning of its repatriation by Royle and Edemsor. The merchants' wrath turned on the British culprits, who "in great dread of suffering from their Resentment," went into hiding for several weeks. Finally, the fugitives approached Bond for protection, and, in Royle's case, for money to secure passage back to England. Shocked by the fanatic zeal of "the American Seduction of British Machines and Artisans" and convinced of the real danger of violence his compatriots faced from the leading men of Philadelphia in their quest to acquire "the industrial secrets of the Old World," Bond paid the fare for Royle and his family out of his own pocket. When the society learned of Royle's and Edemsor's escape, its leaders publicly rebuked and insulted the British consul.

Not intimidated, Bond set about investigating the incident. His inquiries led him to focus on the slippery character of Hague, who had left the city and was rumored to be back in England attempting to procure more equipment for illegal exportation to America. He notified the British Foreign Office that Hague might be found for arrest in Derbyshire, but by the time the magistrates arrived there Hague was gone. He reappeared in Philadelphia the following spring, having successfully smuggled over a new cotton-carding machine.[1] Adding insult to injury, the Pennsylvania legislature awarded him a prize of one hundred dollars on October 3, 1788, for having succeeded in his piracy. The Manufacturing Society trumpeted the achievement in the press and showed little concern for the subject of intellectual property. "It is with great pleasure we learn," it announced,

> that the ingenious Artizan, who counterfeited the Carding and Spinning Machine, though not the original inventor (being only the introducer) is likely to receive a premium from the Manufacturing Society, besides a generous prize for his machines; and that it is highly probable our patriotic legislature will not let his merit pass unrewarded by them. Such liberality must have the happy effect of bringing into Pennsylvania other useful Artizans, Machines, and Manufacturing Secrets which will abundantly repay the little advance of the present moment.

The Society urged leading men in other towns to procure protected British textile machines, declaring that the development of home manufacturing was the way "the manufactures of the United States must succeed."[2]

This incident illustrates the volatility involved in the diffusion of technical knowledge across the Atlantic in the years immediately following the Revolution. In the battle over industrial skill and technology, agents of piracy in one incident would appear as protectors of patents in another. One of the protectors of British industrial secrets in the 1787 incident, Henry Royle, had offered his services to Franklin as part of the Stockport group earlier in the decade. Now Royle's life was in danger because he had participated in the return of Phillips's and Hague's machine to England. Royle's inconsistency, change of heart, or newfound loyalty to Britain demonstrates the fluidity of a situation in which ideas about national ownership of innovation depended on the geographical perspective of the beholder.

The transfer of protected European technology was a prominent feature of the economic, political and diplomatic life of the North American confederation from its first moments as an independent political entity. In the decades before the Revolution, European commentators who wondered what could account for the phenomenal demographic, territorial, and economic boom in the colonies attributed it to the transfer of social and cultural capital, in the form of the European approach to the application of knowledge.[3] The simultaneous timing of severing the political ties with Britain and the boom in British industrial innovation complicated the agendas of the revolutionaries bent on striking a new and independent course. Governments, companies, and individuals actively sponsored industrial espionage in hopes of using the lower costs of raw materials and the higher wages in the New World to propel the young republic into a prominent position in the emerging competitive industrial world market.

In the political vacuum created by the Revolution and its immediate aftermath, however, private voluntary initiatives by individuals and ad hoc organizations played an inordinately large role in this process. The impotence of governments to even feed and provide clothes for Washington's troops during the Revolution, and their helplessness in the face of the economic depression that followed, undermined public confidence in their ability to deliver services, let alone initiate complex policies to develop American manufactures.[4] Hence it was private proponents of industrialization that undertook the project of importing forbidden European technology to the United States. In some sense, these Americans acted as if they subscribed to Franklin's rejection of politically bounded intellectual property. After all, their efforts to lure artisans and smuggle machines openly flouted rivals' efforts to block the diffusion of industrial knowledge across the Atlantic and challenged the intellectual property laws of other sovereign nations. Yet, these voluntary activities had little to do with a universalist ideological commitment to the free dissemination of knowledge. The psychologies of the efforts to appropriate Europe's forbidden know-how in the post-revolutionary era were particularist, protectionist, and nationalist. They affirmed rather than challenged the confinement of ideas and innovations within political entities and foreshadowed the direction of American thinking about international intellectual property in the decades to come.

The Industrialists' Agenda

The events of November 1787 in Philadelphia reveal a fundamental aspect of the psychology of technology transfer in the aftermath of the American Revolution. The activities of Hague and the prominent citizens of the Pennsylvania Society for the Encouragement of Manufactures reflected their conviction that smuggling British technology to the United States was indispensable to American industrialization. The energetic response on the side of Bond reflects a similar attitude in England. But were these sentiments well founded? Could the young nation have developed its manufacturing independently? Was English technology indispensable? Most historians of the economy of the early republic have rejected the myth of North American technological inferiority vis-à-vis Great Britain. True, the young republic had neither the industrial economy nor the factories, experts, and sophisticated machinery of Britain. But in the American context the specialized skilled mechanic in charge of a specific stage in the production process was hampered by the labor shortage. Such a worker would have had difficulties finding the necessary skilled helpers. The specialized mechanic was in the American context less useful than the jack-of-all-trades.[5]

Indeed, some Americans believed that the new nation could carve its own path to industrialization and that the home manufacturing already taking place in America in the postrevolutionary era answered most of the country's industrial needs. A Philadelphia man returning in 1789 after two years in Europe wrote an enthusiastic essay about the improvements in American manufactures during his absence. Given such immense progress in such a very short time, he argued, the need to emulate European technology had ceased to be urgent. The popular image of American workers in the early republic—excellent at performing multiple basic tasks yet far behind their European counterparts in expert innovations—is inaccurate. Many American artisans honed specialized skills and some developed technological breakthroughs that were hitherto unknown to Europeans. Nathan Sellers of Philadelphia, for example, developed in the 1780s a method of making wire screen molds needed by papermakers for turning their pulp into paper—a process that was to be emulated in England some ten years later. Oliver Evans of Newcastle, Delaware, developed a machine that dramatically improved wool carding. Whereas before each household spinner had to produce by hand the cards necessary to align the fibers of wool before spinning, Evans's device spared women this tedious labor, thereby making the "American age of homespun" possible. And newspapers occasionally published reports of industrial successes that eliminated the need to import goods from the Old World. The *New Haven Gazette* informed its readers in 1787 that "the manufacture of nails is brought to such perfection throughout the United States, as to stop the importation of that article." The paper predicted that America would soon rival "Great Britain in many other branches of manufacture."[6]

For all the impressive accomplishments of individual Americans, the Industrial Revolution was characterized by mechanization, the factory, and increased production, and in all three the English textile industry blazed the trail. Contemporaries surely saw it this way. Foreigners traveling through England were struck by the higher standard of living that ordinary women and men enjoyed in comparison to those in the rest of Europe. They understood the causal relationship between technological development and a higher standard of living. Eighteenth-century economists explained that replacing human labor with machinery increased productivity and made for higher wages; that disposable income in the pockets of consumers increased demand for manufactured items; and that the rise in demand made for greater prosperity. American and European eighteenth-century political leaders and manufacturers clearly believed England was the technological leader of the Industrial Revolution. The extent of the foreign espionage effort in England decisively demonstrates the intense international desire for English technology. Contemporaries believed in the centrality of the new technology to successful industrialization and conceived of creative ways to snatch it away. The American press openly celebrated the successful appropriation of forbidden British textile technologies. Silas Deane, in trouble with the Continental Congress and somewhat disenchanted with the Patriot cause, wrote Robert Morris in June 1781 that even after the American victory, the superiority of British industry was so overwhelming that the young nation would "take at least three-fourth of all the European articles she wants from Great Britain." Deane explained that everyone "who has had an opportunity of comparing the manufactures of one nation in Europe with another, or observing the different modes and principles of transmitting business, will at once give England and her merchants the preference."[7] And American consumers expressed their appreciation and admiration of English manufactures. The end of the Revolutionary War ushered in frantic purchasing of English imports. In fact, simply knowing that an item had been manufactured in England was enough to make it desirable to the former colonists.

Even the most patriotic Americans realized that habit and structural economic patterns originating in colonial relationships fostered dependence on European imports and hindered the young nation's technological development. Revolutionary calls for cutting off all connections to the Old World were contradicted by the recognition that for all the patriotic pride and talk of self-sufficiency, the United States had to emulate European discoveries. Just before he called for severing all ties with Europe, David Rittenhouse praised the value of scientific discoveries made "by our Philosophic brethren in Europe." Americans admitted that much of their knowledge of their geographical surroundings was acquired "at the great expence of the British Government." Deane toured British factories in the aftermath of the Revolutionary War to learn "their late, & new inventions, & machines of various kinds." The American Philosophical Society, a staunchly patriotic organization, asked clockmaker Owen Biddle in 1781 to give a "historical sketch on those capital inventions and discoveries, which have led to all the subsequent improvements in useful knowledge." Biddle complied with an oration that emphasized the international nature of the accumulation of technical knowledge. He argued that "discoveries have succeeded each other, by a flow and gradual advancement, and that one invention is linked in with and leads to many others, which are remote and unforeseen." The meaning of Biddle's words to the flagship of American intellectual life was clear. Political separation must not be followed by intellectual isolationism.[8]

The anti-British rhetoric of the postrevolutionary era went hand in hand with calls to industrialize. Patriots warned that if the new republic remained dependent on imports from the British empire, the political success of the Revolution would be rendered hollow. Writers bemoaned the "general prevalence of luxury and dissipation, and the decay of public virtue among us," and proposed to break America's dependency on English products by establishing home manufacturing. American addiction to British manufactures meant, wrote Hugh Williamson, that "we have expended more money since the peace, than we have gained." "Cease to import

Goods from that imperious, insolent, debauched and intriguing Kingdom of *Great Britain,*" cried the *Boston Gazette.* "Abstain from British luxury, extravagance, and dissipation, or *you are an* UN-DONE PEOPLE." In this context, respect for Britain's intellectual property laws was out of the question. "If we intended to maintain our independence we must try to counteract their machinations" to prevent the dissemination of industrial technology, and appropriate the necessary technology for American industrial development. The emerging consensus was best expressed by an anonymous writer who declared that political independence would not be truly secure until Americans could replace British imports with American manufactured goods.[9]

Independence was thus followed by calls for disseminating European industrial technology, the export of which was prohibited. Benjamin Rush openly celebrated the successful appropriation of a "machine lately brought into this city for lessening the expence of time and hands in spinning." Robert Bell published in the midst of the Revolutionary War a collection of practical information drawn from European sources regarding various technical issues related to agriculture and manufacturing. Local newspapers followed suit, publishing technical information about British machinery. Philadelphia political economist Mathew Carey argued that these technical descriptions were being disseminated for patriotic reasons. Publishers hoped to "induce some patriotic persons to undertake a line of manufacture so likely to be of essential benefit to the country." Ambivalence about the morality of appropriating the fruits of the intellectual efforts of foreigners was nowhere to be found. As the *Pennsylvania Gazette* declared, "Machines appear to be objects of immense consequence to this country." It was thus the new republic's right to "borrow of Europe their inventions."[10]

James Watt's improvement of the steam engine, in particular, fired up the American imagination. Audiences received their first full description of Watt's new engine in the July 1788 issue of the *Columbian Magazine*. The first steam engine, developed by Thomas Newcomen in 1705, was wasteful of energy and its main application in England, pumping water out of coal mines, was of little use in the colonies which did not rely on coal for energy. Watt's initial innovation, developed in 1768 and patented the following year, found a more efficient and more powerful way to address the problem of water in mines. After Watt successfully converted the energy from the steam engine to a rotary motion, Richard Arkwright and his assignees bought Boulton and Watt steam engines to run cotton spinning machinery in Manchester. The introduction of steam power sharply lowered the cost of spinning cotton into yarn and weaving yarn into fabric. The adaptation of the steam engine to other industries had the potential to dramatically increase the production capacity of North American industries, which were heavily dependent on human and animal energy. Deane reported that the new steam technology enabled English manufacturers to produce cheaper products despite the high cost of labor, and he offered, if given sufficient reward, to introduce the steam engine into the United States. James Rumsey and John Fitch set out in the second half of the 1780s to apply a steam engine to marine transportation. Fitch enlisted English immigrants to try and duplicate the Watt engine in America. Although several leading Americans lent their financial support to his cause, Fitch failed to produce an economically viable steamboat because he insisted on using American-made rather than British-made engines, while Rumsey spent several years in Britain and France consulting various engineers but never succeeded in building a boat.[11]

Machine importation, however, was problematic. Americans could not build European machinery from manuals since most inventions were kept secret. Even those published in magazines were not translatable into actual machines because descriptions and drawings generally lacked specificity and clarity.[12] In theory, the public in the London patent office could access patented English inventions during the term of the patent, but the knowledge required to conduct an effective search rendered copying specifications all but impossible. In fact, Arkwright intentionally registered his 1782 patents in an incoherent manner to "guard against foreigners." Seventeenth- and eighteenth-century technical improvements originated in individuals' responses to specific situations that involved thinking about a mechanical problem in a nonverbal manner. Manufacturing processes were connected to those that preceded them and those that followed, and all links in the manufacturing chain were closely dependent on local sources of energy and raw materials. Moreover, once a machine arrived in the New World, only those who had worked on a similar one in Britain could put it together and operate it. The various subsidized iron factories of the Revolution faltered because of the lack of skilled laborers. The carding machines Bond had acquired and sent to England sat idle in Philadelphia for more than three years because no one knew how to assemble them and put them to work. Successful acquisition of prohibited English industrial knowledge depended on the emigration of skilled operators and managers of English factories. [13]

As soon as American entrepreneurs began to establish factories in the 1780s they realized that the absence of skilled operators, for a water frame in New England or a spinning mule in Philadelphia, hindered their efforts. Samuel Wetherill, patron of the failed United Company of Philadelphia which tried to establish textile manufacturing from 1775 to 1778, reflected years later that the biggest hurdle "which occurs in so arduous an undertaking, as attempting to establish manufactures in a country not much acquainted with them," was "finding artists and making machines without models." For the nascent American industries of the 1780s, labor shortages created two problems. First, the shortage of skilled workers hindered successful emulation of British manufactures. Second, the scarcity of skilled workers allowed the few capable artisans to demand and receive high wages that undermined the price competitiveness of American manufacturing. A New Haven newspaper published "Hints to Manufacturers" that warned potential industrialists that the cost of "labour is from about twelve to twenty percent higher in Connecticut, than in England." And William Barton explained in a widely read treatise that the high cost of labor in America "would be a considerable obstruction to the establishment of domestic manufactures." The new nation was not naturally inclined toward manufacturing, declared an anonymous writer "because nature has not formed us artists and mechanics, and given us from our birth all the wisdom and experience of old countries and taught us the mystery of being industrious and working cheap."[14]

Champions of industry turned their attention to recruiting skilled artisans and machine operators. The first issue of Mathew Carey's *American Museum* ran a letter that elaborated on the connection between national interest, industrialization, and the promotion of emigration. "As it is the wisdom of America to discourage the importation from Europe of those things she is able to make—so it is equally her wisdom to encourage emigrations from Europe." The emigrants America needed were "the industrious poor" who were "chiefly bred to trades and mechanical business." Another essayist emphasized the importance of attracting to America artisans who would continue to practice their trades in the United States, thereby contributing to the economic development of the nation.[15]

Successful recruitment depended on the construction of a local industrial base where these workers could be employed and ensuring that the wages and working conditions in American factories were sufficiently lucrative to discourage industrial immigrants from abandoning their trades for agriculture. Some suggested offering eight to ten acres of land to prospective industrial immigrants. The "small quantity of Land" appropriated to each would prevent them from turning to Agriculture and "be sufficient for all the purposes of manufacturing." Artisans who came to America, wrote a proponent of manufacturing, "are turning their attention to other occupations." Unless American manufacturers acted quickly, "collected" them in urban settings, and created employment opportunities for the "many artisans and tradesmen now among us," their precious industrial skills would be forever lost to the manufacturing sector. Benjamin Rush wrote that by establishing "woolen, cotton and linen manufactories in this country, we shall invite manufacturers from every part of Europe, particularly from Britain and Ireland, to come and settle among us." The goal was to attract skilled artisans who in turn would improve American capacity for industrial production: "we stretch forth a hand from the ark to invite the timid manufacturers to come in." At the same time, industrial development, by the employment it would offer, promised to "encourage thousands to come and settle in America." Twelve years later Rush's idea was endorsed by another champion of American manufacturing who argued in the *American Museum* that if industrial emigrants could "be assured of employment and encouragement in coming to America, I am persuaded that some thousands would soon visit these shores. We should soon have a competent number of workmen to carry on most kinds of manufactures. There would, in a short time, be no necessity to import a single article" of manufactures.[16]

In order to attract skilled workers, then, industrialists needed to establish factories. Yet, these factories could not be established without specific instruction from those who had worked in them in the Old World. Many Americans did not want to wait for the arrival of workers with the necessary knowledge and experience and argued for taking active measures to induce immigration. The most popular suggestion was to sponsor the cost of the Atlantic voyages of skilled workers. Others suggested providing "ample provisions" to "mechanics and artizans migrating hither from Europe."[17] Some sent recruiting agents and others hoped that the popular press and word of mouth would spread the news of the opening of industrial opportunities in America.

Entrepreneurs recognized, however, the need to ensure that even after industrial immigrants set foot on American shores they did not opt for nonindustrial employment. After all, labor scarcity plagued all sectors of the postrevolutionary United States. If the states were to industrialize, then, more workers, skilled and unskilled, had to turn to manufactures. However, the dominant economic sector in North America—agriculture—was also thirsting for laborers. Promoters of American industry understood that the agricultural interests would oppose national sponsorship of competing employment in manufactures. Indeed, prominent politicians envisioned the new nation without manufacturing altogether. John Dickinson announced in his widely circulated *Letters from a Farmer in Pennsylvania* that "this continent is a country of planters, farmers, and fishermen; not of manufacturers." This view persisted; former physician in chief of the Continental Army John Morgan wrote as late as 1789 that manufacturing was suited to a country "fully stocked with inhabitants." But the labor shortage meant that industrialization would have to come at the expense of agriculture, the real source of national wealth.[18]

To make industrialization politically possible its proponents had to persuade the agriculturalists that the labor pool available to them would not be depleted by the introduction of manufacturing. Societies for the development of American technology often paid more attention to mechanical innovations in agriculture than to those in manufacturing. Agricultural societies were equally interested in emulating European innovations. Proponents of American industrial developments were careful to position manufacturing and agriculture as complementary rather than competing sectors.[19] One popular suggestion was that at least at the unskilled stages, manufacturers employ women and children, who commanded much lower wages. But this approach would have done little to ameliorate America's technological disadvantages. The workers who could industrialize the United States would come from Europe. As one South Carolinian writer explained in 1786, developing manufacturing was necessary to stop the drain of specie that had followed peace and the resumption of purchasing of English products. After proposing the traditional mercantilist measures to develop manufacturing, tariffs and bounties, he went on to assure readers that American industrialization would not compete with agriculture for the limited supply of American laborers. "I only wish to encourage," he wrote, "European tradesmen to come and reside here; their numbers will add strength to us, and enable the planters, without danger, to keep a greater number of hands in the field."[20]

Champions of industrialization succeeded in making overcoming American technological backwardness a national priority. Sponsorship of manufacturing skill, declared the *Pennsylvania Gazette,* by either the private or the public sectors, was the "duty of every friend to America, at home and abroad." At stake was not only the economic well-being of the residents of the newly independent states, but the entire republican experiment. Rush, who like many of his contemporaries believed that the interests of the United States and the cause of human freedom were one and the same, explained that he favored encouraging industrial workers to cross the Atlantic not only as a way to develop American manufactures, but also as a humanitarian gesture by the messenger of republicanism, reaching out with a helping hand to the suffering masses of Europe. "By bringing manufacturers into this land of liberty and plenty," he declared, "we recover them from the torpid state in which they existed in their own country and place them in circumstances which enable them to become husbands and fathers, and thus we add to the general tide of human happiness."[21] In the eyes of patriots, the particularist interests of American manufactures merged with the universal language of the Revolution in a manner that took little account of the rules and regulations of others.

Voluntary Associations for Acquiring Technology

Proponents of American development emerged from the Revolution with heightened awareness of the nation's technological backwardness. The zeal for developing American manufactures was organized and expressed by voluntary industrial associations. The Continental Congress, spurred on by John Adams, called on the legislatures of the various states in March 1776 to establish societies "for the improvement of agriculture, arts, manufactures, and commerce." It encouraged these societies to communicate their developments to each other to make sure that the "rich and numerous natural advantages of this country, for supporting its inhabitants, may not be neglected," and specifically urged them to consider "ways and means of introducing the manufactures of duck and sail cloth, and steel."[22]

The period from the mid 1780s to the early 1790s saw the formation of societies for promoting American manufactures in towns from Burlington to Wilmington. "Every well-wisher of his country," declared one enthusiast, "ought to rejoice, when he is informed, that not only great men, but great associations also, do their utmost, to favour and assist the establishment and progress, of the Manufactures of their country."[23] Some associations actively participated in establishing factories in America and in recruiting European artisans to migrate to the United States. Most required their members to pledge publicly to wear only American-made clothes. Upgrading American industrial technology was at the top of their priorities.

The American associations were modeled after London's Society of Arts, established in 1754, which sponsored fine arts as well as improved techniques in industry and agriculture. The London society was interested exclusively in knowledge that could be applied to practical uses. Its principal method of sponsorship was awarding premiums to individual innovators who improved output. Prior to the Revolution, the London society offered premiums to American innovation, dispensing money to various colonial agricultural products from Massachusetts to Georgia. The Connecticut physician Benjamin Gale, for example, received a gold medal from the society in January 1770 for inventing a drill plow.[24]

Initial colonial efforts to form manufacturing societies did not get very far. As early as 1727 Franklin proposed to establish an American Society for the Promotion of Useful Knowledge. He gathered a small group of Philadelphians around him and tried to launch the organization. But the idea failed to take root. In 1743, together with naturalist William Bartram, he drew up a plan for establishing an Academy for Promoting Useful Knowledge among the British Plantations in America, but after initial successes the attempt folded. In 1750 Franklin assembled around him in Philadelphia a group of twelve men committed to the promotion of the pursuit of science and technology in America, but their sporadic meetings ceased altogether by 1762. Then, in 1768, the American Society for Promoting and Propagating Useful Knowledge was established to promote "the Advancement of useful Knowledge and improvement of our Country." It encouraged the introduction "from Abroad, new Species of Plants, Trees, Fruits, Grain &c., suitable to our own Soil and Climate." Aware of the possible negative reaction to its founding among the British manufacturing and mercantile elite, it announced that "Such Discoveries will not only be a Benefit to ourselves, but they will render us more useful to our Mother Country. They will give full Scope to our Industry, without exciting her Jealousy, or interfering in the least with her Manufactures."[25] In 1769 the society merged with the American Philosophical Society, a union dominated by the Philosophical Society's emphasis on theoretical learning. Those interested in practical applications of science to industry formed separate groups, like the Silk Society (1770), and the United Company of Philadelphia for Promoting American Manufactures (1775).

The imperial crisis and the separation from England infused the American technological efforts with cultural nationalism and turned American leaders against the intellectual internationalism of the prerevolutionary era. Virginia's Arthur Lee, for example, resigned from the Royal Society because membership in it was incompatible with his American patriotism. The general sentiment was, as the constitution of the Delaware Society for the Encouragement and Promotion of Manufactories of America declared, that in order "to complete the great fabric, the progress of which has already astonished the world—it becomes the duty of the sons of America to promote the arts and sciences" and that "the attainment of these objects requires various and extended exertions, beyond the power of a few individuals." American voluntary associations for the promotion of manufactures, free from the constraints of the Empire, pursued a nationalist agenda.[26]

The American societies attracted the social and political elite— leaders who saw an intimate connection between industrialization and political independence. New York's Society for Promoting Useful Knowledge, launched in 1784, was led by Samuel Bard, an Edinburgh-trained physician, and included prominent politicians like New York State's governor, George Clinton, New York City's mayor, James Duane, and the Confederation's secretary for foreign affairs, John Jay. The Virginia Society for Promoting Useful Knowledge was composed of slave-owning planters. The leadership of the Pennsylvania Society for the Encouragement of Manufactures and the Useful Arts, the most prominent of these organizations, included Benjamin Franklin, George Clymer, Tench Coxe, Mathew Carey, Samuel Miles, Benjamin Rush, and Samuel Wetherill.[27]

Patriotic rhetoric abounded in the proceedings of the Pennsylvania Society. In announcing its formation in 1787 the board explained that developing manufactures was the premier national task because Americans must now take charge of "promoting and establishing manufactures among ourselves." Wetherill bemoaned "our late dependence on foreign nations for many of the most useful articles in life," and called for "great exertions of virtue and industry" to lift America out of its current "disadvantageous situation." The commercial crisis of the mid 1780s, triggered by the closure of the markets of the slave colonies of the West Indies to American agricultural imports, necessitated the development of home manufacturing. "We feel an hourly diminution of our wealth; and the support of our artificers and labourers is become precarious and difficult," explained the officials of the society. Should America fail to develop its manufacturing, they warned, "our population will be diminished; our strength as a nation destroyed; and our country reduced to poverty, insignificance and contempt."[28]

The society openly declared its intention to appropriate forbidden technology from Europe. Indeed, technology piracy occupied a central role in its program to develop American industry. And the nationalist rhetoric used to persuade Americans of its value justified the violation of the British intellectual property laws. The manufacturing committee of the society devoted much of its effort to acquiring English machines and attracting the skilled artisans who could build and operate them. The "want of proper bleach yards and the difficulty of procuring persons well skilled in bleaching," for example, undermined American ability to manufacture sufficient quantities of linen.[29] It was therefore essential to find a way to bring such knowledge to America.

The society underwrote the establishment of a textile factory in Philadelphia.[30] Its officials declared that in the context of the high cost of labor in America "the acquisition of machines must be a capital advantage."[31] Technological piracy was the chosen route "to obtain some of those machines, which, by a substitution for manual labour, enable the most agricultural countries to manufacture to very great advantage." Two years after the society's founding a writer in the *American Museum* praised it for fostering "the spirit of emulation" and credited it with the successful birth of American manufacturing.[32] And the society was quite energetic in its efforts. Within a year of its founding it operated a large cotton factory. To be sure, the factory relied for the most part on the labor of two to three hundred women who used hand spinners and jennies to produce linen and yarn. The men, however, used smuggled British machinery, acquired through the efforts of Tench Coxe and his agents, to make British-model carding engines and spinning machines. The first year was declared an economic success and at the parade celebrating the adoption of the new federal constitution members and workers proudly wore their American-made clothing. That the entire operation rested on pirated technology seemed to have mattered to no one.

Tench Coxe became the society's most prominent spokesman. Philadelphia emerged in the last quarter of the eighteenth century as the center of the American efforts to catch up with British technology. The city developed into a magnet for thousands of British skilled artisans who brought with them not only the know-how but also the new capitalist industrial psychology that had developed in English manufacturing towns. Coxe, who became the society's secretary, saw the connection between the arrival of new technologies and the rise of his city. He dabbled in technological piracy as early as 1775 when he was one of the patrons of the failed United Company of Philadelphia. In the early days of the Revolution Coxe entertained

FIGURE 4. Tench Coxe (1755–1824). Portrait by Jeremiah Paul, 1795. Coxe was the leading advocate of industrialization in the young republic through the illicit appropriation of foreign technology. Courtesy of The Historical Society Collection, Atwater Kent Museum of Philadelphia.

some loyalist sympathies. His dubious patriotic credentials, however, did not hinder his postrevolutionary ascent in Philadelphia's social, political and economic elite. By the late 1780s Coxe was widely recognized as the most prominent and active advocate of American manufactures.[33]

Coxe believed that European manufactures were technologically superior and argued that imported machinery "will give us immense assistance" in launching an independent industrial economy.[34] In the second half of the decade Coxe campaigned in behalf of state and federal support of industrial piracy. He made sure that America's technological backwardness was on the minds of the men who convened in Philadelphia to form the new constitution in the summer of 1787. On May 11, three days before the delegates to the Philadelphia convention were scheduled to begin their deliberations, Coxe addressed the need for government-sponsored industrialization in a passionate talk at the home of Benjamin Franklin. Then, on August 9, while the convention was in session, he explicitly called for importing technology in his inaugural address to the society at the University of Pennsylvania.

The new national government, he told the men gathered at Franklin's house, must support industrialization efforts to provide employment for the many who "will probably emigrate from Europe, who will chuse to continue their trades."[35] Artisans would cross the Atlantic because tyranny, unemployment, low wages, and civil wars in Europe, contrasted with freedom and opportunity in America, "will bring many manufacturers to this asylum for mankind. Ours will be their industry, and what is of still more consequence ours will be their skill." Many of the society's leaders speculated that among the men already arriving in the United States each month there were skilled artisans who could lift the level of American industrial technology. "Is it not, then, a melancholy consideration," asked one member, "that many tradesmen of these descriptions, after coming to America, are obliged through want of work, to return home again—while many of those who stay, must commence labourers to produce a morsel of bread?" Coxe proposed that a committee of the society "visit every ship arriving with passengers from any foreign country, in order to enquire what persons they may have on board capable of contributing useful machines, qualified to carry on manufactures, or coming among us with a view to that kind of employment."[36]

Coxe sang the glories of his homeland and predicted that Europeans would see things similarly and vote with their feet. But he was not content to let the virtues of the United States gradually cause the desired population movement. He implored his listeners and the men devising a new form of government in the summer of 1787 to "Carefully examine the conduct of Other countries in order to possess ourselves of their methods of encouraging manufactories." He made two specific proposals: (1) Grant federally protected exclusive rights over inventions to introducers of technology; (2) Award land grants to skilled Europeans who introduced European machinery to the United States. America's industrial virginity would work in its favor for, if Europeans continued to improve their machinery, "their people must be driven to us for want of employment, and if on the other hand, they should return to manual labor, we shall under work them by these invaluable engines." It is time for the young nation, he declared, to "borrow some of their inventions." [37]

A year later, in the pages of the *American Museum,* Coxe was even blunter. American industrialists had recognized long ago that the "want of workmen, and the high rate of labour" had delayed the development of American manufactures. They resolved to obtain "machines which were said to be in use in foreign countries" since the new machinery required fewer workers to produce greater quantities. This was particularly appropriate in a country like the United States, which suffered chronically from labor shortages. Thus far, "notwithstanding the impediments which the natural jealousy and self interest of mankind have thrown in our way, acquisitions of the utmost consequence have been made." We are not ashamed of our efforts to acquire Europe's industrial secrets, Coxe declared. Americans "heartily rejoice in the early success of our endeavors to obtain them."[38]

Emigration of skilled workers from Europe, Coxe argued, was the optimal solution to America's labor problems. Agriculture, Coxe insisted, would remain the primary sector in the nation's economy. The farming interests need not worry that industrialization would come at the expense of agricultural labor: "there is another grand source from which supplies of manufactures may be obtained— Emigration from foreign Countries. To this end our laws must be made to countenance, assist and protect them." Coxe hoped that the adoption of the new federal constitution would calm those who feared the disorder of the years of the Confederation. He declared: "the door is opened wide, and the call is made in a loud and friendly voice, upon the whole body of European manufacturers, to come out, and sit down among us. The present circumstances of this country, and the universal disposition of the people of the united states, must strongly persuade and encourage them; and we can have no doubt, that very many of this new and valuable class of emigrants will every year repair to America, and make it their home."[39]

When Coxe was writing of technological rivalry, he had only Great Britain in mind. During the colonial period "it was the unvaried policy of Great Britain to discourage manufactures," and after the separation it continued to suffocate the westward flow of technology. When the United States was but a colonial outpost of the British Empire "our progress was very slow, and indeed the necessity of attention to manufacture was not so urgent, as it has become since our assuming an independent station." He believed that Britain was determined to suffocate American manufacturing attempts just as it blocked the development of manufactures in Ireland.[40]

Coxe saw in the involvement of Phineas Bond in the return of the carding and spinning machines that had been smuggled out of Britain an indication that Britain was determined to keep America technology-deficient. Unlike the enraged citizens of Philadelphia who surrounded Bond's home, Coxe saw the events as a natural extension of the international competition over technology. While he bemoaned the loss of machines that could save "the labour of no less than 120 workmen, daily," he understood that Bond had "acted in perfect confidence with the dictates of national and commercial rivalship." In Virginia, British agents bought and burned stocks of cottonseed "to avert the injurious effects, which the extension of the cotton manufactures in America, must produce on the importation of Manchester goods." Such actions, Coxe hoped, should wake American industrialists to the realities of the worldwide all-out competition for technology, and he urged other states to adopt a "prudential spirit of jealousy and circumspection" and follow the example of Pennsylvania that had enacted legislation "to prevent exportation of machines and enticing away artizans." [41]

Coxe did not confine himself to words. In the summer of 1787, he recruited Andrew Mitchell to return to England and pirate English textile technology. Mitchell was to go to England, buy models of machinery, and transport them to France through a French middleman who was to ship them to Philadelphia. The scheme was exposed, British officials seized the trunk containing the illegally obtained models, and Mitchell was forced to escape to a safe haven at Copenhagen.[42] In the same year Coxe entered into a partnership with a Philadelphia clockmaker, Robert Leslie, who was known as a collector of "every model, drawing or description" of European machinery. In 1788 Coxe, together with John Kaighan, reported that the process of coloring leather, while attempted in America, "has not yet been obtained here." They published the process "as communicated by Mr. Philippo, a native of Armenia, who received from the society for the encouragement of arts in London, one hundred pounds sterling, and also the gold medal of the society, as a reward for discovering this secret."[43]

Coxe embodied the new American attitude. In the aftermath of independence the United States and Great Britain became political and economic adversaries. American political independence was founded on economic self-sufficiency, which in turn depended on the ability of the young nation to reduce its vast consumption of English imports and manufacture industrial goods at home. The new mood, heightened by wartime demands for military and industrial goods and the postwar desire to prove the compatibility of republican government and a high standard of living, viewed technology piracy as the premier tool to industrial development. The weakness of the national government left the initiative for American industrialization in the hands of voluntary associations like the Philadelphia society and aggressive individuals like Coxe who, capriciously, and without considering the wider implications of their actions, cast a wide net in their effort to lure artisans and technology to the new nation. The intellectual internationalism of the Enlightenment gave way to an exclusive technological nationalism.

CHAPTER 5

Official Orchestration of Technology Smuggling

On June 3, 1790, the first Congress under the newly ratified Constitution faced the question of subsidizing the transfer of technology. A group of glassmakers from New Bremen, Maryland, requested compensation for the cost of traveling from Germany and setting up a factory in the United States. A Congressional committee considered the matter and recommended lending John Fried Amelung, the group's leader and primary investor, eight thousand dollars. The money was to compensate him for the costs of bringing hundreds of European glass workers, reasoning that "a manufactory attended with so much difficulty in its commencement, so important in its consequences to the United States, and of such general utility to the whole Union, ought to receive the assistance and protection of the United States." Amelung, however, never received a penny from the Federal government. Congressional opponents of the subsidy prevailed, establishing thereby an important precedent as to the manner in which the young republic would deal with the importation of European technology.[1]

The affair began shortly after the signing of the Anglo-American peace accord in Paris. Seizing on what he perceived was an opening up of opportunities in the newly formed nation, Amelung set up a company with leading Bremen merchants "to establish a Glass-House" in the United States. Benjamin Crocket of Baltimore was visiting Bremen at the time, and he told the Germans that materials for the production of glass were both cheap and abundant in Maryland. Crocket also led the group to believe that the state would take effective measures to support the venture. The group therefore chose to set up its factory in Maryland, expecting "that the Government of this State would encourage and assist to utmost" by allocating the necessary land, giving the enterprise priority over other manufacturers in procuring supplies, and subsidizing the building of the factory, because it "certainly deserves the patronage of the Public."

Amelung advertised for skilled glass blowers interested in migrating to the United States and practicing their trade there, and his campaign lured many artisans who headed to the state of Hanover, where Bremen was located, from all over Germany. The harsh winter of 1784 caused a crucial delay. Some could not travel because the rivers froze and others arrived so weakened that "they could not be directly transported." The delay complicated matters. British sea captains and merchants in Bremen at the time wrote to their officials about it and "this jealous Nation, who look on the glass trade as an important one, desired the Government in Hanover, to do all that was in their power to frustrate a plan which they feared, would be to their loss, and greatly to the benefit of this country." The German states of Hanover, Brunswick, and Hesse, and the smaller neighboring principalities responded to the English demand and, according to Amelung, "all possible obstacles were partly by intrigue, partly by force and despotic behavior thrown in my way—the workmen I had engaged were detained, and nothing left untried to oppose me." The government at Hanover prohibited further recruiting and tried to stop the group. Amelung, however, quickly left for America with the workmen he had already assembled, because "I would not expose myself and family, to the rage which then took place."[2]

Meanwhile, Herman Heyman, another glassmaker from Bremen, approached Benjamin Franklin with a familiar request. Having heard that American manufacturing was still in its infancy, he informed the American minister that a group of glassmakers from Bremen was interested in emigrating to North America. "It can't but be very advantageous as well to your good Country as likewise to the Commoners," Heyman explained, "to Erect a Glass-Manufactory in some part of the United States." The group headed to Maryland. Their leader was planning to take the first vessel to Baltimore in the spring and personally supervise the establishment of a glass manufactory. Amelung, Heyman reported, "carries besides him 80 more Families all Experienced to our Purpose in the vessel for Baltimore." Heyman asked Franklin what kind of help they could expect from Maryland, and requested letters of introduction to the state's elite so that the German glass workers would receive an "agreeable Reception."[3] While there is no record of Franklin's response, apparently he did provide the group with letters of introduction.

As Amelung told it, a British vessel bent on detaining the glassmakers miraculously failed to catch up with their ship. In August 1784 he and sixty-eight German workers disembarked at the port of Baltimore. In November, fourteen additional workers arrived via Holland. Once in America, carrying letters of introduction from Franklin and Adams and aided by three Maryland gentlemen, Amelung purchased land and erected his factory.[4] He was instantly successful. In fact, the demand for his glass was so great that he sent an assistant back to Germany to recruit more artisans and open another factory.

In 1787 Amelung wrote *Remarks on Manufactures* to promote his product, factory, and cause. He boasted that his "glass is cheaper, and of better quality, than a great deal of what is imported." Even though he already employed nearly 350 workers at his shop, he was still looking for experienced glassmakers and encouraged recent arrivals to turn to him. He promised handsome rewards to anyone who referred an artisan to him. By the following year, however, his fortunes took a turn for the worse and he looked for public support.

Finally, and most importantly, Amelung had spent twenty thousand pounds out of his own pocket bringing the first group to the United States and now was spending more on sending a recruiting agent to Germany to bring over the new group. He first applied to the State of Maryland for financial assistance in 1788, explaining that he had brought glass manufacturing to perfection at heavy personal cost. His application was favorably received, and he was given a loan of one thousand pounds and a tax exemption for five years.

The Maryland subsidy proved insufficient. Early in 1789 the factory was destroyed by fire and on May 26, 1790, Amelung turned to the first federal Congress which had just convened in New York. He boasted of his contribution to the nation in the previous years and couched his request in the context of the national struggle against British domination. Congress should help him because "measures are now taking in England to prevent the success of the Manufactory; so that the Works, which bid fair to become of great and lasting Utility to the United States, are in danger of being rendered totally useless." He believed that the quality of his product and his service to the United States entitled him to expect "the attention of the Government and the patronage of the Public."

Amelung had powerful allies. President Washington wrote enthusiastically to Jefferson about the project and saw it as another pillar of his plan to make the Potomac a major commercial artery. Congressman Charles Carroll of Carrollton, one of the richest men in Maryland and Amelung's neighbor and powerful ally, urged the federal government make him the loan. Carroll reasoned that Amelung had provided a valuable service to his country. He had brought

FIGURE 5. Sugar bowl with cover, ca. 1785–95, manufactured by John Amelung's glass manufactory in New Bremen, Maryland. The bowl was custom-made for Christina Geeding (1779–1814) and inscribed on its front: "To Miss. C. G. / In Washington City." Amelung's imported technology established the standards of quality and beauty for glass manufacturing in America. Courtesy of the Winterthur Museum, Winterthur, Delaware).

over workers and introduced hitherto unknown technology. Congress, however, declined to make the loan, though hardly because it was taking a stand against technology piracy. William Loughton Smith of South Carolina argued that the federal government did not have the power to loan money to individual entrepreneurs. Theodore Sedgwick of Massachussetts pointed that that many "manufacturing enterprises" were "languishing" in the United States "for want of encouragement." In 1790, before America's finances were secured, the federal government was not in a position to subsidize the project regardless of how just the plea sounded. [5]

The story of how a group of German glassmakers came to the North America expecting governmental subsidy illustrates the complex terrain and multiple levels on which the transfer of technology took place in the aftermath of the American victory over Britain. Amelung had to circumvent European restrictions. In search of support he moved back and forth between representatives of the Confederation and state governments. Ultimately, he came close to enlisting the aid of the newly established federal government, only to be turned back at the last moment by a Congress not yet up to the task of supporting the introducers of new technology to the United States. Amelung's travails demonstrate that the contest over the diffusion of industrial technology went beyond the activities of private individuals, businesses, and associations. The relationship between political authority and the ownership of ideas and inventions was caught in two competing unstable relationships: between the states and the central government under the Articles of Confederation, and between the new collective American political entity and its former colonizer. This chapter explores the same period studied in the previous one, focusing on the way the American states and ultimately the U.S. Constitution came to formulate a unique national information policy.

Launching Anglo-American
Technology Competition

The international perspective takes the discussion back to London in 1783, where the surprising British defeat at the hands of the American rebels and their hated European allies soured John Baker Holroyd, earl of Sheffield. A devout proponent of British imperialism and mercantilism, he was appalled by the 1782 Shelburne ministry's appeasement of the United States. Holroyd determined to influence Minister of State Charles James Fox to stiffen the British attitude toward the former colonists—to show them the disastrous consequences of their foolish independent course. While Shelburne dreamed of reconstructing the Anglo-American connection in all but name, his political rivals in London, led by Fox, Holroyd, William Jenkinson, and William Eden successfully toppled his ministry and embarked on a confrontational path.

Holroyd wanted to make sure that Parliament and the ministry remained true to the mercantilist principles of the Empire. In 1783 he published a long polemic, *Observations on the Commerce of the American States*, arguing against taking a conciliatory approach toward the Americans. Sheffield argued that the balance of trade between the two nations, which heavily favored England, was likely to remain unchanged for the foreseeable future. American producers could sell their products only through British channels because they could find no viable alternative to the Empire's markets, goods, and credit. Sheffield saw no threat to continued British domination of the American markets because of the lower price and superior quality of British goods. Moreover, the prerevolutionary cultural habit of American consumers disposed them to prefer British manufactured goods over all competitors. Excluding American ships from the Empire promised to benefit British shipping and mercantile interests. The ministry followed Sheffield's recommendations. New orders in council were issued on July 2, 1783, which placed Anglo-American relations on the same footing as Great Britain's relations with its European mercantile rivals.

The policy could backfire. Trade restrictions risked reducing Anglo-American commercial traffic, thereby raising the price of English manufactured goods in America and prompting the development of local industry. But Holroyd was certain that it would "be a long time before the Americans can manufacture for themselves." The high cost of labor in America would discourage investors. Skilled immigrants, tempted by the affordability and availability of land, would abandon their trades; "they will not work at manufactures when they can get double the profit by farming." The progress of American industrialization would "be stopped by the high price of labour, and the more pleasing and more profitable employment of agriculture." Furthermore, the urban setting necessary to industrialization was unlikely to develop "while the spirit of emigration from New-England provinces to their interior parts of the continent rages full as much as [it] has ever done from Europe to America."[6]

Trying to make sure that this forecast would come true, Sheffield went on to discourage emigration. Rosy pictures from the New World were deceptive. "The emigrants from Europe to the American States will be miserably disappointed." They write glorious stories of life in America because, "having got into a scrape, they may wish to lead others after them." They do not come back to Britain primarily because they daily exhaust their resources trying to survive in the unforgiving environment of the New World. What keeps them in America is often "the difficulty and shame of returning home." Other writers echoed Holroyd's sentiments. James Hughes, an English cotton artisan from Manchester who was contemplating a move to the United States, reported to Franklin of "the general opinion entertained here by the great Manufacturers and Merchants of the impossibility of manufacturing among you for a Century or two to come. The great and I think almost only argument of consequence against your manufacturing arises from the high price of Labour." A loyalist who had fought with the British during the Revolutionary War went on an American tour and reported that he saw nothing but misery—a country "without artisans" and "without manufacturers." Sheffield himself concluded his discussion by declaring: "Emigration is the natural resource of the culprit, and those who have made themselves the object of contempt and neglect; but it is by no means necessary to the industrious."[7]

Such polemics echoed across the Atlantic. The decades of the imperial conflict conditioned Americans to expect such hostile tones from the British mercantilist sector and former Tories. But much to their chagrin, the predictions of America's enemies materialized. The post-Revolution United States economy seemed to regress. The Confederation plunged into an economic recession fueled mostly by the closure of the West Indian markets to American agricultural exports. And patriots admitted that for all the nationalist hyperbole of the struggle for independence, the years of conflict had retarded the growth of American science and technology.[8] The separation from the Empire had come home to roost.

Some Americans felt the need to discredit Sheffield's *Observations*. The banker William Bingham, who had a first-hand knowledge of the workings of the Empire since he served in the 1770s as Britain's, and later, the United States' consul in Martinique, argued that England's economy depended on selling its manufactured products overseas. Unfriendly policies toward the United States would precipitate measures that would curb American buying of British products. Declining demand for British products would force factories to lay off workers. The unemployed, Bingham predicted, "in their own defense, will emigrate to America." Bingham warned that American partiality to British goods was eroding and the migration of skilled men from all over Europe was likely to change American purchasing habits away from British goods towards continental European and American products. Bingham predicted that the immigration of industrial workers and scientific men would quickly help Americans catch up with English industrial technology.[9]

Tench Coxe had a somewhat different response. Less concerned with the exclusion of commercial shipping from the West Indies, he saw in the British policy an opening for the development of American industry. The United States should learn from Britain. Before continental artisans brought over dyeing techniques, for example, that art did not exist in the British Isles. A century later English textiles dominated the world market. Coxe believed that a similar process would take place in the United States. Artisans' migration would quickly turn a nonindustrialized country into a leading exporter of industrial goods. High wages and liberal government were already attracting "manufacturers and artizans in the manual branches." The scarcity of labor was hastening the pace of American industrialization because new machinery "yields the greatest profit in countries where the price of labour is the highest." American entrepreneurs were already investing "great sums towards the introduction of cotton mills, wool mills, flax mills, and other valuable branches of machine manufacturing." Sheffield's gloating over the superiority of British industry, he argued, was outdated. The end of the Revolution meant that British artisans could "now emigrate with the greatest convenience" to the United States. Sheffield was wrong, Coxe argued, because he failed to see that American manufactures were on their way to becoming "the most successful competitors with those of Great Britain in the American market."[10]

Prohibitions on the emigration of artisans and the exportation of machinery from the British Empire had been in effect throughout the eighteenth century. In the mid 1770s, as the imperial conflict took shape, Parliament ruled that all people leaving for the North

American colonies from the British Isles and Ireland with intent to settle there must pay fifty pounds per head. In the period following American independence, however, growing anxiety in Britain over industrial piracy prompted stronger legislation and stricter enforcement. Exporting industrial equipment for the manufacture of textiles, leather, paper, metals, glass and clocks was prohibited in the 1780s. The restrictions were particularly comprehensive regarding everything connected with the textile industry, covering existing as well as future developments. Robert Owen, recalling his early days in England's textile industry, reported that in the 1780s the "cotton mills were closed against all strangers, and no one was admitted. They were kept with great jealousy against all intruders: the outer doors being always locked."[11] A two-hundred-pound fine, forfeiture of equipment, and twelve months' imprisonment (or a five-hundred-pound fine, forfeiture, and imprisonment in the case of textile machinery) were laid down for the export or attempted export of industrial machinery. The export of steam engines was prohibited temporarily in 1785.

No one was more attuned to these anxieties than England's most successful eighteenth-century patentee, Richard Arkwright. When Arkwright thought Parliament and the ministry did not show sufficient appreciation for his technological contributions, he threatened to "publish descriptions and copper plates of all the parts, that it might be known to foreign nations as well as our own." Arkwright's patent monopoly was invalidated in 1785, however. The restrictions on its exportation nevertheless remained. In fact, embittered by rulings against him by British courts, Arkwright may have disclosed his industrial trade secrets to William Pollard, fully knowing he was on his way to the United States.[12]

Prohibitions on the export of machinery, then, did not apply exclusively to items still protected as patented inventions. Innovations belonged to individual inventors for the prescribed number of years only within the confines of the British state. From an international perspective, ownership of knowledge rested with the state. After the term of patents expired, ownership of industrial innovations became part of the public domain, subject to the mercantilist regulations of the Empire. Before the American Revolution intellectual property policy in the peripheries was subservient to the needs of the metropolis. Most colonies did not establish an organized patent system of their own. The ultimate decision about the validity of colonial patents resided in London. In the colonial period, then, individuals' intellectual property in the Empire was conceived in the broader context of a mercantilist national information policy. After U.S. independence was secured, most British officials followed Sheffield's lead and belittled American industrial potential. They believed that emigrants to the United States would end up regretting their move, and their reports to their relatives back home would curtail the enthusiasm to emigrate. When large-scale emigration to North America recommenced, some tried to calm anxious mercantilists by assuring them that the professional caliber of the emigrants was rather low. A customs official from Newry, Ireland, reported to the government in August 1783 that the passengers on the three ships that just left for America were not the most skilled workers, but "the lower order of tradesmen." He added that the reports immigrants send back home were "very discouraging, and will probably continue to damp the spirit of emigration."[13]

As migration to the former colonies picked up steam, officials began to voice concern that many of the emigrants possessed skills that could quickly transform the United States into an industrial competitor of Great Britain. Loyalist William Smith, who left for England in 1783 and later served as chief justice of Canada, published in 1784 an anti-emigration pamphlet in which he repeated Sheffield's prediction of continued domination of the American market by British manufacturing. He warned against reaching any form of understanding with the United States because it might open the door for "that crafty people, under the specious pretense of opening their ports by a commercial treaty to our manufactures, to decoy our artificers, and make Englishmen do what the whole house of Bourbon were never able to accomplish by the sword." Every emigrant to the United States, he warned, "is lost to Great Britain." If the Empire wished to maintain its international position it must stop the flood of emigrants and "find employment for her people." The cries of Sheffield and his allies were heeded in London. By 1788 the government decided to ask its consuls in the United States to report whether the immigrants arriving had paid for their trips or arrived as indentured servants, and what inducements were offered to prospective migrants. Penalties on emigration became stiffer than those on machine smuggling, reflecting the greater official concern with the flight of skill. Under the new laws artisans and manufacturers were prohibited from leaving Britain and Ireland for territories outside the Empire. Textile workers were not even allowed to migrate within the Empire outside the British Isles. Illegal emigrants lost their nationality and property, and if apprehended could be convicted of treason. [14]

Americans roamed England in the 1780s looking for recruits. Abel Buel of Killingworth, Connecticut, a convicted counterfeiter who was pardoned on account of his appropriation of European methods of grinding and polishing crystals because it was "a great saving and advantage" to the state, went to England to copy the latest developments in textile production. Hartford's mercantile houses of Wadsworth and Colt, for example, who later were among the owners of Hartford's first textile factories, recruited about one hundred English migrants in 1784 to settle in Connecticut. British authorities, in turn, tried to crack down on American industrial espionage. American agent Thomas Digges reported to Jefferson from Dublin that his recruiting of "useful mechanics" had gotten him into trouble, and that two of the men he had recruited were "under rigorous trial in the Courts here for attempting to ship themselves with their Tools implements &ca &ca." Later in the same letter Digges asked Jefferson to help facilitate the migration of Franklin's old acquaintance, Henry Wyld. He instructed Jefferson, however, to communicate to Wyld through him because "as a Citizen and tradesman He may be much injured if the substance of this correspondence should become known." English authorities, indeed, tightened restrictions on foreign recruitment in the 1780s. Recruiting agents could be fined five hundred pounds and imprisoned for twelve months for each emigrant they enticed. Thomas Philpot, for example, was convicted in 1788 of inducing men to migrate from Ireland to America. He was fined five hundred pounds and jailed for a year.[15]

The English ports were naturally the last line of defense. Ship captains were required to submit lists detailing passenger occupations to customs officials before departing. Shipmasters were liable to a pay a fine of one hundred pounds for each passenger who was illegally migrating to North America. At least in one instance the Royal Navy seized an illegal emigrant on an American ship, the *Union*, as it was leaving Liverpool.[16] A guide for emigrants published early in the nineteenth century reported that before an emigrant could pass the custom house at Liverpool or at other British ports, he had to furnish the following certificate:

> We, the undersigned Churchwardens and Overseers of parish of the county of —— do hereby certify and declare unto the officers of his Majesty's customs, and all other whom it may concern, that we have known A. B. of the parish of —— aforesaid, for several years last past; and that the trade or business of the said A. B. during all the time we have known him, hath been that of a ——. And we do further particularly certify and declare that the said A. B. is not, nor hath ever been, a manufacturer or artificer in wool, iron, steel, brass, or any other metal, nor is he,

or has he ever been, a watch-maker, or clock-maker, or any other manufacturer or artificer whatsoever. And we do further certify that the said A. B. is about—years of age, stands—feet and—inches, or thereabout, in appearance.[17]

The British efforts to stem the outflow of machines and artisans failed. Americans rarely had difficulty appropriating the knowledge and machinery they sought. Industrial espionage overcame public and private restrictions. Had individuals engaged in covert appropriation of English technology at their own risk, the matter would have been strictly a question of local law enforcement. The activities of official American agencies and their representatives, however, transformed the technology piracy of the 1780s into an all-out economic contest between the United States and its former ruler in which respect for individuals' and nations' intellectual property took a back seat to the nationalist developmental impulse. Concurrent with the feverish activities of entrepreneurs, promoters, and voluntary associations to pirate forbidden know-how, the 1780s saw officials of the federal and state governments engage in similar activities. On both levels, independence forced Americans to define their policies toward intellectual property in the local, national, and international contexts. Before there was some order, however, there was chaos. [18]

Diplomats in the Service of Technology

The United States emerged from its war for independence not as a coherent political entity, but as a loose coalition of competing states. The political mechanism established under the Articles of Confederation provided for a government by a national legislature, but left authority over the national purse and all final power to make and execute laws entirely in the hands of the states. Conflicts between the states over western claims, commercial regulations, national tariffs, and navigation of the Mississippi underscored that the Confederation could not speak with a unified voice. Foreign policy was the only arena where the central government could exercise initiative and authority under the Articles of Confederation. Only in Europe could representatives of the United States speak and act on behalf of the whole. In fact, they were practically the only people who consistently behaved as if the United States existed as a single cohesive entity in the 1780s.[19]

The subject of American industrialization came up in diplomatic negotiations even before American independence was secured. During the peace negotiations Robert R. Livingston instructed John Jay to impress upon the European nations that America would remain agricultural "while a market shall be afforded for our produce. But if that market [primarily the slave colonies of the West Indies] is shut against us; if we cannot vend what we raise, we shall . . . from necessity, manufacture for ourselves." Similarly, John Adams declared in 1783 that "it will be a long time before the Americans can manufacture for themselves" as "the high price of labour, and the more pleasing and more profitable employment of agriculture" discouraged industrialization.[20] For Livingston and Adams, developing American manufacturing was a matter of last resort. The United States would industrialize only if its agricultural exports were checked by mercantilist regulations.

America's leading diplomat in the second half of the 1780s, Thomas Jefferson, gained a reputation as its most outspoken anti-industrialist. Jefferson, who spent half of the decade in France working to improve Franco-American trade relations as an alternative to British commercial domination, associated industrialization with the ills of English society. His only book, *Notes on the State of Virginia*, published while he was in Paris, blasted manufacturing with typical eloquence. He rejected the notion that "every state should endeavor to manufacture for itself." His ideal America was an agrarian society: "let us never wish to see our citizens occupied at a work-bench, or twirling a distaff. Carpenters, masons, smiths, are wanting in husbandry: but, for the general operation of manufacture, let our workshops remain in Europe."[21]

This passage belongs to the republican rhetoric of the Revolution, which depicted virtuous agricultural political economy as valiantly resisting the worldwide onslaught of an unjust and corrupt commercial and industrial order. Developing American manufacturing and duplicating the inequality and exploitation of England threatened to undermine the essential goal of the Revolution—namely the preservation of republican simplicity and equality. Persuading European artisans to immigrate so that they could develop American industry was incompatible with this attitude. At times, Jefferson expressed similar sentiments to people approaching him in Paris. A Frenchman claiming he had discovered a new method of preserving flour requested a subsidy from the American government for introducing the method to the United States. Jefferson replied that "every discovery which multiplies the subsistence of men, must be a matter of joy to every friend to humanity." Yet, the United States does not offer any inducement "for its communication. Their policy is to leave their citizens free, neither restraining nor aiding them in their products." He nevertheless suggested that the inventor turn to other governments who may be "sensible to the duty they are under of cultivating useful discoveries, as to reward you amply for yours." And to Henry Wyld, who was still offering to migrate so as to industrialize the United States in 1785, Jefferson wrote: "It is impossible that manufactures should succeed in America from the high price of labour" caused by "the great demand of labour for agriculture." Any industrial worker who emigrates is likely to change his vocation upon arriving in America, "tempted by the independence in which that places him."[22]

While Jefferson was the best-known of the Americans in Europe, the sentiments expressed in *Notes on Virginia* and the letter to Wyld were not the dominant point of view among them. On the contrary, American representatives of all ranks, including Jefferson himself, shared a commitment to the development of American industry. The other leading American in Europe at the time, John Adams, appreciated the importance of industry to the survival of the United States. To be sure, Adams shared his contemporaries' preference for the republic not to "manufactures enough for her own Consumption, these one thousand years." Yet, he believed that the technological developments of his time were an integral part of launching the new American experiment, and his *Defense of the Constitutions* praised them for the "Changes in the condition of the World and the human character" they have occasioned. "Emulation really seems to produce genius," he wrote in 1790, and "next to self preservation will forever be the great spring of human action."[23]

Like Franklin before them, American representatives in Europe were besieged by artisans who offered to bring hitherto unknown technologies to the United States in exchange for special privileges. Some of these were the very same men who had earlier approached Franklin. Henry Wyld, for example, wrote Jefferson that so long as the United States "are beholden to a foreign country for Artists, your manufactures are precarious." He explained that since he was informed of the "real wants" of the people of the republic, he would endeavor to procure help on his own and cross the Atlantic. Wyld reminded Jefferson that his efforts would amount to a net acquisition of skill and manufacturing for the United States and only asked for "a Vessel in which we could stow bulky substances, and bring over few hands without expence."[24]

Wyld's approach was not unique. Many European artisans similarly turned to American officials and private citizens with similar requests. These advances reveal the emergence of a new kind of player in the battle over industrial technology—the artisan who had illicitly made his way out of the British Isles and was looking to sell his trade to the highest bidder. One Joseph Fielding approached Jefferson saying that he initially migrated from England to France and planned to go no farther, but the political turbulence there persuaded him to look elsewhere. He claimed to be an assignee of Arkwright who understood "the making of all kinds of machinery for the Spinning as well as the Manufacturing." He was willing to consider America, but inquired of Jefferson "what encouragement wou'd be given, if I was willing to Establish such a Manufactory as the Manchester Manufactory?"[25]

Some artisans skipped the diplomatic middlemen in Europe and wrote directly to the Continental Congress. William McCormick of Ireland claimed to have known the cotton manufacturing techniques practiced at Manchester, and asked the Continental Congress to subsidize his passage to Pennsylvania where he could establish a factory. The count of Beaufort wrote the Continental Congress in October 1785 that the technological disparity between Europe and the United States made it essential for the latter to look for ways of closing the gap. If Congress gave him a huge tract of land with rivers and waterfalls, he promised to use American waterpower "to establish therein a number of new arts and manufactures" by bringing over the finest European artisans. Congress considered the proposal but declined to pursue it, primarily because it could grant neither the land nor the political autonomy Beaufort demanded.[26]

American officials on both sides of the Atlantic declined these direct appeals. Charles Thomson, secretary of the Continental Congress, declared in 1784: "The ports of the United States are open to all foreigners and the several states are ready to receive any men of science or abilities who may be willing to settle among them, but the sovereign body of the Union do not seem to think it necessary to give any particular encouragement to any nation or to any individuals." And Jefferson told Wyld that it was "not the policy of the government in that country to give any aid to works of any kind . . . . I must add that I have neither the authority nor the means of assisting any persons in their passage to that country."[27] Officials of the American government under the Articles of Confederation repeatedly stated that the United States would not actively sponsor the appropriation and smuggling of European technology.

These emphatic refusals were hardly the last word on the subject. Individual Americans recruited artisans and offered inducements for immigrating. Moreover, these private capitalists often turned to American officials for support. Silas Deane, convinced that machinery enabled English manufacturers to produce cheaper products despite the high cost of labor in Great Britain, offered, if given sufficient reward, to introduce the steam engine into the United States. Thomas Digges wrote William Carmichael, the American chargé d'affaires in Madrid, that he was about to travel to observe English manufactures in northern England and Scotland, and reported "a great appearance of *vast* Emigration to America, & I encourage it all I can." Needless to say, Carmichael did not respond urging him to stop his activities.[28]

Jefferson and Adams themselves, whatever their published views, were also not averse to promoting industrial espionage. Adams's official position as the American minister to the court of Saint James did not prevent him from transmitting for publication in the United States instructions written for the Admiralty for converting cast iron into malleable iron.[29] Adams also armed English immigrant John Noyes with a letter of introduction asking the leaders of Massachusetts to assist him in establishing an ironworks in the commonwealth. Noyes included Adams's letter in his petition to the General Court for a patent monopoly for the production of iron using imported steam engine technology. The Massachusetts legislature complied, and granted Noyes and his partner Paul Revere the patent even though the commonwealth already had water-powered ironworks.

Jefferson was even more active. He participated in the American efforts to procure Arkwright's technologies when he tried to acquire carding and spinning machinery built by immigrant English artisans in France. He was involved in Coxe's attempt to get Andrew Mitchell and his pirated machines smuggled through France to the United States. Even while rejecting Wyld's request for a subsidy, Jefferson was careful not to discourage him from migrating altogether. In fact, he went on to propose Virginia as the ideal cite for the establishment of a modern American textile industry.[30]

Jefferson apparently saw little connection between the miserable living conditions of English industrial workers whom he was so eager to leave in Europe, and the new industrial technology. The man who wanted workshops to remain in Europe went on to advise American travelers to examine "Mechanical arts," so that they could duplicate them in America. In 1785, not knowing of Watt's steam engine, he wrote the Reverend James Madison that he was not aware of the "new method of raising water by steam." During a 1786 visit to England Jefferson was transformed. He enthusiastically praised a steam engine–operated mill he saw near London and commended in the strongest possible words the application of the Boulton and Watt technology to American surroundings. America's most prominent agrarian spokesman admitted that "the mechanical arts in London are carried to a wonderful perfection."[31]

The Marshaling of Governmental Resources

While representatives in Europe labored on behalf of American industries, the states and the Continental Congress struggled to define the meaning and limits of intellectual property in the new nation. The Articles of Confederation addressed neither intellectual property nor patents, and the weakness of the central government stood in the way of forming a unified American information policy.

Indeed, inventors and importers of technology who turned to Congress did not know what to expect. James Rumsey was a successful and well-connected Maryland millwright whose connections with some of Virginia's leading families earned him the position of chief engineer for the Potomac Company—an enterprise the commonwealth established to build canals in hopes of making the Potomac the chief commercial artery to the west. Rumsey was also engaged in developing a jet-propelled steamboat and, supported by his financial backer George Washington, applied for a patent from the Continental Congress. Congress rewarded Rumsey's ingenuity with thirty thousand acres in the west rather than with a production monopoly. The form of reward attests to Congress's lack of authority under the Articles to protect intellectual property in all the states. In other words, lacking the power to grant a monopoly, Congress rewarded an inventor out of its only asset, western land. [32]

The 1780s did see a rather more concerted effort to address the question of the rights of authors to profit from their intellectual labor. Connecticut's General Assembly enacted a copyright legislation in January 1783 stating that "every author should be secured in receiving the profits that may arise from the sale of his works, and such security may encourage men of learning." At the urging of Oliver Wolcott of Connecticut, Congress picked up the matter shortly thereafter. A committee composed of Hugh Williamson, Ralph Izard, and James Madison, formed in March 1783, was assigned to consider the issue. Two months later the committee submitted a report declaring that "nothing is more properly a man's own than the fruit of his study, and that the protection and security of literary property would greatly tend to encourage genius, to promote useful discoveries and to the extension of arts." The Continental Congress thereupon recommended that the states pass copyright laws granting a fourteen-year ownership of books written by citizens of the United States. The resolution explicitly denied protection to foreign authors, thus encouraging the unauthorized reprinting of mostly British authors in North America. [33]

State legislatures turned their attention to authors' rights soon after. Some went further than merely supporting copyright, and made declarations of principle in support of other forms of intellectual property. North Carolina, for example, affirmed that "nothing is more strictly a man's own than the fruit of his study, and it is proper that men should be encouraged to pursue useful knowledge by the hope of reward; and . . . the security of literary property must greatly tend to encourage genius, to promote useful discoveries, and to the general extension of arts and commerce."[34] The state's legislature employed both natural rights and utilitarian reasoning to justify its support for intellectual property, even though the two perspectives were somewhat incongruent. On the one hand it declared the fruit of the mind to be private property, and on the other it insisted that bestowing exclusive rights over ideas and discoveries upon individuals would in the long run benefit all members of society. This dual reasoning became the principle foundation of American support for intellectual property.

The copyright movement of the 1780s was triumphant. By 1786 all states, with the exception of Delaware, passed acts that in principle established their commitment to protecting the intellectual property of authors. The copyright movement owed its success, however, less to Congressional concern for the well-being of authors than to the energetic campaign of Noah Webster, whose *Grammatical Institute of the English Language* was a best-seller. Webster feared that pirated versions of the book would deprive him of profits. He therefore lobbied each state legislature to protect his ownership either through the application of the common law, or by acts specifically protecting his book. He enlisted the support of well-respected revolutionaries like Thomas Paine and Joel Barlow to speak out in support of copyright legislation. And he associated his cause with patriotism. His 1783 *American Spelling Book* set out from the outset to establish the legitimacy and distinctiveness of American English. The book that was to replace English-made spellers in American elementary schools included words that were uniquely American such as "rattlesnake," reversed the English *re* ending with an American *er* for words like "theater," and dropped the *u* from the English spelling of words like "labour." Webster's tireless efforts, political connections, and patriotic symbolism made his campaign for the notion of property in authorship highly successful.

The campaign demonstrates the obstacles facing those who looked for the young nation to enact a unified information policy under the Articles of Confederation. Congressional action in favor of the rights of authors consisted merely of a nonbinding resolution indicating the sense of that body, but nothing more. All that Congress could do was make a recommendation. Whether a policy was enacted or not remained up to the states. Similarly, the right to issue patents to reward a mechanical innovation or the introduction of a useful technology from Europe resided exclusively with the states. The underwhelming authority of the central government under the Articles of Confederation meant that much of the pursuit of technological advancement took place at the state level.

Before 1775 the information policy of the colonies was subsumed under the mercantilist relations with the metropolis. Given colonial subservience, local patents for innovation were of limited value and not much in use. Colonial legislators occasionally awarded manufacturing grants to encourage invention or duplicate English machinery. Once independent, however, the states took up the promotion of technology by issuing patents to inventors and introducers of technology. The old manufacturing grant symbolizing dependence upon the English economy gave way to a rush of patents aiming to construct a free American economy. Pennsylvania, New York, Massachusetts, and Connecticut led the way in offering loans to introducers of hitherto unknown technologies, while Massachusetts acquired models of textile machinery and encouraged industrialists to copy them and put them into operation.[35]

Spearheaded by the rapidly industrializing Philadelphia region, Pennsylvania took the lead. As a colony it had not granted a single patent, but in the 1780s it led all other states in issuing exclusive patents for discoveries and introductions of industrial technology. The Pennsylvania legislature began offering premiums and bonuses to introducers of new technology as soon as the separation from the Empire became permanent. The provincial assembly voted fifteen pounds to an immigrant weaver who promised to build English-style jennies in Philadelphia, and forty pounds to an English threadmaker for his promised contribution to American technology. And in 1788 it gave Joseph Hague one hundred dollars for successfully pirating textile machinery. The Pennsylvania legislature further showed its support for American appropriation of forbidden knowledge by voting to buy one hundred shares of the Pennsylvania Society for the Promotion of Manufactures—an organization explicitly committed to smuggling technology to America.[36]

Senior state officials and legislators in other states openly championed the appropriation of protected industrial technology from Europe, where the "spirit of discovery and improvement" originated. The Massachusetts General Court supported the establishment of the American Academy of Arts in 1780, reasoning that the state had a responsibility to support "Men of Genius and Learning" who would diffuse knowledge throughout Massachusetts. Governor James Bowdoin, the society's first president, was far more interested in the promotion and dissemination of technology than in the theoretical promotion of science. "Every wise government has encouraged mechanics, labourers, and new settlers, to emigrate into it," wrote a Massachusetts advocate of industrial self-sufficiency. "It is particularly the interest of a young country like America so to do."

The writer went on to call on the commonwealth's legislature to "repeal all laws restricting the emigration of foreigners, and make a new one, excusing for a certain number of years, all industrious labourers and servants and artists and mechanics, who may come and settle amongst us, from paying any kind of tax whatever. Further, as an encouragement to the owners of ships it is proposed that every one who may bring any such persons into the state, shall have, for each one so brought in, two tons of the vessel's burden excused from the tonnage duty." Similar sentiments generated similar concerted activities in all the New England and Mid-Atlantic states.[37]

Immigrant artisans like Amelung found sympathetic ears and open wallets in the state legislatures. Two Englishmen, James Leonard and Thomas Somers, looked in the mid 1780s for public or private support for establishing a textile factory. At first, these efforts yielded no governmental response. Just before they were about to give up and return to England they met the prominent Massachusetts politician George Cabot. Cabot was concerned with the state's reliance on imported textiles and recognized the value of developing local manufacturing in Massachusetts. He decided to patronize the enterprise and led the formation of an investment group set on establishing a textile factory in the town of Beverly. Somers and Leonard, however, were dissatisfied with private investment and looked for more support from the state. Somers, claiming he was a "perfect master of the weaving in the speediest manner" and of other modern textile skills, petitioned the Massachusetts legislature in February 1787 for financial assistance as a reward for introducing textile technology to America. He had gone to England "at his own risque and expense . . . to procure the machines for carding and spinning cotton," and thought it was appropriate for the state to compensate him for his risk, investment, and effort. Members of the General Court were persuaded, and decided the following month to "encourage the aforesaid manufactures," and grant Somers "twenty pounds, lawful money, to be applied to the purposes aforesaid." Hugh Orr, a Scottish immigrant who became a member of the Massachusetts Senate in the 1780s, was appointed to oversee the enterprise. In January 1789, some of Massachusetts's most prominent men, including Somers, Leonard, John and George Cabot, and Henry Higginson, submitted a new petition to the legislature extolling the Beverly factory and declaring that the project "has reached that point in population and agriculture that it becomes necessary to establish manufactures. That no kind of manufactures appears to them more practicable, at present, or more useful than that of cotton. The principal part of the labor is performed by machinery." The petitioners argued that because the entire community stood to benefit from the creation of local textile manufacturing in the commonwealth of Massachusetts, it was "absolutely necessary to the establishment of such a manufacture as this that the Legislature should grant some particular favors to the first adventurers." A detailed account of the expenses was enclosed, which included the purchase of English machinery and £220 to cover the cost of moving to Beverly and living expenses for the two British artisans and their families. The commonwealth's legislature complied in February 1789; it incorporated "The Proprietors of the Beverly Cotton Manufactory," subsidized its initial cost of operating, and exempted the foremen from paying the state's poll tax. The General Court declared that it was "essential to the true interest of this Commonwealth, to encourage within the same, the introduction of such manufactures as will give the most extensive and profitable employment to its citizens, and thereby, instead of these emigrations which are ruinous to the State, increase the number of manufacturers, who by consuming the productions of the soil will add to the value of it."[38]

At times, legislators looked for creative ways to finance technology piracy. Connecticut passed An Act for the Encouragement of Certain Manufacturing in the State in 1788, which exempted a number of woolen companies from state taxes. The following year the state granted a tax-free status to buildings used for cotton, linen, and wool manufactures. In order to encourage men to work in these factories the legislature exempted all their employees from the poll tax for two years. Hugh Orr sponsored the Atlantic passage of Robert and Alexander Barr, who established a cotton carding, roving, and spinning machinery on the model of Richard Arkwright's water frame. The Massachusetts legislature showed its support for such illicit operations by sponsoring the importation of three of the four machines used in the Barr operation. A special committee of the General Court examined the machines upon their arrival and recommended that a two-hundred-dollar loan be made "to enable them to complete the said three machines and also a roping machine, and to construct such other machines as are necessary for the purpose of carding, roping, and spinning of sheep's wool." The following year the Barr brothers were exempted from repaying the loan. The generosity of the General Court reached new levels when it granted the corporation six tickets in the state's lottery, none of them blanks. The Connecticut General Assembly resorted to similar measures to support technology piracy. It sponsored a state lottery in December 1790 to finance the operations of the Hartford Woolen Manufactory. Daniel Hinsdale, the company's agent, explained that "the grant of a Lottery, for the purpose of raising the sum of One Thousand Pounds" would finance the "purchase [of] further useful Machines" to enable the company to build a factory to "the general advantage of the Public." The following year the General Assembly ran another lottery that raised some thirty-two hundred pounds for the construction of a woolen factory in New Haven by William McIntosh, an immigrant from London.[39]

Much of this activity on the state level was justified on patriotic grounds. Silas Deane, whose reputation came under attack during the war for actions he took while serving as the American representative to the court of Louis XVI, went back to Europe to prove his patriotism and reported from there that "nothing would be of more or greater service to the Country, than the introduction" of new machinery. Governor Bowdoin of Massachusetts wrote that the American Academy of Arts and Sciences was founded because "the balance of advantage will always be in favour of that people whose skill, industry, and cheapness of labour, enable them to manufacture, and export, the greatest quantity of commodities . . . And that balance . . . will give them a national superiority in riches, influence and prosperity." "Machines appear to be objects of immense consequence to this country," declared the editors of the *Pennsylvania Gazette.* "It is the duty of every friend to America, at home and abroad, to keep a vigilant eye upon everything of that kind which comes his way."[40]

Efforts by individuals, associations, and states to import European technology altered the economic landscape of North America. State governments awarded monopolies, granted bounties, exempted from taxation, and handed out cash gifts to attract skilled artisans to settle in their midst. Proponents of American industrialization, however, were frustrated by the slow pace and inconsistency of the process. While states increasingly erected a system to grant and regulate patents, the shortcomings of the system were readily apparent. The need to import machines, processes, and skills from Europe, and the absence of an effective federal system of enforcement, undermined the potential effectiveness and value of patents granted in individual states. Inventors and introducers who wanted to ensure continued exclusivity over machinery had to file for patents in each and every state. James Rumsey, for one, followed his successful campaign for a patent with the Continental Congress by filing for patents for his jet-propelled steamboat with the various states. His great rival in the contest over exclusive rights to steamboat technology, John Fitch, tried the same strategy but had less success. Fitch filed a petition with the Continental Congress the same year as Rumsey, but as he lacked Rumsey's political connections his request was denied. Like Rumsey, he realized that success with the Continental Congress was meaningless and turned to campaign in the state legislatures where the real battle over exclusive rights to the steamboat invention took place.

Introducers of forbidden technology faced a similar ordeal. Silas Deane was very impressed with the impact of the new steam engine on mills and ironworks in England, and decided to introduce the Watt engine to America and claim exclusive rights to it. A business associate, Jacob Sebor, assured Deane that the fact that he was not the original inventor of the steam engine would not impede his ability to get a patent for it. "You would find no difficulty in obtaining a patent here or for any other new invention that could possibly be useful in America," Sebor wrote. In order to make sure that he had the exclusive rights over the engine, however, Deane bypassed the central government and turned directly to the states. He applied and received a patent for Watt's engine in seven states: Virginia, North Carolina, Maryland, Connecticut, New York, New Jersey, and Pennsylvania. In securing the patent monopoly in those states, he sought to prevent "larger capitalists" from jumping on the steam engine wagon once they realized how useful it would be in America. Deane hoped that securing a patent in the various states would enable him to take an English partner who could ensure the technical and financial viability of the enterprise.[41]

For all the energy on the state level, the absence of a national mechanism to reward innovation and importation of technology was highly problematic. Production monopolies were unenforceable and inapplicable across state lines. Deane continued to push for the introduction of the Watt engine in America. But his American correspondent, Frederick William Geyer of Boston, doubted the prospects of using steam engines in American mills because such an innovation "must turn out profitable in a Country that has a fixed & Settled Government," and this was not the state of the young nation under the Articles of Confederation. A "patent can be of no use," Geyer continued, "unless it is from Congress, and not from them till they are vested with much more authority."[42] The ineffectiveness of states' granting patents, and the burdensome process of multiple applications by competing applicants to rival political bodies, highlighted the need for crafting a centralized system of patents.

Political divisions and the absence of an effective central authority stood in the way of industrial development and undermined its attractiveness to potential immigrants. Virginia's representative to the Continental Congress, William Grayson, worried that as long as the current system was in place "we shall have no emigrants from beyond seas, and the want of inhabitants is perhaps our only calamity."[43] American efforts to foster the importation of European technology, wrote Coxe in a piece published in the Philadelphia publication *American Museum* in May 1787 just as the delegates were assembling to devise a new plan of government, proved only partially successful because the union, "scarcely held together by a weak and half-formed federal constitution," had a central government "unequal to the complete execution of any salutary purpose." The "present state of things," he argued, "instead of inviting emigrants, deters all who have the means of informing and are capable of thinking." And as the movement to replace the ineffective loose Confederation with a strong central government gathered steam in the second half of the 1780s, some looked for the new national government to "invite emigrations from the rest of the world and fill the empire with the worthiest and happiest of mankind."[44]

Backers of American industrialization expected the men working on the new constitution to devise ways for the federal government to direct the effort at closing the technology gap between the United States and Europe. Echoing revolutionary rhetoric, they equated the sorry state of manufactures with the imperial crisis and spoke of their struggle to develop American industries as the indispensable second chapter of the American Revolution. American industrial backwardness served the interests of British mercantilists who profited handsomely from American dependence on British imports. Moreover, Britain could exploit the skewed balance of trade between the two nations and exclude American vessels from the Empire's ports while the United States had no way of retaliating. "We have nothing to give her which she *esteems*," that withholding which would force England to open its colonial ports to American vessels, complained an American patriot. "We must make her less necessary to us by becoming our manufacturers." Such a situation required that the government should actively introduce unknown industries. It should also attract foreign artisans as the "high price of labor operates equally against exporting as against manufacturing." Nations should " 'spare no expense in procuring the ablest masters in every branch of industry, nor any cost in making the first establishments; providing machines, and every other thing necessary or useful to make the undertaking succeed.' "[45]

Champions of industry backed the constitutional movement that gathered steam in the second half of the 1780s. Concerned with the seemingly insatiable American consumption of imported manufactured goods from Britain, they eagerly anticipated the creation of a central government capable of promoting innovation and creativity in a unified and effective manner. A Connecticut businessman reported that in his circles "Great expectations are formed from the convention that is to meet this day from the different states at Philadelphia," that it would establish a government capable of giving encouragement to innovative manufacturing.[46] Such optimism was well founded. After all, the intellectual force behind the unification movement, James Madison, was on the Congressional committee that urged the states to pass copyright laws in 1783. In 1785 Madison

authored a Virginia bill that generously secured exclusive copyrights to authors over their creations for a period of twenty-one
years. Even future opponents of the Constitution like George Mason
believed that the new central government would be dedicated to the
encouragement of American manufactures. Industrialists thus expected that the Constitutional Convention would establish unified
principles applicable to all forms of intellectual property.[47]

The Constitutional Convention did not disappoint these expectations. On August 18, 1787, Madison and Charles Pinckney of South
Carolina recommended that the Constitution include a clause rewarding creativity in both theoretical and practical realms by granting exclusive rights over creations for a specified period of time.
Madison suggested in addition to "encourage by premiums and
provisions, the advancement of useful knowledge and discoveries."
The subject was forwarded to the Committee of Eleven. We know
nothing of the debates over the issue within the committee. But on
September 5, 1787, the convention unanimously approved the inclusion of a paragraph in the United States Constitution, which in
Article I, section 8 instructed the new government "To promote the
progress of science and useful arts, by securing for limited times to
authors and inventors the exclusive right to their respective writing
and discoveries." The Founding Fathers decided to provide a mechanism by which individual inventors and authors were rewarded for
enriching American society with new devices or writings. Inventors
and writers were the only occupational groups given special benefits
in the United States Constitution.[48]

Why did the United States Constitution specifically instruct the
new central government to promote the progress of useful arts? The
framers have left us little by way of explaining their reasons. Why did
they not specify banking policy or internal improvement, both of
which would fall under the "necessary and proper" clause, yet insist
on promoting knowledge, and even specify doing so by securing

exclusive rights for inventors for a limited time? The presence of the intellectual property clause in the Constitution is all the more remarkable because it is the only place in the document where specific benefits are promised to any group. The patent provision in the United States Constitution was the first ever legal affirmative recognition of the property right embodied in the process that produced innovation.[49]

The inclusion of the intellectual property clause in the Constitution had many possible origins. American constitutional thought originated in British law and practice, in which the principle of intellectual property was firmly established. Local circumstances in Philadelphia may have forced the delegates to pay close attention to the issue. The city was by 1787 the center of the American industrialization effort. The local elite had concluded that technological deficiencies undermined the region's ability to develop local manufacturing and supported the improvement of American know-how by means that were not always kosher. Leading the way, of course, was Tench Coxe who by then had established himself as the preeminent champion of American manufacturing. Coxe had great faith in "European inventions of labour-saving machinery," but recognized that they were "very imperfectly understood, and not possessed in the United States." He wrote Franklin in June about the positive impact of imported machinery and declared that "Emigration from foreign Countries" could fuel American industrialization. On August 9, 1787, nine days before the delegates formed the committee that was assigned to compose the intellectual property clause of the Constitution, Coxe spoke at the University of Pennsylvania and publicly urged them to "examine the conduct of other countries in order to possess ourselves of their methods of encouraging manufactures." Cognizant of the fact that land was just about the only asset the federal government could freely dispense, Coxe proposed rewarding innovation and importation of technology with unsettled parcels of one thousand acres. "By offering these premiums for useful invention, to any citizen of the union, or to any foreigner, who would become a citizen," Coxe suggested, "we might often acquire in the man a compensation for the land . . . of more consequence to the state than all the purchase of money." Another prominent Philadelphian, Benjamin Rush, suggested that the new Constitution establish an office of professor of economy whose duties would be to "unfold the principles and practice of agriculture, and manufactures of all kinds: and to enable him to make his lectures more extensively useful, congress should support a traveling correspondent for him, who should visit all the nations of Europe, and transmit to him from time to time, all the discoveries and improvements that are made in agriculture and manufactures." Such statements by leading men set the stage for the Convention's deliberations on the subject.[50]

The Convention's discussion of the intellectual property clause did not take place in the abstract. The battle between John Fitch and James Rumsey over who would receive governmental backing for his version of the steamboat was a prominent feature of the era's politics, and whatever course the Convention were to take with regard to intellectual property was bound to have ramifications on that contest. Just about every leading American seems to have taken side with either Fitch or Rumsey. On August 22, three days after the intellectual property issue was first raised at the Convention, the delegates took a break from their deliberations to observe Fitch's first attempt to use a steamboat on the Delaware River. We don't know what transpired between Fitch and the delegates as they stood on the riverbank. Fitch, however, had been campaigning to be recognized as the sole inventor of steam-powered boats in America for some time, and it is likely he used the opportunity to promote his cause.

The consensus in favor of the clause suggests widespread cultural acceptance of the measure. No one in particular had to push the delegates to include it in the Constitution. The prevalence of intellectual property clauses in the state constitutions suggests that most American leaders recognized by the 1780s the need to promote literary and industrial creativity in the new nation. In unifying the patent grants on a national scale the Constitutional Convention created an apparatus that spared authors and patentees the chore of having to secure grants in each of the individual states. The Constitution made the state patent systems obsolete.[51]

The clause attracted little attention in the heated battles over ratification of the Constitution. In *Federalist* no. 43 Madison argued that the "public good coincides" in the case of intellectual property "with the claims of individuals. The states cannot separately make effectual provision," and thus this issue merited the action on the national level. At the Pennsylvania ratifying convention Thomas McKean, speaking in support of the Constitution, addressed the clause in the context of championing the virtues of economic unity. The current system, in which authors and inventors had to get patents from thirteen states, he argued, was harmful not only to individuals, but to "science in general."[52]

Some anti-Federalists seized on the incompatibility of the natural rights and utilitarian reasoning that was embodied in the clause. They attacked the Constitution's intent to grant monopolies that would restrict public access to information and innovation as a manner of promoting the general welfare. Maryland's Samuel Chase feared that the restrictive monopoly given to individuals would allow Congress to "destroy the liberty of the press." In Virginia, anti-Federalist George Mason attacked the Congressional power to grant monopolies embodied in the clause as an infringement on liberty. Monopolies, after all, represented privilege, and the Constitution's explicit support for such policies confirmed anti-Federalists' suspicion that the new government was set to serve the few at the expense of the many. Federalists retorted that modern civilized nations protected the rights of authors and inventors because they recognized that such a policy promoted the arts and sciences. North Carolinian James Iredell declared that Mason was "a gentleman of too much taste and knowledge himself to wish to have our government established upon such principles of barbarism as to be able to afford no encouragement to genius."[53]

A strong dissent against the clause originated in Paris. Jefferson, who had some reservations about the proposed Constitution, initially opposed the wording on patents. He dismissed the argument that having "no monopolies lessens the incitements to ingenuity," and declared to Madison his opposition to "monopolies in all cases." Madison replied that patent and copyright monopolies were justified because they fell under the category of rights of the few needing protection from the tyranny of the majority. Monopolies, he conceded, are "among the greatest nuisances in Government. But is it clear," he asked rhetorically, "that as encouragements to literary works and ingenious discoveries, they are not too valuable to be wholly renounced?" Jefferson backed off and softened his position, acknowledging that for the sake of progress some monopolies should be allowed. Yet he continued to insist that intellectual property should be limited to a number of years and be restricted to individuals "for their own production in literature, and their own inventions in the arts."[54]

The Constitution was sufficiently vague to allow patents of importation. To be sure, its mention of authors and inventors seemed to exclude introducers. Yet the wording did not challenge centuries of practice in the metropolis, colonies, and states of granting patents of introduction. Piracy of intellectual property could be accommodated. Because the Constitution provided no clear standard for what qualified an innovation to receive a federally mandated patent, the first Congress and administration were left with the task of defining. What was an invention? Did it have to be wholly original? Did prior use in another country proscribe an invention from being protected in the United States? And how did the republican hostility to monopolies and principled opposition to piracy coexist with a national consensus that the young republic must industrialize, and that it could do so only by the emulation of prohibited technologies? Policies and principles were en route to collision. [55]

Philadelphia was festive on July 4, 1788. The city sponsored a large parade to celebrate the adoption of the Constitution, and the Pennsylvania Society for the Promotion of Useful Knowledge took the thirty-ninth division in that procession. The division's motto was "May the Union Government protect the manufacturers of America." The float also featured workers operating a carding machine and a spinning machine—both of which had been smuggled by Joseph Hague. Another smuggler of technology, John Hewson, was given the honor of being seated with his wife and four daughters in the center of the float together with another immigrant artisan from London, William Lang. The Hewsons and Lang were dressed in cotton cloth they had manufactured in Philadelphia with pirated equipment and skills. That smuggled machinery and known violators of British restrictions on technology diffusion occupied center stage symbolized the expectation that the new government would endorse technology piracy. As the *Pennsylvania Gazette* declared: "We may invent, and we may borrow of Europe their inventions."[56]

CHAPTER 6

Constructing the American Understanding of Intellectual Property

When Thomas Attwood Digges was twenty-six years old, he sailed from the British colonies to Europe in hopes of gaining fame and fortune. Born in 1742, this son of one of Maryland's most prominent Catholic families thought he was destined for greatness. After some early troubles in his teen years— Digges was somewhat of a kleptomaniac—he moved to Europe in the late 1760s, settled in Portugal, and engaged in international trade. At the same time he began working on a novel. In 1774 Digges moved to London; legal troubles with Portuguese authorities provided the push and love for an Englishwoman provided the pull for the change of residence. The following year he published his largely autobiographical novel, the first ever written by an American, *Adventures of Alfonso*.

The literary career of this American expatriate took a political turn during the Revolution. His close relationship with George Washington—the Digges estate was located just across the Potomac from Mount Vernon—made him a natural choice for enlisting with the revolutionary effort in England, and he took part in illegal shipping of munitions to the America rebels. But Digges's involvement in the American cause was highly controversial. He aroused the suspicion of almost all the American representatives in Europe, who believed he was a double agent. His reputation plummeted when it was discovered that he had embezzled charitable funds aimed at arranging the escape or ameliorating the conditions of American prisoners. Benjamin Franklin, for one, wrote that "If such a fellow is not damn'd it is not worth while to keep a devil."[1] Franklin's rival, John Adams, however, trusted the controversial Marylander. Digges arranged the publication of Adams's revolutionary propaganda in London and sent him numerous reports of British thinking about the war. The diplomatic stature Digges attained is evident by the fact that the British prime minister Lord North chose Digges to be the bearer of his 1782 peace overture.

With the war over, Digges turned to technology piracy. In the decade following American independence he traveled through England and Ireland in search of artisans willing to violate British laws and migrate to America with their advanced machinery. By taking such personal risks in violation of English law Digges hoped to profit handsomely while rehabilitating his patriotic credentials. His most successful recruit was William Pearce, a mechanic from Yorkshire who settled in Belfast in 1790. The ambitious Marylander called his prized recruit a "second Archimedes" and claimed Pearce "was the inventor of Arkwright's famous Spinning and Weaving Machinery, but was robbed of his invention by Mr. Arkwright." Pearce was also, according to Digges, the innovative force in the Cartwrights' mill, "which dresses the Wool, spins, and weaves Broad Cloth by force of Water, steam, or by a horse." After Pearce failed to get premiums from the Irish Parliament for a variety of mechanical innovations, he warmed up to Digges's overtures and agreed to emigrate to the United States. Digges proudly reported to Secretary of State Jefferson that "a box containing the materials and specifications for a new In-vented double Loom" was about to depart for America and that Pearce and two of his able assistants would follow it there, reassemble

FIGURE 6. Thomas Digges of "Warburton Manor" (1742–1821). Portrait possibly by Sir Joshua Reynolds, ca. 1775–81. Whether or not Reynolds painted this portrait is in dispute. I thank Ken Bowling for alerting me to this fact. The family lost custody of the portrait following the resolution of an estate dispute in 1957 and the painting's current location is not known. This reproduction is of a duplicate in the custody of the Historical Society of Washington, D.C.

the machinery, and put it to work. "It gives me great pleasure," he concluded, "to have been the means of getting so valuable an Artist to our Country." Alas, Pearce's journey did not go smoothly. Digges reported that an English cutter "pursued & searched His Vessel twice for His double Loom & they would have brought him back had He not entered & given in a different name."[2]

While reading a New York newspaper Digges came across Alexander Hamilton's *Report on Manufactures*. Submitted to Congress on December 25, 1791, the secretary of the Treasury's thorough analysis of the state of American industries was followed by a call for an aggressive policy of technology piracy. Digges was delighted to read that Washington's closest lieutenant had endorsed his goals and methods, and believed that this was an excellent time to plunder European technology. By offering inducements and developing opportunities for employment, Hamilton wrote in the report, the United States could immeasurably "increase the extent of valuable acquisitions to the population, arts and industry."[3]

Digges could not have agreed more. He wrote Hamilton that in the industrial regions of Belfast, Liverpool, and Manchester, newspapers would not publish any favorable account of American manufactures, fearing that it might "lead the people to Emigration." He had one thousand copies of Hamilton's *Report on Manufactures* printed in Dublin in 1792 and spread among local societies for the promotion of manufactures in Britain and Ireland. He believed the report would "induce artists to move toward a Country so likely to very soon give them ample employ & domestic ease." The Dublin edition was "distributed and Sold cheap," reported the Edinburgh bookseller Samuel Peterson to Hamilton. Yet the encouragement given in the *Report on Manufactures* to "the poor distressed Subjects of these States to flock to America" antagonized "the great people & Landed Interest" who sought to discourage emigration.[4]

Digges's proclivity to steal, not pay his debts, and engage in industrial espionage landed him in a British jail for some time in the mid 1780s, in 1792, and probably in 1795.[5] His many American detractors were not impressed by his activities in England and continued to distrust him. In the eyes of at least one American, however, Digges's clandestine efforts in behalf of American manufacturing proved his patriotism. Responding to Digges's critics, President George

Washington declared that all along he had believed that the conduct of "Mr. Thomas Digges towards the United States during the War . . . has not only been friendly, but I might add zealous." And those who doubted his devotion to the republic should look no further than "his activity and zeal (with considerable risque) in sending artizans and machines of public utility to this Country I mean by encouraging and facilitating their transportation."[6]

Digges was not the only American industrial spy in England. At least four others traveled around the English countryside in the late 1780s and early 1790s looking to recruit artisans and transport industrial technology to the New World. An anti-emigration pamphlet, published in London in the mid 1790s, declared that "there are plenty of agents hovering like birds of prey on the banks of the Thames, eager in their search for such artisans, mechanics, husbandmen, and labourers, as are inclinable to direct their course to America." The pamphleteer went on to warn potential immigrants that these agents were hired "at a considerable expense" by American manufacturers, "expressly for the purpose of inveigling them to quit their friends and connections" and seek "ideal romantic happiness, in a solitary uncultivated waste, little calculated, and still less capable of conferring the comforts and benefits of society." Digges, the pamphlet declared, was the worst of these offenders, though he was not the only one engaged "in such nefarious practices." The American industrial spy had approached an English gentleman and asked to be informed of "any persons desirous of emigrating to America" and offered to pay two guineas for each artisan and one for each immigrant laborer. Digges was a "designing villain" and a "very dangerous character," and prospective immigrants should shy away from this "artful" confidence trickster who preyed upon the "credulity of his audience."[7]

Digges's financial fortunes improved after his brother, who died in 1793, left him a handsome estate. He nevertheless continued to engage in industrial espionage. When he heard that Jefferson was working on establishing an American mint he offered to help secure the assistance of Matthew Boulton who "is by far the neatest and best Coiner and has a more excellent Apparatus for Coining than any in Europe." He hoped that his activities would rehabilitate his reputation in the United States. Yet his trials and tribulations in behalf of American industry neither restored his reputation in the eyes of the American elite nor earned him the gratitude of his countrymen. Digges, who returned to his Maryland estate in 1799, lived the remaining two decades of his life in relative obscurity.[8]

The industrial spying career of Thomas Digges stands for the crucial transformation in American ideas about technology diffusion and technology piracy that took place in the 1790s. The first decade of national existence saw the most intense pursuit of English technology on the federal and state level. Initially, the constitutional provision to promote the useful arts was interpreted as a mandate to use the mechanism of the new national government effectively to appropriate forbidden European technology. These efforts were particularly successful in the textile industry as small-scale capacity to build and operate the newest mule spinning and Arkwright technologies sprang up in a variety of spots in the northeastern urban centers.

At the same time, however, a new understanding developed about the proper arena for technology piracy. A self-respecting government eager to join the international community on an equal basis could not flaunt its violation of the laws of other countries. Patterns established under the semi-anarchic circumstances of the Revolution and Confederation were inappropriate behavior for a respected member of the international community. This was all the more important for the nascent Washington administration, whose chief task was establishing legitimacy at home and abroad. To be sure, clandestine appropriation of English technology not only persisted but also intensified. Every major European state engaged in technology piracy and industrial espionage in the eighteenth century, and the United States could not afford to behave differently. Yet, there was etiquette to this piracy. It was undertaken in secret and officials would deny any connection to such practices.

The young republic embraced a Janus-faced approach. The government of the United States, after briefly considering sponsoring such activities, formally disengaged from technology piracy. Officially it disavowed the practice and Congress passed a patent law founded on a principled commitment to worldwide originality as the foundation of intellectual property in the United States. Covertly, federal officials winked as they disavowed any connection to the theft of knowledge. The constant influx of immigrants lessened the necessity for recruiting skilled artisans in Europe. Moreover, the wars of the French Revolution created a large demand for American agricultural products, unleashing an unprecedented economic boom. In this context the impetus to create a self-sufficient industrial economy in order to secure American independence was no longer urgent. In a sense, federal policy toward technology piracy signaled the coming of age of the republic.

A Vigorous Spirit of Acquisition

The formation of an effective government and the ascent of George Washington to the presidency inspired widespread optimism among nationalists and champions of industry. The president was a known advocate of economic development who had invested his own money in technological and industrial projects. Washington was delighted that a "spirit of industry and economy" had already begun to transform the nation, pointing out to an English correspondent that the establishment of the federal government had already delivered the desired effect. "More Manufactures of cotton, wool, and iron have been introduced within eighteen months past than perhaps, ever before existed in America." He promised the Delaware Society for Promoting Domestic Manufactures that the "promotion of domestic manufactures," would be "among the first consequences which may naturally be expected to flow from an energetic government."[9]

Many Americans shared their new president's sentiments and agenda. Private and public discourse abounded with boasts of the coming new age of American industry. A group of tradesmen and mechanics from Baltimore asked "that the encouragement and protection of American manufactures will claim the earliest attention of the supreme Legislature of the nation." The United States, they declared, has all the natural resources necessary to make it "a great manufacturing country, and only want the patronage and support of a wise, energetic government." A writer from Hartford declared: "Our people are industrious and intelligent; they are possessed of uncommon genius for mechanical inventions, and of such versatility, that they can, with great ease and quickness, turn their hands to those arts which are introduced among us from abroad." Another essayist explained that during the colonial era American technology had "laboured under the unjust imputation of inferiority," but that the new government would set local industry on a course that would prove it could be equal to and even better than foreign rivals. And Coxe expected many manufacturers to "migrate into this country" following the establishment of the federal government. "Many have already come," he observed, "and as fast as encouragement may be offered or prospect of success appear, so fast will the manufactories of the United States be supported by foreign workmen."[10]

Calls to develop American manufacturing showed complete disregard for the intellectual property laws of European nations, particularly those of Great Britain. An essayist in *American Museum* celebrated the widespread abuse of European intellectual property as a sign of culture and cosmopolitan society. Pro-emigration tracts published in London elaborated on the favorable opportunities for artisans in the New World. In the United States, meanwhile, promises of assistance to foreign artisans emanated from many sources. A Philadelphia pamphlet declared: "MECHANICS and MANUFACTURERS, of every description, will find certain encouragement in the united states." The constitution of the Germantown Society for Promoting Domestic Manufactures pledged that it would never "use its influence with government, to prevent foreign manufacturing from being introduced; but on the contrary, shall exert itself to promote" the acquisition of technical knowledge from abroad, "which is the true interest of every country." The *Philadelphia Monthly Magazine* did not find it "improper" to publish exact "Specifications of British patent" issued to Samuel Ashton for his new method of tanning.[11]

Optimism did not blind proponents of industrialization to the persistence of American technological deficiencies. Following Congress's request in January 1790 that the secretary of the Treasury prepare what became the *Report on Manufactures*, Hamilton, who lacked expertise in these matters, turned for information to leading industrialists and to the local societies for the promotion of manufactures that had popped up in many cities in the 1780s. The responses that trickled back to New York over the next year had much in common. They described growing industrial activities and at the same time elaborated on the obstacles to manufacturing in the United States.

Success depended on manufacturers' overcoming the nation's technological backwardness. Correspondents from all states told Hamilton of their difficulties in attracting and holding on to foreign workers. Manufacturers from Charleston, South Carolina, blamed their industrial underdevelopment on the shortage of skilled labor. One Connecticut industrialist complained that the price of hats had fallen significantly in the past few months because of "Bad Work done which goes to Market & has injured the Credit of American Hats very much, & must in time ruin it entirely." Glass manufacturing in Massachusetts was delayed in getting started because entrepreneurs "wait only for Workmen which are engaged & probably on their passage to commence making Sheet and other Glass." Textile manufacturing in Massachusetts was "destitute of the necessary information," as local investors were being "misled by every pretender to knowledge."[12]

Americans, however, were determined to overcome the technology gap. Individuals, voluntary associations, state legislatures, and the federal government set out to attract immigrants and their machinery to the New World. Spying for new products or better ways of producing known ones had been going since the early days of English colonization and had intensified following independence. The early 1790s nevertheless stand out because of the scope of the American effort and the manner in which it was conducted. Secrecy was abandoned as the battle over industrial technology raged in the open. As an anonymous writer explained, "The Europeans, by introducing a variety of machines for abridging the quantity of labour employed in manufactures, have taught us a lesson which we may improve greatly to our advantage and in their detriment." In Europe, he went on, new technologies have been "profitable to the proprietors of manufactories, but not advantageous to the European nations; because they have such numbers of indigent workmen that need employment." The shortage of labor in the United States meant that new technologies would benefit both workers and industrialists. Moreover, because raw materials were both plentiful and cheap in America, the acquisition of modern machinery promised to "enable us to out-rival the Europeans even in their own markets." American success at pirating English technology was so well known that continental rivals turned to American industrial spies rather than to

English artisans. In the heyday of its bloody revolution, the French government recruited two American artisans and paid them six thousand livres to establish cloth manufactures in France modeled after the English ones.[13]

Successful industrialization depended on manufacturers' ability to pirate British technology primarily through enticing skilled British artisans to emigrate. The "spirit of manufacturing has begun to make considerable progress in South Carolina," reported a writer in the pages of the *Universal Asylum and Columbian Magazine,* following the arrival of a "gentleman of great mechanical knowledge" from Europe. In the new factory the "clothes are dyed, pressed, and finished, with great neatness, by artisans from Great Britain." Button production in New Haven picked up following the arrival of an English worker who "has the Skill perfectly, who is a Gentleman who is able, and has Engaged to instruct and teach us every thing Necessary in the making of them." The machinery of the textile manufactory in Norwich, Connecticut, was imported from England. Elisha Colt, manager of the Hartford Woolen Manufactory, emphasized the crucial role played by British artisans in the success of his factory. When the company was first established, it knew nothing of the division of labor necessary for industrial production and was "destitute of every kind of Machinery and Labourers for executing such a project." News of the enterprise reached the ears of workers who had worked at "the Woolen & Worsted Business in England." They came to work for the factory and since then, Colt boasted, "every part or branch of the Business is managed in the same manner as practiced in England."[14]

Nearly every branch of American manufactures of the 1790s was founded upon imported skill. Irénée E. Du Pont imported gunpowder technology from France, directed the construction of a factory in the Brandywine region of Pennsylvania, and supervised production there. The testing equipment and the production machinery were also imported from France. Later on, Du Pont went to France and negotiated with officials of the *Administration des Poudres* who promised to send to him skilled workers they felt they could spare. Likewise, Joshua Gilpin, founder of the Brandywine Paper Mill, traveled through England and Scotland in the 1790s and wrote detailed accounts of English production methods, aided by a "gentleman" from Edinburgh who informed him about the entire process. A European traveler noted that "A large proportion of the most successful manufacturers in the United States are persons who were journeymen, and in some instances foremen in the workshops and manufactories of Europe, who having been skilful, sober, and frugal, and having thus saved a little money, have set up for themselves with great advantage in America, and few have failed to succeed." The same author also declared that "Master workmen in every manufacturing and mechanical art . . . with their journeymen and labourers, must succeed here."[15]

The development of American industrial technologies depended on transatlantic communication. Most of the men who experimented with building steam engines in the 1790s, for example, were either immigrants from the British Isles, or Americans who worked in cooperation with English emigrants. Even after settling in the United States, mechanics continued to look to England for instruction. Some went to visit and learn of new developments while others tried to keep up with innovations via letters to friends and family members. British immigrants linked the United States to technological developments in Europe and taught local artisans how to operate sophisticated machinery. In the first two decades of independent American national existence, they were the messengers of the Industrial Revolution.

Most of all Americans coveted textile manufacturing techniques. The founders of the American woolen industry sought to emulate British technology. Mechanization in wool was slower than in cotton, and the process by which fibers were straightened and made ready for spinning was mechanized only in the late eighteenth century in England. The Hartford Woolen Factory hired a few British deserters and former prisoners of war in the late 1780s who had some experience in the English woolen industry. These workers, however, were absent from Britain in years in which critical breakthroughs were accomplished. Thus they did not know of the most recent developments in the trade, particularly the improvement in carding technology. More English workers were hired and yet the company floundered. The case of the Hartford Woolen Manufactory illustrates that failure often followed successful appropriation of foreign technology. Even though the company was embraced by the city's elite, its building was subsidized by the state of Connecticut, and its product was toasted by George Washington, it had to shut down in the mid 1790s, plagued, among other things, by the scarcity of skilled dyers and finishers.[16]

The collapse of the Hartford Woolen Manufactory did not discourage other importers of English woolen technology. Americans remained committed to the idea of industrializing through the recruitment of skilled immigrants. Britain had passed laws to restrict the migrations of artisans, wrote one confident pamphleteer, because "jealous Britons [are] justly fearful lest they themselves should lose their wool mart." These laws, however, were not terribly effective. An English traveler reported that William McIntosh of Essex, England, opened a woolen factory in New Haven with "many English workmen engaged at great wages." Another attempt to build a British-model woolen factory was launched in Newburyport, Massachusetts, in 1793 by John and Arthur Schofield of Yorkshire. The brothers employed fellow immigrants who built and operated the machinery. The enterprise, however, could not compete with the cheaper and better English imports. In 1799 the Schofields sold their interest in the mill and moved to Connecticut, and four years later the factory was converted to cotton manufacturing by an English investor.[17]

The most sought-after technologies involved the processing of cotton. Americans targeted Arkwright's spinning machine, in particular, because it offered a significant saving in labor. It allowed a single operative to spin several threads at once and produce yarn that was strong and uniform. Initially powered by horses or water and later by a Boulton and Watt steam engine, this innovation was particularly suited to an economy suffering from chronic labor shortages. A number of British artisans who came to the United States claimed to have been personally trained by Arkwright. Three British immigrants, George Parkinson, William Pollard, and William Pearce, battled over the exclusive right to the Arkwright technology. Parkinson advertised in 1791 that he had obtained a United States patent for spinning flax, hemp, and combed wool by methods that represented "improvements upon the mill or machinery of Kendrew and Porthouse of the town of Darlington in Great Britain." Parkinson declared that he was the originator of this "entire new invention" which would be "of general utility to the United States." His American partner, Tench Coxe, however, confessed that he and Parkinson were "not the inventors" and that they considered Arkwright "the inventor and ourselves the introducers" of the machinery. They nevertheless deserved the patent because no "model or drawings" of this machines were available in the United States.[18] Pollard, meanwhile, obtained a patent in December 1791 and in June of the following year his factory was in full operation. Pearce failed to get a patent but opened a competing factory in Philadelphia. He did not go unsupported, however. No less than George Washington himself came to show his support for the factory. As the *Gazette of the United States* reported, "The President of the United States, and his Lady, attended by the Secretary of State, and the Secretary of the Treasury and his Lady, visited Mr. Pearce's Cotton Manufactory. The

President attentively viewed the Machinery, &c. and saw the business performed in its different branches—which received his warmest approbation."[19]

The decade's spirit of enterprise was founded upon imported technology. The Englishman Henry Wansey, who toured the United States in 1794, was chagrined by the ease in which Americans circumvented British restrictions on emigration and dissemination of technology, and acquired the most closely protected industrial secrets. In New York he inspected a factory where "twelve or fourteen workmen from Manchester" used "all the new improvements of Arkwright and others." All the machines "were made on the spot from models brought from England and Scotland." Everywhere Wansey visited he found evidence of successful industrial espionage.[20] A young and confident nation led by an effective visionary administration was rapidly gaining on its European competitors.

Flirting with Official Sponsorship of Technology Piracy

Shortly before taking office as the first president of the United States, Washington outlined to Thomas Jefferson, his future secretary of state, who was still in France, the goals of his administration. The promotion of American manufacturing and the development of inland navigation, Washington wrote his fellow Virginian, were "the greatest and most important object of internal concern." He reported a discussion he recently had at Mount Vernon with "an English Gentleman, who has been many years introducing those [cotton] manufactures into France" in which they agreed that the young nation had great manufacturing potential that would materialize upon the introduction of efficient modern industrial technologies. The "introduction of the late-improved Machines to abridge labor," he informed Jefferson "must be of almost infinite consequence to America." The president's first State of the Union Address was equally explicit. "I cannot forbear to you the expediency of giving effectual encouragement as well to the introduction of new and useful inventions from abroad."[21]

Washington had been a proponent of importing European technology since the end of the Revolutionary War. In the 1780s, determined to make the Potomac a major commercial artery in the economic life of the new nation, he tried to recruit a French engineer to come to Virginia and employ modern technology to dig a system of canals linking the river to the commonwealth's plantations. He had supported James Rumsey's efforts to develop a steamboat as part of the Potomac canal works.[22] And in his public addresses the president articulated the expectations of proponents of American industrialization.

Washington was voicing the widespread expectation that the federal government would devote its energies to industrial development. The president and captains of industry set the tone by symbolic acts. In the fall of 1789 Washington traveled through the New England states in a highly celebrated affirmation of federal legitimacy. The people of the region showered him with joyous orations, parades, and dinners. Washington, in turn, made a point of wearing clothes made at the Hartford Woolen Manufactory. "I hope it will not be a great while," he wrote, "before it will be unfashionable for a gentleman to appear in any other dress."[23] Hartford's entrepreneurial elite was naturally delighted that the "President expressed great satisfaction at the progress which had been made in that useful undertaking," for it demonstrated the "prospects of happiness that we are becoming as independent of the Manufactures of Great Britain."[24] Ironically, revolutionary republican criticism of British society was redirected in the 1790s toward the importation of English know-how to the republic. The prewar rhetoric about British oppression was replaced with talk of making political independence real by replacing industrial dependence on England with home manufacturing. Industrial undertakings, both private and public, were fused into the newly imagined notion of national interest. Addressing the technology gap between the two nations assumed great national importance.

When the first Congress convened in New York in 1789, disagreements between the future leaders of the Federalists and Jeffersonians surfaced almost immediately. The crux of the disagreement centered on relations with Great Britain. Both sides were alarmed by American economic dependence on British imports and by the exclusion of American ships from the British West Indies. Madison and Jefferson proposed charging a higher tariff on goods arriving in British vessels in American ports. They believed that British anxiety over the migration of artisans to America made that nation particularly susceptible to economic coercion by the United States. "The raw and bulky exports of the United States," Madison explained, "employ her shipping, contribute to her revenue, enter into her manufactures, and enrich her merchants, who stand between the United States and the consuming nations of Europe." Any interruption of that trade would cause substantial losses to British merchants, middlemen, and manufacturers, which in turn would lead to mass unemployment, social unrest, and emigration, and thereby ultimately "hasten the establishment of American Manufactures."[25]

Enticing foreign immigrants was on the founders' minds. Coxe, in his capacity as secretary of the Pennsylvania Society for the Encouragement of Manufactures and the Useful Arts, approached Madison with the suggestion that Congress should allocate a million acres of "the nearest, least broken, & most valuable land in their western Territory as a fund to reward the introduction of Machinery inventions, arts, and other things of that nature from foreign Countries, and Inventions and discoveries first communicated to us by Natives of foreigners the benefits of which . . . should be useful to the United

States." Madison replied that the idea of setting a parcel of land to reward "imported inventions is new and worthy of consideration." All the same, the plan could not be enacted under the existing Constitution because "Congress seem to be tied down to the single mode of encouraging inventions by granting the exclusive benefit of them for a limited time, and therefore to have no more power to give a further encouragement out of a fund of land than a fund of money." Madison told Coxe that he had proposed a land grant clause to this effect in Philadelphia, but his proposal had been "expressly rejected."[26]

Madison and Jefferson integrated their support of American acquisition of European technology into their larger vision of American diplomacy. In their minds, the young nation's consumption of English imports undermined its political independence and allowed England to pursue anti-American commercial regulations. They advocated an open trade war against Great Britain and proposed in Congress a set of discriminatory retaliatory tariffs on English imports. The primary goal of commercial coercion was to force Great Britain to rescind its restrictions on United States trade with the British West Indies. In a roundabout manner, however, retaliatory tariffs benefited the technologically starved American industries. Raising the cost of buying British imports in America, they reasoned, would reduce demand, leading to production cuts and rising unemployment in English industrial towns. Unemployed workers could be expected to emigrate to the New World where their skills were very much in demand.[27]

Their rival Alexander Hamilton, however, doubted the young nation's ability to force Britain to rescind its policies and feared that the United States would be the one devastated by such a contest. Instead, he proposed to liberate the American economy by developing large-scale American manufacturing. When Congress, following the president's lead, asked Hamilton in January 1790 to prepare his *Report on Manufactures*, the secretary of the Treasury seized the opportunity to outline his vision of American industrialization. He appointed Coxe his assistant and charged him with drafting the report. The appointment of America's most vociferous advocate of technology piracy to draft the blueprint of American industrialization signaled the future policy recommendations of the document.

Before he joined the administration Coxe published a pamphlet arguing that promoting industrialization must be the first task of the new government. A nation whose industry was lagging should "view as its first object, the supplying itself with all its necessaries." Should the United States persist "in the habit of importing their manufactures, the States will remain dependent, impoverished, and embarrassed." Coxe suggested that the federal government give "special encouragement for the introduction of such manufacturing arts" by emulating European technology piracy practices so that smugglers "would introduce into the States, every manufacturing secret in Europe." Coxe also suggested that the government help industries that failed to attract skilled immigrants by buying imported finished articles in order to analyze and reproduce them. [28]

In writing the first draft of the *Report on Manufactures*, Coxe elaborated on themes he had been promoting since the mid 1780s. American manufactures were plagued by labor problems. Labor was scarce, wages were high, and the United States did not have competent operators versed in modern techniques. He proposed three remedies. First, the United States should import modern machinery that used fewer workers, thereby reducing competition for laborers and bringing wages under control. Second, women and children, who earned much lower wages, should do the unskilled work. Third, the United States government should campaign aggressively to persuade European artisans to emigrate.

Inducing emigration was pivotal to the program's success. Yet how could a nonmanufacturing, capital-starved economy attract skilled workers? Coxe modified the proposal he had made to Madison a few months earlier: instead of a million acres he now proposed that the government allocate "five hundred thousand acres, of a good quality and advantageously situated, land" to grant to "the first introducers or establishers of new and useful manufactories, arts, machines, & secrets not before possessed, known or carried on in the United States." He also proposed setting up a fund under the direction of the president of the United States to make cash payments to introducers of items or ideas that "will not yield an immediate or adequate benefit" in the market. Persons who brought in "manufacturing Machinery and secrets of great value" that had an immediate market applicability should be rewarded by "granting to the introducers such exclusive privileges for a term of years as would have been secured by patent had they been the inventors." Coxe concluded the draft by explaining that "these great Instruments of Manufacture in the European Nations, labor-saving Machines" were crucial to American industrial development and that the present state of American manufacturing made governmental efforts to help secure such machines politically and economically prudent.[29]

Hamilton reworked and expanded Coxe's draft five times before submitting the document to Congress in December 1791.[30] The revised report echoed Coxe's sentiments. Hamilton deplored American dependency on European imports. Only the development of an indigenous industrial economy could liberate the nation's economy from the British hold. He ascribed the difficulties of American manufacturing to technological deficiencies and wrote that the gap between Europe and the United States would diminish "in proportion to the use which can be made of machinery." He called on the federal government to establish some "auxiliary agency" to coordinate the piracy of European technology. He proposed to market America's industrialization in Europe so that skilled workers might be induced to circumvent national restrictions on artisans' immigration. He endorsed Coxe's proposals for encouraging industrial immigration, such as travel subsidies for artisans and exemption from customs for their implements of trade, and household goods. The "public purse must supply the deficiency of private resources," he declared, for "as soon as foreign artists be made sensible that the state of things here affords a moral certainty of employment and encouragement—competent numbers of European workmen will transplant themselves, effectively to ensure the success of the design." The industrialization of the United States, Hamilton concluded, would "in a great measure trade upon a foreign stock." [31]

The *Report on Manufactures* and its brainchild of late 1791—the Society for Establishing Useful Manufactures of Patterson, New Jersey, represent the high water mark of federally sanctioned technology piracy. The secretary of the Treasury proposed to set up a federally orchestrated program aimed at acquiring the very industrial secrets rival nations sought to protect. Most manufacturing nations, he explained, "prohibit, under severe penalties the exportation of implements and machines which they have either invented or improved." The United States government must circumvent the efforts of industrially advanced nations to frustrate and prohibit the international diffusion of industrial know-how. In order to compete with the British textile industry, Americans must have a better-qualified work force. Skilled workers were "an essential ingredient" of American industrialization, yet thus far efforts "employed have not generally been adequate to the purpose of procuring them from abroad." He called on the society "to procure from Europe skilful workmen, and such machines and implements as cannot be had here in sufficient perfection."[32]

Hamilton did not have the patience to wait for Congress to act on the report's recommendation and began to recruit skilled workers on his own. During 1791 he interviewed new immigrants in order to identify potential introducers of English technology who were already in the United States. He sent a Scottish stocking weaver back home to recruit men for a factory in America. English artisans heard of the secretary's interest in their technology and expected assistance upon arrival. Roger Newberry, for example, believed Hamilton should help him find a job in the United States because he possessed plans for two "most ingenious & very beneficial" new English textile machines. In December 1791, Hamilton reported to the directors of the Society for Establishing Useful Manufactures about an understanding he had reached with one Mr. Mort, who agreed to "go to Europe, to bring over Workmen, at his own Expense in the first instance; but with the assurance of reimbursement and indemnification." The society's directors approved the agreement unanimously, and promised, "to carry the same into Effect on their part."[33]

Hamilton, Coxe, and their associates, however, were increasingly out of touch with the emerging approach to addressing the nation's industrial deficiencies. Drawing on the experience of the Old World, they envisioned an activist government directing specific programs of economic development to the benefit of the general public. Hamilton was committed to importing equipment and artisans because he believed that American economic growth must follow the route taken in Europe. For him, if the United States was to become a major economic power it must follow in England's footsteps and establish large-scale centralized enterprises, such as the Society for Establishing Useful Manufactures, founded upon imported machinery and skill. Hamilton, however, failed to comprehend that rather than follow the English model, American manufacturing would develop in a uniquely dispersed and disorganized manner.

American industrial development did not follow the mercantilist European model where the central government took the lead in subsidizing, regulating and protecting industries. Early attempts to orchestrate an aggressive federal sponsorship of technology piracy, exemplified by Hamilton's *Report on Manufactures*, failed to take into account the powerfully dynamic impact of the rising market capitalism on the form and pace of American industrialization. These early efforts were intellectually grounded in the precapitalist world, when human mobility was regulated and when the threat of famines and epidemics was ever present. Governmental direction of the economy made sense in an era when periodic economic disasters required that societies prepare for such emergencies, and was made possible by a stable social and economic hierarchy. However, the market economy, the breakthrough in agricultural productivity, and the consumer revolutions of the second half of the eighteenth century ushered in unprecedented prosperity and liberated men and women from the fear of the future that had once ruled their daily lives. The emerging capitalism of the late eighteenth century allowed men to imagine they could leave behind the cautious and measured ways of yesterday and expect a future of sustained and uninterrupted economic growth.[34] To be sure, the new economy exacted a heavy price and many were left off the path of progress. Yet, the improved material conditions inspired an optimistic expectation that the fruits of the market's new productivity would trickle down to all sectors and classes. A new idea of a naturally growing economy took hold. Governmental regulations, even when they overtly attempted to favor the industrial sector, stood in the way of growth and prosperity. The promise of capitalism ushered in a new age of acquiring forbidden technology.

The Janus-Faced Federal Information Policy

When Samuel Slater was fifteen years old, his father got him a management apprenticeship with Jedediah Strutt's mills in Milford, England. The Milford mills were at the forefront of technological innovation in textile production. Strutt, who became one of Arkwright's backers and partners, centered the production process on Arkwright's recently developed water frame which turned cotton into high-quality yarn in a fast and consistent manner. Slater was a quick learner, rose in the ranks, and became an overseer. He began thinking of emigrating to North America after learning of the "anxiety of the different state governments here to encourage manufactures." He was particularly excited by reports that "a liberal bounty (£100) [was] granted by the legislature of Pennsylvania, to a person, who had imperfectly succeeded in constructing a carding machine." Slater decided to take the risk and cross the Atlantic to try his luck. Aware of the rules against the diffusion of technology in general, and against the emigration of men of skill like himself, he presented himself as merely a farmhand and kept his apprenticeship papers as his only proof of identity. He left without any drawings or machinery, trusting to his memory to emulate British textile technology. Once in the United States, Slater first tried his luck in a New York workshop. Meanwhile, in Rhode Island, the entrepreneur and merchant Moses Brown was trying to emulate British industrial technology without much success. When Slater heard that Brown, who had earlier purchased a British machine to spin cotton, was looking for someone who could operate it, he contacted him and offered his services. Brown wanted to hire Slater merely to fix and operate the machinery, but Slater knew that he was indispensable to the operation and demanded to become a full partner. Cornered, Brown improved his offer and Slater moved to Pawtucket, Rhode Island, to lead the project. [35]

Because Slater relied exclusively on his memory, it took a great deal of tinkering with the machines Brown had smuggled out of England to construct in Pawtucket a factory similar to the one he had left behind. The mill succeeded in producing thread at the end of 1790. Slater cemented his position in the family business, became a partner, and built up the firm until it owned a few such factories in Rhode Island. Slater's mills became a model of modern family-owned machine textile production in the United States. Whereas

Arkwright's prestige was damaged when his originality was challenged in court, Slater's standing as the founder of American industry remained intact. By the second decade of the nineteenth century Slater had established his reputation as the most successful technology pirate in American history. A British traveler through Rhode Island noted "that the cotton trade had been introduced here by a gentleman from England, a pupil of Arkwright, who had been very successful; that other people were following this example, and that this branch was likely to increase to a great extent in this district."[36]

Pearce, Parkinson, and Pollard enjoyed the support of the elite. Pollard and Parkinson received a patent for their imported technology and Pearce was supported by Washington and later was recruited to lead the work on Hamilton's most ambitious project, the Society for Establishing Useful Manufactures. The subsequent career of these well-connected artisans, however, was marked by failures and disappointments. A similar fate awaited the factory established by the Pennsylvania Society for the Encouragement of Manufactures and the Useful Arts. Despite legislative and financial support of technology piracy from the Pennsylvania legislature, the factory's coarse cloth was no match for the superior and cheaper British imports. The factory closed its doors following a fire early in 1790. Well-connected artisans backed by the nation's top politicians and large-scale publicly funded enterprises floundered whereas Slater succeeded. Slater and thousands of other smaller entrepreneurs and household producers rather than large-scale government-backed enterprises were the ones who sparked the republic's industrial take-off.[37]

Clandestine technology piracy did not abate. On the contrary, recruiting and smuggling of artisans and machinery intensified. And yet, contrary to the expectations of many, direct federal involvement did not materialize. The Constitution instructed Congress to enact legislation to promote the progress of the arts and sciences by grants of monopolies over inventions for a limited time. A few petitions for such protection were presented during Congress's first session in 1789, though the distinction between American and worldwide originality remained unclear. The most prominent applicant was John Fitch, who requested an exclusive patent for "the improved state of steam engines." Fitch claimed he was "totally ignorant" whether his invention "is similar or not to those in England." He urged Congress to follow the British practice of granting patents of importation to introducers of technology, pointing out that Parliament had granted Sir Thomas Lombe a patent for a silk mill he had obtained in Italy and had added a fourteen-thousand-pound monetary reward. In other words, Fitch believed he deserved a patent monopoly whether he was the actual inventor or merely the emulator of the machine. What entitled him to this privilege was not originality, but the "important advantages" his steam-powered boat would bring to the United States.[38]

A bill to establish a patent system was introduced at that first session of the United States Congress, but it did not reach the floor. The initial proposal followed the English system enacted to attract superior European craftsmen to the kingdom. Men who introduced technological innovations hitherto unknown in England were rewarded with production monopolies. Likewise, in the proposed American bill introducers received patents of importation and enjoyed all the privileges of original inventors. The president, eager to expedite matters, addressed the issue in his first annual message in January 1790. Washington requested the enactment of legislation encouraging "skill and genius" at home and "the introduction of new and useful invention from abroad."[39] In the subsequent Congressional session the House of Representatives complied with the request and produced a bill granting introducers of pirated technology the monopoly privileges accorded to original inventors. The Senate, however, amended the bill to grant patent monopolies only to inventors of machines "not before known or used," and deleted the location qualifier of the House version—"within the United States." The first United States Patent Act, then, broke with the European tradition of patents of importation. It restricted patents exclusively to original inventors and established the principle that prior use anywhere in the world was grounds for invalidating a patent. This criterion is particularly puzzling because the young nation needed to import technology to develop its industrial base. Moreover, the two most important members of the Washington administration, the president and Alexander Hamilton, supported granting patents of importation.[40]

The 1790 act authorized the creation of a cabinet-level Patent Board, composed of the secretaries of state and war and the attorney general, to decide on the merits of each application. This requirement became too burdensome, particularly for the secretary of state, who was put in charge of the entire project. Jefferson, who fancied himself as a scientist and inventor, initially put great effort into examining the usefulness of the applications. From 1790 to 1793, some sixty-seven patents were granted. The task of examining each application, however, proved overwhelming. Jefferson complained to Congressman Hugh Williamson of North Carolina, chairman of the committee charged to prepare a new patent law, that the current system "cuts up his time into the most useless of fragments." Jefferson, who preferred to have others make confrontational declarations for him, indicated his displeasure with the act in the pages of the *National Gazette*. Phillip Freneau, the paper's editor and Jefferson's personal mouthpiece in the partisan battles of the early 1790s, published critiques of the act in the issues of July 11 and 14, 1792, authored by Jefferson's ally Joseph Barnes.[41]

The sheer volume of applications made the first patent act an administrative nightmare.[42] In 1793 Congress relieved members of the cabinet from wasting their time examining individual patents and assigned the duty to a clerk in the State Department. A patent became a registration of a claim anyone could make provided he or she paid the thirty-dollar fee, and that no similar claim was previously registered. Acquiring a patent depended exclusively on prompt completion of the necessary bureaucratic paperwork. The revised system maintained the dual demand for novelty and originality by requiring each patentee to take an oath that he or she was indeed the first and original inventor. The disputes likely to arise from this strictly bureaucratic registration were to be resolved by a board of arbitrators and the courts. A revision in 1800 added the requirement of an oath by all applicants to the effect that their "invention, art or discovery hath not . . . been known or used either in this or any foreign country."[43]

Textual examination of the law might give the impression that the young republic rejected technology piracy and established a new intellectual property code of behavior. Reality, however, was different. The statutory requirement of worldwide originality and novelty did not hinder widespread and officially sanctioned technology piracy. William Thornton, who administered the United States patents for much of the life of the 1793 act, did not insist on the oath of international novelty. It is indeed entirely possible that most of the applications received at the Patent Office were for devices already in use. In fact, since acquiring a patent involved little more that successful completion of paperwork, the Patent Act of 1793 permitted patentees to receive patents that infringed on the intellectual property of others. Moreover, the act explicitly prohibited foreigners from obtaining patents in America for inventions they had already patented in Europe. This meant that while United States citizens could not petition for introducers' patents, European inventors could not protect their intellectual property in America. The American patent system, then, sanctioned technology piracy as long as imported technology was not restricted exclusively to any particular individual introducer. Intellectual property in the early republic favored operators, internal developers, and entrepreneurs at the expense of investors and inventors.

Proponents of patents of importation lobbied Congress to revise the law in accordance with the English model. Coxe argued with Madison over the latter's contention that the Constitution's promotion of arts and science clause could not be extended to imported inventions. He reported that Parkinson was about to apply for another patent for his version of Arkwright's machine, and declared that the American duplication was superior to the one the Milne brothers had erected in France. Coxe did not doubt "the talents of my Countrymen & their ability to attain these things by their native strength of mind," yet he thought it was wiser to create a legal mechanism by which the republic could "draw upon that great fund of skill & knowledge, particularly of the useful Arts, wch. Europe possesses." In the *Report on Manufactures,* submitted to Congress in December 1791, Hamilton urged Congress to revise the Patent Act of 1790 in a manner that granted introducers of technology the same rights it granted original inventors. The United States, he declared, must employ the same methods "which have been employed with success in other countries."[44]

Proponents of patents of importation tried once again to amend the Patent Act. Congressman Williamson introduced a revised patent law in the House of Representatives on March 1, 1792, that proposed to use revenue from fees paid by patent applicants to import useful inventions from abroad.[45] Later that month, however, Coxe's and Hamilton's vigorous efforts on behalf of American technology were disgraced. The Treasury secretary's own favorite creation, the Society for Establishing Useful Manufactures, killed his program. Hamilton's authorship of the society's business plan and his involvement in its operations were public knowledge. The revelations that the society's directors had lost most of the company's funds in the financial crash of March 1792 discredited Hamilton's program and his efforts to revise the Patent Act.[46]

In spite of impressive political backing from the president and the secretary of the Treasury Congress refused to sanction patents of importation. This stand, however, had little to do with principled commitment to the rights of authors and inventors regardless of their citizenship. Indeed, statesmen began to wonder whether it was either necessary or prudent to take an official stand on the subject of international intellectual property. The new nation would adopt a two-pronged approach; a formal policy in which the government of the United States distanced itself from technology piracy, and an informal practice of facilitating it.

The following episode illustrates the delicate change in the American position. It began in the summer of 1789 when the Englishman Thomas Howell wrote Washington that in 1788 he had tried "transplanting a manufactory" to America, but had abandoned the idea until political stability was secured. After the new Constitution went into effect he offered his "service to the state of Virginia, to introduce the Woolen Manufactory on the present plans now working in England." Howell proposed to invest one thousand pounds of his own capital and "import Engines for cording and machines for slabing and spinning with every other apparatus necessary for the business." The absence of skilled and unskilled laborers had undermined previous efforts to develop manufacturing in the commonwealth. Howell suggested turning to "Gentlemen who are disposed to emancipate their Negroes [who] would appoint some of their younger ones for that business and give them their freedom after a service of seven years as an Apprentice." He promised to bring over "a sufficient number of my best Workmen to take under their care these young people" and train them in all aspects of the trade.[47]

Howell's petition was similar to ones submitted by European artisans and entrepreneurs, and Washington initially supported the scheme. It was, after all, in line with sentiments he had expressed both publicly and privately for much of the previous decade. He forwarded the proposal to Beverly Randolph, governor of Virginia, pointing out that in his recent tour of New England he had seen how technology transfer could rapidly increase industrial production, and declaring that he wanted his home state to follow suit. Aware of the questionable legality of the proposal, the president urged Randolph to keep Howell's name secret so that he could avoid "the most distressing consequences" in England.[48] The Virginia legislature formed a committee to look into the matter and recommended subsidizing the enterprise to the tune of one thousand pounds. The commonwealth's House of Delegates was even more generous and approved a twenty-five-hundred-pound subsidy, but the Senate refused to go along. In November 1790, the Virginia legislature reversed itself and instructed Governor Randolph to reopen negotiations with the federal government on the subject.

The president turned to his attorney general and secretary of state, asking what could be done to help the project. Jefferson initially supported it, writing that "Presidential intervention seems necessary till the contract shall be concluded." Jefferson soon changed his mind, however, and recommended that Washington stay out of the affair. Attorney General Edmund Randolph opposed the scheme from the outset. He warned Washington that Howell's action violated English restrictions. With his secretary of state and attorney general both opposed, the president backed off. "I am told that it is a felony to export the Machines which it is probable the Artist contemplates to bring with him," he wrote Governor Randolph, "and it certainly would not carry an aspect very favorable to the dignity of the United States for the President in a clandestine manner to entice the subjects of another nation to break its laws." [49]

The president's reply was, to say the least, disingenuous. The illegality of technology piracy was hardly news to him. In the previous decade he had campaigned for the importation of European technology to the United States without contemplating the legal dimension of the issue at all. Neither did Washington's response in early 1791 mean that the president no longer supported technology piracy. On the contrary, in the same letter to the governor of Virginia Washington urged the commonwealth to give serious consideration to the offer, declared that he was "impressed . . . with the utility of such an establishment" and promised, "to give it every aid that I can with propriety."⁵⁰ The goals and views of Washington remained the same. What changed was the office he held. No longer the leader of a revolutionary struggle against an oppressive colonial power or a leading Virginia planter, he now stood as the leader of a young republic struggling for international legitimacy. Becoming an accepted member of the international community required that the United States officially refrain from openly violating the laws of other nations.

The strong British reaction to American technology piracy made federal promotion of the practice inadvisable, particularly in the eyes of those who increasingly came to see England as the great protector against French imperialism. British representatives in the United States kept their London superiors informed about American appropriation of British technology. Phineas Bond dedicated much of his official correspondence to it. Major George Beckwith, who discussed the possibility of an Anglo-American alliance with Hamilton in 1790, alarmingly reported the arrival of a model of Arkwright's machine in America and worried about technology piracy's "ultimate effects upon the interests of the Empire."⁵¹ When Hamilton's call in the *Report on Manufactures* for overt piracy became public, British officials urged their superiors to show greater vigilance in protecting the country's industrial secrets. Bond recommended assertive implementation of laws "against seducing manufacturers and conveying away implements of manufacturing." The first British minister to the

United States, George Hammond, warned the Foreign Office that the federal government intended to fully support the proposed program because "Mr. Hamilton's reputation is so materially involved in the result of the experiment." England must now energetically enforce the prohibitions on technology export, he wrote to the foreign secretary, Lord Grenville, "to prevent the emigration and exportation of machines necessary to the different branches of manufactures."[52]

Leading American officials learned of Britain's reinvigorated effort to block the outflow of industrial technology. Samuel Peterson of Edinburgh wrote Hamilton that in "Britain the Penalties are 500 Str & 6 Mo Imprisonment for every person Indented to goe out of the Kings Dominions." He suggested that bounties for smuggling artisans be given to European shippers because the "Penalties & Forfeitures, are so very heavy & so easily incurred, that no person Unacquainted with the Laws durst Venture upon Such a Measure— But the European Captain & owners know how to agree with Passengers so as to Escape the Penalties." Another correspondent told the secretary of the Treasury that he had come to the United States without documentation of his skill, the "Laws of England being very severe against the Emigration of Mechanic's." Digges informed the secretary of state that the British government was "making Laws and trying all possible means to stop the Emigration of Artists and their tools. I need not tell you," he added, "that it is not only difficult to get such away, but highly dangerous to those concerned; Therefore, the more secret it is kept the better." Digges also informed Washington that "they are watchful in England as well as here for any going to America that upon the slightest suspicion they stop & search the Ship."[53]

The British authorities' renewed efforts focused on blocking emigration to the United States. A London newspaper reported on two hundred workers from Manchester "seduced" to migrate to America and establish a cotton factory in the New York area, and called for "laws [to] be put in force to prevent these emigrations." Concerned Englishmen enlisted to persuade potential emigrants that they stood to lose much by transplanting themselves to the United States. Thomas Clio Rickman, in response to the "mania of emigration to the United States," published letters "written by a gentleman who visited America, with the intention of emigration thither; but who, upon a year's residence in various parts, and close observation on the country, its climate, and the manner and morals of its inhabitants, relinquished all such intention." Rickman hoped to "save others the trouble of making a similar experiment."[54] The campaign to discourage emigration failed. As long as artisans believed that better opportunities lay across the ocean they continued to circumvent the British regulations and immigrate to the New World.

The outbreak of European hostilities following the French Revolution heightened British concerns. Foreign nations, bent on raiding English industries, offered a variety of incentives to lure superior technology and artisans. Many more artisans were tempted to take the risk and migrate. One writer warned that failure to protect industrial secrets would spell the Empire's doom. William Radcliff of Stockport, whose contribution to improvements in weaving technologies is comparable to Arkwright's contribution to the art of spinning cotton, decided in 1794 for patriotic reasons not to sell cotton yarns or warps for export so as to not assist foreign competitors. It was similar fears that impelled various associations of English manufactures to adopt resolutions calling for export restrictions. The Privy Council decreed on April 8, 1795, that captains of foreign vessels must submit a list of passengers' names, ages, occupations, and nationalities before leaving. British artisans trying to depart were to be promptly arrested. In 1797 the Privy Council even agreed to subsidize the return of James Douglas, a wool specialist, to England.[55]

The wars of the French Revolution, which engulfed Europe from 1792 to 1815, rendered aggressive American official promotion of industrial piracy unnecessary. In the *Report on Manufactures*, which was submitted to Congress shortly before France took to exporting its revolutionary message to its neighbors, Hamilton speculated that the "disturbed state of Europe" would incline "its citizens to emigration." Every independent nation has the right "to pursue its own interest, in its own way." He admitted that "to find pleasure in the calamities of other nations would be criminal," yet to benefit "by opening an asylum to those who suffer, in consequence of them, is as justifiable as it is politic." Hamilton believed that the early 1790s were an excellent time to plunder European technology because the bloody political crisis there would dispose "the requisite workmen" to emigrate.[56]

Proponents of American industrialization were indeed ready to pounce on the continent's distress. Thomas Marshall, who feared that "unless God should send us saints for Workmen and angels to conduct them" the Society for Establishing Useful Manufactures would falter, argued that to avert such a calamity the United States must capitalize on the European crisis and "Engage as many manufacturers in as many different Branches to Emigrate to this country." The first American edition of Davies's *One Thousand Valuable Secrets* urged Americans to capitalize on the state of war in Europe and catch up with the mechanical and scientific knowledge of the Old World. In the introduction to the book, which aimed to disseminate the latest innovations throughout the country, the publisher declared: "Whilst the inhabitants of Europe are distracted by the din of arms, and their principal employment is to contrive the most expeditious means of destroying one another, let the happy citizens of these infant states" learn European discoveries "until we no longer stand in need of their supplies, or remain exposed to the fluctuations of their fortunes."[57]

Some proponents of American manufacturing did not share Hamilton's view that to take pleasure in the European bloodbath was criminal, and celebrated out in the open. At the meeting of the Rhode Island Manufactures Society in Providence in 1794, the officers recited the following verse:

> But shall in Europe and the East
> Mechanic Arts prevail,
> And not their flight into the West
> Promote Columbia's weal?
>
> Already hither do they fly
> Here sheltered from the storm
> Crushe'd by despotic wars they die
> And here secured from harm."

The following year the society sounded a similar theme:

> But while on Europe's clouded sky
> Fair virtue drop the pitying tear
> The Arts in quick succession fly
> And find safe asylum here. . . .
> Here may we follow virtues star
> And rise to greatness unconfin'd
> While no proud despot dares to bar
> The gates of glory on mankind."

And in 1800 a speaker to the Providence Association of Mechanics and Manufactures asked rhetorically: "Will you not lure improvement from the embattled shores of Europe?"[58]

The Anglo-American rapprochement, initiated by Hamilton in 1790 and officially sanctioned by the Jay Treaty in 1795, combined with the rapid pace of American industrialization, altered the technological relations between the two nations. In fact, the movement of technology was never only in one direction. Some European mechanics spent time in the New World and doubtlessly learned from local artisans. The Frenchman Marc Isambard Brunel, for example, escaped Robespierre's terror, spent most of the 1790s in the United States, and left for England after learning over dinner at Hamilton's house in 1798 about the Royal Navy's need for a better supply of pulley blocks. He collaborated with Samuel Bentham, inspector general of naval works, and the gifted machine builder Henry Maudslay to design a set of machines for making pulleys, and even received an English patent for one of them. American mechanics who secured their patents in the United States recognized that if they wanted to protect their inventions abroad they had to register their patents in London. Amos Whittemore registered a patent in June 1797 for a machine that automated the entire process of making carding combs for cotton or wool: piercing the leather handles, cutting and bending wires to form the teeth, inserting them through the pierced holes, and bending them again to fasten them to the leather. To reap the profit from his invention, Whittemore traveled to London in 1799 and registered his innovation, and it "soon became fully appreciated" in England.[59]

There were prudent economic considerations behind the retreat from the attempt to attract British artisans and from the use of patents of importation. First, rewarding imported patents could undermine local innovations. As one writer put it, "childish dependence on the supposed bounties of a reputed parent, damped the rising efforts of inventive genius" in America. Second, it was no longer necessary to entice artisans to migrate. By the summer of 1793 Americans learned that the British entry into the European war was "occasioning great emigrations from Britain to America," mostly of "manufacturers, the most valuable part of our labourers." The State Department's partial list of British immigrants living in America during the War of 1812 confirmed that the wars of the French Revolution had lent momentum to the influx of industrial immigrants from Britain to the United States.[60] Finally, by virtue of their migration to the New World, British artisans cut themselves off from the source of their knowledge. While improvements and innovations continued to take place in England, the migrants' knowledge rapidly became outdated. In an ironic twist, immigrants threatened to slow down the pace of development because their standing in the United States was founded on the state of knowledge in Europe before they immigrated. Any innovation in Europe therefore undermined their privileged status in the New World.

Writers addressing prospective immigrants alerted them to the new mood in America. Thomas Cooper warned that those "imagining that America must be in want of them, and that Congress would probably be disposed" to granting their demands "of having their passage paid, lands given, salaries appointed, exclusive privileges for terms of years &c" should realize that under the new Constitution Congress had no such powers and that even state governments were moving away from such practices. Massachusetts, for example, granted a piece of land to the Scholfield brothers to help them establish a woolen factory in Newburyport. Yet, by the mid 1790s, the General Court no longer saw the need to use the public purse to promote English-style industrialization. Twice, in 1795 and 1797, it rejected petitions for the property of the workmen in the factory to be exempt from taxation.[61]

Even staunch supporters of offering inducements moved from promises of subsidies to singing the praises of freedom and opportunity in America. In 1794 Coxe published *A View of the United States of America*, which extolled the many virtues of the republic, from religious and political tolerance to cultural diversity. He promised prospective immigrant workers "constant employment, and better wages, than in the dearest countries in Europe," and declared that "master workmen in every manufacturing and mechanical art . . . must succeed here." The Coxe of 1794, however, sounded a tune very different from the one he had played just a few years earlier. Whereas in the 1780s and early 1790s he had promised state subsidies, patents of importation, and land grants, by the middle of the decade he tied the success of European artisans in America to "having been skilful, sober, frugal," and having invested their savings in setting up factories in the United States. Absent were promises of governmental programs to reward the importation of forbidden industrial technology.[62]

Americans increasingly spoke of competing effectively and mastering modern technology without resorting to open advocacy of technology piracy. Becoming "*independent of Foreign Countries,* for Articles which form the Necessities, or the Comforts of Life," remained a national priority. "Nine hundred of every thousand dollars paid by us for imported manufactures," explained one patriot, "rewards the superior skill of the foreign artist." It was therefore "the undoubted duty of every Citizen of the United States," declared Jeffersonian politician George Logan to the New York Tammany Society, "to give encouragement to the Mechanics, and Manufactures of our Country; not by promoting prohibitory laws against the importation of Foreign Fabrics, but by calling our own manufactures into use."[63] Support for local industry took precedent over the importation of foreign skill.

While Hamilton continued to believe that the United States should follow the English developmental model, the rising Jeffersonian opposition abandoned its earlier hostility to manufacturing and argued that the English model could not be followed in the American context. Efforts like that of the Society for the Establishment of Useful Manufactures to establish large factories similar to the ones in England failed precisely because economic conditions in America were so radically different. Whereas English industrialists relied on easy access to capital, cheap labor, and markets, American industrialists had none of these advantages. The best representative of the new confident faith in the unique American path to industrial development was a recent immigrant from Geneva who in the second half of the 1790s rapidly rose in the ranks of the Jeffersonian opposition. Albert Gallatin first came to national prominence as one of the principal leaders of the Democratic-Republican Society of western Pennsylvania, whose reputation was tarnished by its connection to the Whiskey Rebellion. In 1794 Gallatin was elected to the Senate from Pennsylvania, only to be unseated by a Federalist majority on the grounds that he had not been a United States citizen for nine years, as required by the Constitution. The following year Gallatin was elected to the House of Representatives and quickly emerged as the most effective Republican spokesman on economic matters. The only national leader of the decade who owned and managed a factory as his primary occupation, Gallatin had firsthand experience with the emerging industrial economy.

In 1796 Gallatin published a scathing criticism of Hamilton's program, *A Sketch of the Finances of the United States*, in which he challenged the fundamental assumptions of Hamiltonian economics and articulated a highly sophisticated counter vision. Gallatin disagreed with Hamilton's premise that American manufacturing was plagued by capital shortages and technological backwardness. He argued that industry and exports in the United States were growing "greater, in proportion to their population than those of any other nation." While only a "few manufactures are yet carried on upon a large scale in the United States," he believed that small-scale and home manufacturing were up to the task of supplying the nation with "the most essentially necessary articles." Gallatin was not concerned that American technological backwardness would hinder industrial development. He maintained that "every further increase of population, in many of the states, diminishes the relative quantity of land and of produce raised, and promotes the establishment of manufactures." Gallatin's experience as a manufacturer and his reading of the emerging demographic and economic realities of the war-torn world persuaded him that American dependence on foreign manufactures was decreasing and that federal intervention to acquire European know-how was unnecessary.[64]

The Jeffersonians equated state intervention in the economy

with abuse of power, and contrasted Federalists' promotion of large-scale government-sponsored manufactures with their own reliance on individual entrepreneurs. The economic prosperity of the second half of the decade inspired faith in the nation's economy. The boom had little to do with industrialization. The European war created a vast demand for American agricultural products and for neutral shipping capable of transporting goods during wartime. The United States, as the most important neutral commercial power, was the main beneficiary of this demand for goods and for a neutral carrying trade. The prosperity brought about by the wars of the French Revolution inspired great confidence in the economy of the nation. Americans ceased to look to Europe for models of industrialization. The United States should industrialize not by "that baneful system of European Management which dooms the human Faculties to be smothered, and Man to be converted into a machine."[65] American industries would rise and compete with those of Great Britain without emulating the latter's economic strategies, nor its political corruption and social injustice.

The requirements of novelty and originality in the American patent law emerged in the 1790s as the official American position regarding the problem of international technology piracy. The United States, however, did not turn its back on importing protected technology from Europe. For all the grandiose insistence on originality and novelty, technology pirates filed for and received patents from the United States government, even when it was known, as in the cases of Pollard and Parkinson, that they had pirated rather than invented the machinery. The Patent Board declined to examine for themselves how American claims differed from European patents. Patentees were required to present a petitions to the board in which they specified in writing the function of their devices and how they differed from previously known and used ones. The board, however, never made a concerted effort to establish the universal originality or novelty of an application. When the patent law was revised in 1793, even the appearance of scrutiny of the legitimacy of claims was abandoned.

After a brief flirtation with technology piracy, then, the federal government withdrew from active participation in the practice. It was unnecessary to invest in recruiting of skilled artisans because the nation proved sufficiently attractive to European immigrants. All the same, no legal restrictions were placed on immigrants like Samuel Slater who established factories in the New World using pirated British technology, but who did not file for patents. The prosperity brought about by the wars of the French Revolution boosted economic activity in all sectors of the economy. The more backward the economy, the more fundamental state activity becomes to acquiring technology. The spectacular growth of the American economy in the 1790s allowed the federal government to play a passive role in the project of catching up with European industrial technologies.

CHAPTER 7

The Path to Crystal Palace

In 1804, seventeen years after its launching, the Pennsylvania Society for the Encouragement of Manufactures and the Useful Arts asked its most prominent founder, Tench Coxe, to prepare a report on the state of manufactures in the United States in general, and in Pennsylvania in particular. The public career of the preeminent champion of American manufacturing, which had looked so promising from the mid 1780s through his tenure as assistant secretary of the Treasury under Hamilton, had reached a dead end. In the heated partisan struggles of the 1790s Coxe left the Federalists for the Republicans. In the election of 1800 he campaigned for Jefferson, assuring industrialists that the election of the author of *Notes on Virginia* would not harm their interests. Coxe assumed that a grateful new president would reward his services with a senior appointment. Jefferson, however, initially ignored Coxe and only after much lobbying relented sufficiently to offer him a low-level patronage position which Coxe declined to occupy. All but finished politically and in a rather philosophical mood, Coxe used the report to reflect on the accomplishments of the society and on the past and future of American manufacturing.

In the early years, he wrote, the society had devoted itself to importing "labor-saving machinery" from England because "we were, at that time, destitute of these invaluable machines, and of many labor-saving secrets, devices, and processes, then known and since greatly improved in Europe." Before the society was founded in 1787, American manufacturers, devastated by a decade and a half of economic dislocations and political uncertainties, had lagged far behind Europe in most matters of industrial know-how. Thus, the society determined to improve American technology by importing modern machinery and encouraging the emigration of skilled artisans from Europe. The effort was highly successful. "With regard to machinery," Coxe reported, "great information and acquisition have been obtained during the last ten years." As for skilled artisans, the "acquisition and actual [arrival] of *a very great number and variety of foreign artists, tradesman and manufactures*" ready to practice their trades in America had made up much of the technology deficit. While much had been accomplished, Coxe warned that the era of American dependence on European know-how had not come to an end. The United States was still far behind England in most matters pertaining to industrial technology. Nevertheless, aggressive acquisition of European machinery was no longer a national priority. Technology piracy would be relegated to individuals and businesses. The states and the national government had to find ways to nurture and develop nascent industries.[1]

Jeffersonian Technology Policy

The Jeffersonians who controlled American politics for most of the first three decades of the nineteenth century did not share Hamilton's taste for centralized and planned development and did not consider American technological inferiority a national concern. A confident and optimistic outlook replaced the Federalists' anxiety-driven central planning. As one Virginia Republican

declared, "Europe may soon learn to respect our genius, our industry, and our patriotism, and no longer believe that we are to derive
from her alone, those gifts which Providence has placed within our
reach, and intended for our use."[2] Whereas Hamilton's *Report on
Manufactures* of 1791 devoted many pages to devising strategies to
remedy the know-how deficit, the Republicans' most prominent
economist, who served as secretary of the Treasury under Jefferson
and Madison, Albert Gallatin, submitted to Congress in 1810 a radically different *Report on Manufactures*. Gallatin said nothing of the
technology gap. He argued that the chief obstacle standing in the
way of American manufactures arose from "the vastly superior capital of the first manufacturing nation of Europe, which enables her
merchants to give very long credit, to sell on small profits, and to
make occasional sacrifices." Gallatin suggested that the federal government play the role of England's financial companies by "circu-
lating stock, bearing a low rate of interest, and lend it at par to
manufacturers."[3] Notwithstanding his blindness to the emerging
American stock market, which efficiently channeled private capital
to fuel industrialization, the report conveys Republican confidence
that the nation's manufacturing sector did not need to look for
technical assistance from the Old World. His hostility to the foundations of Hamiltonian economics—federal expenditure, a national
bank, and the stock market—doomed Gallatin's proposal. His rosy
outlook on the competitiveness of American industries overlooked
the facts that they were plagued by technological deficiencies and
persistent labor shortages, and that the cost of manufacturing in the
United States placed American products at a severe comparative
economic disadvantage. Proponents of industry turned to aggressive
advocacy of protective tariffs that would place the burden of assisting fledgling American manufacturing on consumers. However,
their pleas to the Jefferson administration to enact protective tariffs
fell upon deaf ears.

Early nineteenth-century industrial discourse retained the patriotic rhetoric of the revolutionary period. "So long as we remain a nation of farmers and merchants merely," declared an association of mechanics and merchants of New York City, "we shall be tributary to the Europeans; we shall lavish upon them the wealth that may be retained at home." American inventors and engineers associated the fortunes of technology with the success of the American republican experiment. Robert Fulton, for example, explained to Treasury secretary Gallatin that the federal government ought to support his canal building scheme because it would unite the republic socially and economically and instill faith in republican institutions. Nevertheless, ambivalence about the moral and social consequences of industrialization persisted. National leaders no longer spoke about keeping America's workshops in Europe, yet they remained committed to an agricultural political economy as the cornerstone of the republic. The anti-industrial language, so central to the republican rhetoric of the Revolution and the struggle against Hamilton's program, became the domain of social and religious critics of the emerging order. For the political and social mainstream, however, the American system of manufacturing and Yankee know-how would emerge as the primary models of industrial efficiency and ingenuity.[4]

Common language, culture, and leadership in mechanical innovation meant that Britain continued to be the primary source of imported technology. The pace and manner of the diffusion depended on relations between the two countries. From 1805 to 1815, when Anglo-American relations gradually deteriorated into open warfare, the revolutionary rhetoric and confrontational strategies of the 1780s and early 1790s resumed. In 1805, just as the Jefferson administration allowed the Jay Treaty to expire, the European war took a turn that indirectly drew American interests into the conflict. Trying to break the military stalemate, France and England each changed their strategy from attempting a decisive military victory to a policy of starving the enemy. In 1806 and 1807 Napoleon issued the Milan and Berlin decrees which excluded British shipping from the continent, while England responded with orders in council that imposed a blockade on the entire continent. Both measures encouraged seizure and confiscations of neutral vessels, and indeed American ships quickly became the primary victims of these policies. Making things worse for the American economy, the Jefferson administration responded with progressively harsher measures of commercial coercion culminating in the Embargo of 1808 which exacerbated the suffering of the public.

The European war and the Jeffersonian countermeasures sharply reduced American foreign trade. For most Americans the trade war spelled economic catastrophe. Manufacturers, however, gained a needed reprieve from having to compete with cheaper and better-known imports. President Madison wrote William Pinckney, his minister to the Court of St. James, to warn his hosts that American manufactures had made great strides in recent years and that British assaults on neutral trade would aid the "astonishing progress of manufacturing" in the United States. Inventive activity, as measured by grants of patents, grew more than sevenfold in the first decade of the nineteenth century—from 35 patent grants in 1800 to 246 in 1810. Foreign observers noted that "the shackles with which the belligerent powers have obstructed the navigation and commerce of neutrals" had aided the growth of American industries. Prices of imported manufactured goods rose quickly and domestic finished goods took their place. The sharp decline in exports of raw materials, primarily cotton, forced planters to look for alternative markets in the northeast, where manufacturers, emboldened by this unexpected turn in their favor, sought new workers and new technologies to capitalize on their momentary good fortune. They rapidly established new mills whose chief goal was the attainment of national self-sufficiency. For twenty years, wrote Benjamin's Rush's student James Mease, England had dominated textile manufacturing. "If our cotton shall be impeded by the belligerents on its way to foreign markets, we must and shall manufacture many cotton goods, so as to rival foreign woolens."[5]

The flow of industrial immigrants from England to the United States was responsive to the political and economic situation in each country. At Phineas Bond's initiative, Parliament passed an act in 1803 that limited the number of passengers per ton that British ships could carry. This measure, as Lord Castlereagh admitted to John Quincy Adams, was primarily designed to stem the flow of skilled emigrants to America. Such measures were mostly ineffective, however, as the large flow of men and equipment continued. Many artisans emigrated from 1810 to 1812, when the European war, combined with the American restrictions on Anglo-American trade, created hardships for industrial workers in England. Shortly after Congress declared war on Britain in June 1812, the State Department ordered all enemy aliens to register with local marshals. Hezekiah Niles, the publisher and editor of the *Niles Weekly Register,* reported that the number of noncitizen enemy aliens residing in the United States during the war was so great that they composed nearly a third of the population of northeastern seaboard towns. Historians who examined the partial records collected by the State Department about enemy aliens living in the United States during the War of 1812 confirm Niles's observation. Moreover, they found that many resident aliens were artisans claiming to have learned their trades from Crompton, Arkwright, and Hargreaves, and promising to share their know-how with their American apprentices. In July 1814, when British forces invaded the United States, a royal proclamation ordered all British nationals to return home or face the charge of treason. (Since Britain did not recognize American naturalization, this decree threatened many Americans.) All in all, some seventy-five hundred British citizens relocated to the British Isles, nearly 40 percent of whom were industrial workers. The efforts of the British authorities to curtail wartime emigration to the United States were ineffective. Whatever deceptive methods they used to overcome legal obstacles, British artisans who wished to emigrate to America were not prevented from doing so.[6]

Deteriorating relations leading up to the war fired up the patriotic spirit in the battle over industrial technology. Young Henry Clay, whose anti-British stand in those years earned him the reputation of a war hawk, argued that the government should aid domestic manufactures so that it could supply domestic demand with goods of "equal elegance" to and "greater durability" than the British imports. Spokesmen harped on the theme that industrial dependency resulted in political subservience. Debts "incurred for foreign manufactures" had perpetuated the colonial state; "we are too much under the influence, indirectly, of British merchants and British agents: we are not an independent people," explained Thomas Cooper, who migrated from England to the United States in 1795. Only the establishment of a strong industrial base capable of replacing British imports could set American independence on a safe and secure footing.[7] Standing up to the British transcended the abstract issues of neutral rights and national honor, promising to complete the unfinished business of the Revolution, namely economic independence.

The new mood momentarily revived the calls for a patent law explicitly devoted to technology piracy. The principled commitment to worldwide novelty and originality of the patent acts of the 1790s gave way to a renewed interest in patents of importation. In 1810 Thomas Fessenden issued a call for Congress to pass a new Patent Act that would encourage technology piracy by awarding introducers of hitherto unknown machinery the same privileges given to inventors. The Massachusetts Association for the Encouragement of Useful Inventions petitioned Congress in 1811 to make available to the public the most recent European treatises in the arts, sciences, and technology.[8] In a belligerent mood, Congress considered adding the battle over technology to the wartime agenda. On January 22, 1812, the Senate began to discuss revising the 1793 act to promote sciences and useful arts. The new bill proposed that "any person who shall first import, bring or introduce, into the United States any invention or discovery aforesaid, made in a foreign country, shall be taken and deemed the inventor or discoverer of the same, and shall be entitled to a patent for such invention or discovery, to be obtained in like manner, and upon like terms, and subject to like conditions, restrictions, and limitations as are herein prescribed in the case of an inventor." The House of Representatives followed the Senate's lead, formed a committee to study the initiative, and reported back positively. The matter remained dormant from March until June 12, 1812, less than a week before Congress declared war on Great Britain, when Representative Adam Seybert submitted a report on the state of the Patent Office which stated that much in the upcoming conflict "may depend upon our manufactures," and called on the United States to "do all in our power to encourage their ["labor saving machines"] importation from abroad; in this respect England is an example worthy of imitation" as it did "all in her power to invite [her enemies' skilled artisans] emigration."[9]

None of these proposals became law. The issue at hand was neither reforming the patent law nor reconsideration of industrial policy. These initiatives were discussed while Congress was passing legislation to prepare the nation for war against England. They were wartime measures. Britain humiliated United States sovereignty, impressed American sailors, seized American vessels on the high seas, and confiscated their cargo. Congress was in a bellicose mood and the measures encouraging technology piracy proposed to flaunt American violation of English law and weaken the enemy by draining it of its industrial strength.

The Patent Office and the Courts

The reemergence of official orchestration of industrial piracy in the context of the War of 1812 was an aberration. Official American policy regarding patents of importation was not altered even though some American diplomats used their positions to import forbidden technology. Robert Livingston and David Humphreys, for example, circumvented Spanish prohibitions on the export of merino sheep, whose wool was very fine, and transported them to the New World.[10] For the most part, however, elected officials paid little attention to smuggling forbidden industrial technology from Europe during the Jeffersonian era. This vacuum on the federal level allowed William Thornton, the first superintendent of patents who ran the office from 1802 to 1828 almost single-handedly, to shape United States patent policy. Thornton believed that he was the guardian of the rights of patentees. In order to make sure that competitors would not reconstruct protected inventions from the detailed descriptions required for patent registration, Thornton refused, contrary to specific instructions from Congress and the executive, to give the public access to the details of patents. Appointing himself judge, jury, and executor of all matters relating to patents, Thornton was in effect the only one who could deny an application because its claim to international originality was suspect. However, he had neither the will nor the means to monitor this. As he explained in 1811, "there is at present no discretionary power to refuse a patent." In fact, Thornton did not even insist that patentees take the required oath that their application was indeed novel and original. Thus, even though the Patent Act specifically forbade patents of importation, the federal government did little to enforce this provision.[11]

In the early national republican imagination, patents remained associated with the antirepublican idea of monopoly. Early nineteenth-century American juries were disposed to side with local imitators against distant patentees because diffusion of innovation throughout the community promoted the common good. In the context of the growing nationalist consciousness of the era, the interests of national development justified violating the intellectual property of foreigners. On the other hand, concurrent with the rising nationalism of the postwar years, market capitalism emerged as the defining feature of northern economy and society. The budding spirit of capitalism slowly eroded republican hostility to patent monopolies. As Americans looked to the law to encourage economic growth, patents, which supposedly rewarded and thereby encouraged innovation, were seen as a wise development policy. Patents were responsible, as the lawyer Peter A. Browne declared in 1826, for the "wonderful improvements that have taken place within the last half century, in manufactures and the useful arts" and "the happy effects that these improvements have had upon the condition of the human race."[12] To be sure, arguments for the usefulness of patents did not go uncontested. Local juries might still privilege the interests of a locality over the intellectual property of a distant litigant. The judiciary, however, looked more favorably on patent infringement suits and took to the protection of intellectual property. The growing use of equity rather than juries to resolve patent disputes placed decisions about patents in the hands of judges who encouraged industrial development and held favorable views of patent monopolies.[13]

The absence of clear direction from either Congress or the Patent Office left the issue of patents of importation to the courts, where federal and state judges consistently refused to grant introducers of technology the rights of inventors. Supreme Court Justice Bushrod Washington in numerous rulings in the Pennsylvania Circuit during the first two decades of the nineteenth century established the norm that no patent should be granted to inventions imported from Europe. While the federal law was clear, nothing prevented states from granting patents of importation to introducers of new technology, particularly if a state wanted to develop a particular branch of industry. As Supreme Court Justice Joseph Story wrote, while the federal government could not extend the rights of patentees to introducers of new technologies, the states "may grant an exclusive right to the possessor or introducer of an art or invention who does not claim to be an inventor, but has merely introduced it from abroad." While the states could grant such patents, they became useless after the Supreme Court ruled in 1824 in *Gibbons v. Ogden* that state-sponsored patent monopolies were not enforceable beyond state lines. The decision invalidated the power of states to privilege their own manufacturers to produce for the national and international markets.

State courts also declined to support patents of importation. Chancellor James Kent of New York, author of the most important nineteenth-century American legal treatise, *Commentaries on American Law* (1821), wrote in 1812 in *Livingston v. Van Ingen* that Congress had ruled that no exclusive rights could be given to importers of new technology into the United States. In 1824, the Circuit Court of New York, in *Morris v. Huntington,* explained that this restriction did not apply exclusively to immigrants and that American citizens could not get patents for foreign invention. The following year, in Massachusetts, Justice Story ruled that even though English law encouraged patents of importation, they were strictly forbidden in the United States.[14] Thus, by the end of the first quarter of the nineteenth century, American courts took a decisive stand against technology piracy.

Collapsing Barriers

The letter of the law and the consistent upholding of its intent by federal and state judges had little impact on the movement of men and machines across the Atlantic, especially as diplomatic relations between the United States and Great Britain improved in the decades following the War of 1812. The Anglo-American understanding that followed the Ghent peace accord did not signal a period of friendship and harmony between the two nations. Many Americans expected a resumption of hostilities and champions of industry argued that it was prudent and necessary to support American industries "until war or some sudden emergency may render them of incalculable importance."[15] American statesmen continued to view Britain as the United States' chief political and economic rival, and British newspapers continued to toe an anti-American line. Yet, Lord Castlereagh, the architect of the new British approach, was alarmed by the growing strength of the Holy Alliance in Europe and opted to overlook commercial and territorial rivalries in North America. The British government, which tolerated serious American provocations such as the execution of British nationals by Andrew Jackson's forces in Spanish Florida, was not inclined to allow the question of American raiding of British technologies to sour relations between the two countries.

At home, English mercantilists continued trying to prevent the diffusion of industrial technologies. The web of laws and regulations aimed at preventing the migration of artisans and the export of machinery remained on the books, and at times authorities successfully prevented the emigration of some artisans. During the War of 1812, the British government tried to improve enforcement of its prohibitions on the emigration of mechanics and the export of machinery. On July 23, 1814, a royal proclamation was issued giving British citizens four months to go back to England or face the charge of high treason. In 1815, for example, five glass craftsmen were arrested in the port of Liverpool on a ship bound for the United States. The occasional arrest of an emigrant on route to America, however, could not obscure the overall ineffectiveness of the policy. Still, English industrialists who embraced, in the first half of the century, the cause of international free trade in hopes of penetrating protected markets, confined their advocacy at home to the importation of raw materials and agricultural products. The calls for free trade did not extend to technology. British free traders opposed lifting the ban on the export of machinery, fearing that following a short-term boom for English machine building, England would lose its comparative economic advantage because in the long run foreigners would learn how to build the machines themselves, manufacture them at home, and develop home industries which would replace British imports.[16]

Discussion of the impact of the brain drain on the British Isles resumed in full force. In 1816, a year after the Congress of Vienna, an English poet already bemoaned the emigration of skilled artisans, at a "moment when labour is so scarce." While some went to Europe and even to archenemy France, most emigrants headed for the United States. Some English writers echoed eighteenth-century restrictionist sentiments and wrote books to warn their fellow countrymen of the pitfalls of leaving home. Richard Parkinson, for example, published an account of his travels through the United States "to prevent the ruin of many a family" by the foolish act of emigration. He found "no situation of life a man can be subjected to in England which can be much bettered in America; and it is ten times worse for ladies." Parkinson proposed strengthening the law against the emigration of artisans by requiring men who were about to board a vessel to show the customs collector certificates from their parish clergymen vouching for their professions, thereby guaranteeing that skilled mechanics could not leave.[17]

More often than not, however, the British state could not enforce its restrictions on the emigration of skilled artisans. Thus, in March 1811 when customs officials of the port of Liverpool arrested Dennis Manion, a spinner with McConnel and Kennedy headed for America aboard the ship *Union*, they could do little more than delay his departure. Manion skipped his trial date, jumped bail, and successfully absconded to the United States the following June. Emigration of all artisans was banned from 1814 to 1824 by the Privy Council, but enforcement of this prohibition was another matter. Artisans could and did lie about their professions and thus avoid detention. The lure of better pay and higher status in the New World provided plenty of incentive for violating these measures. Letters from friends and relatives and pamphlets on emigration spread the word that anyone "in any vocation, manual or mechanical, may, by honest industry and ordinary prudence, acquire an independent provision for himself and family; so high are the wages of labour, averaging at least double the rate in England, and quadruple that in France; so comparatively scanty the population; so great the demand for all kinds of work; so vast the quantity, and so low the price of land; so light the taxes; so little burdensome the public expenditure and debt." Indeed, from machine builders to spinners, the proportion of immigrants with prohibited industrial skills that took the risk and crossed the Atlantic rose significantly between 1800 and the 1820s.[18]

The dimension of the phenomenon—between two and a half and three million immigrants from British Isles came to the United States before the outbreak of the Civil War—altered the terms of the public debate over emigration in Britain. Realistic observers could neither consider the matter marginal, nor contemplate the possibility of standing in the way of millions on the move. Travelers' accounts of the United States reported an "ascendancy of manufacturing" and numerous success stories of "naturalized" citizens who rose to "eminence" in their professions, and "commanded consideration" from the American public. Some approved of the departure of the "surplus population of England" yet warned skilled workers that they would not find in America comforts of life equal to those they were accustomed to in Great Britain, and would realize upon their arrival that "they have made a mistake and a bad exchange." Others pointed out that emigration led to neither shortage of laborers in English industrial towns nor a significant decline in exports, and that emigration could solve the problem of pervasive unemployment in industrial towns. Finally, many of those who emigrated lacked the skills or the connections to land the best jobs in England.[19] In such a context, what was the use of the anti-immigration laws? As the English guidebook writer Robert Holditch put it,

> The inutility of the law prohibiting the emigration of manufactures or machinists to the United States is so obvious to all acquainted with the interior of that country, that they are at a loss to conceive why it continues to exist. It is still more surprising that it should yet be enforced in a country where excess of population is a subject of complaint,—where means have been devised to check the rapidity of its progress,—and where the classes denied the privilege of expatriation are complained of as being an encumbrance, and are daily adding more and more to the distress of the nation . . . In the eastern and middle states there are many hundreds of factories, abundantly supplied with managers and machine-makers from Britain, of which there is such redundancy, that a very considerable number have resorted to agriculture. Whether manufactories will succeed in America, or to what degree, time alone can determine; but that their progress can be in the least impeded by restrictive laws prohibiting the emigration of manufacturers or machinists from this country, is now absolutely impossible."

Having neither the manpower nor the technical capabilities to stem the tide, the British government acknowledged the futility of its efforts and in 1824 lifted all restrictions on the emigration of artisans.[20]

Smuggled Technology and the Antebellum Industrial Boom

The War of 1812 and its immediate aftermath made Jeffersonian legislators reconsider their industrial policy. In 1815, after being excluded from the American market for nearly eight years, British manufacturers tried to regain their hold on that market by flooding it with items at reduced prices. Following the signing of the Ghent peace accord British merchants and manufacturers, as John Adams put it, "disgorged upon us all their stores of merchandise and manufactures—not only without profit, but at a certain loss for a time—with the express purpose of annihilating all our manufactories and ruining all our manufacturers."[21] Congress responded with a tariff on woolens and cotton, iron, leather, hats, paper, and sugar. Congress would go on to revise the tariff numerous times in the antebellum period as the issue emerged as a persistent source of sectional conflict. For all the political controversies it engendered, the tariff policy shielded American manufacturers from European competition and gave a boost to the development of technology. And proponents of the tariff cited British technological superiority as one of the reasons why the federal government must protect the nascent American industries. Mathew Carey, who replaced Coxe as the leading spokesman of American manufacturers, argued that when "the improved machinery, and the skill of the British manufacturer, protected as he always is by the government, are considered, it ought not to excite surprise that the American manufacturer, without the support of his government, is found unequal to the contest."[22]

Some Americans viewed the normalizing relationship with Great Britain as a wonderful opportunity to intensify their recruiting of British artisans. Samuel Ogden, in a treatise on the future of the American textile industry in the aftermath of the War of 1812, told his countrymen that peace freed the nation to "adopt all attainable means, to facilitate work, to curtail the price of labour by improvements in the mode of working, and to prevent waste of stock." In England, Ogden wrote, the "management or superintendence of the business is mostly conducted by well experienced practitioners, of more than common abilities." In contrast, in the United States "we appoint men . . . who have no knowledge of what they undertake." Ogden urged American industrialists "to imitate" the technological innovations and professional standards of British manufacturers.[23] This sentiment was echoed in the report that Representative John Quincy Adams submitted to Congress in May 1832, which openly advocated emulation of the British model. Adams wrote that the British policy of rewarding the "inventive ingenuity of a few natives of the British islands" while acquiring contemporaneously inventions "made in other parts of the civilized world, and applying them to the exercise of mechanical arts, had placed Great Britain at the head of manufacturing nations of modern times." England's support and acquisition of mechanical improvements and "their application to manufactures," had elevated that nation to international supremacy, and, he urged that the United States must follow that example or be left behind.[24]

The conclusion of Anglo-American hostilities was followed by resurgence in the number of societies established to promote American manufacturing. The societies of the early nineteenth century followed strategies similar to the ones advocated by the societies that had sprung up in American cities in the 1780s. The Shamrock Society of New York published a pamphlet in 1816 on the merits of emigrating from the Old World to the New, letting Europeans know that American artisans enjoy a higher standard of living than their European counterparts because wages in the United States were higher. In an open challenge to Britain's restriction on emigration it declared: "We bid you welcome to a land of freedom: we applaud your resolution; we commend your judgment in asserting the right of expatriation; a right acknowledged and practised by people of all nations." The Pennsylvania Society for the Encouragement of American Manufactures sent an agent to Europe and instructed him to examine reports on European improvements and collect all relevant information about railroads in particular, "to enable our fellow citizens to resort to one of the most valuable internal improvements now in use." The accomplishments of British inventors and industrialists, declared a speaker to the Rhode Island Society for the Encouragement of Domestic Industry, more than made up for the corruption and blunders of British politicians. "The inventions of Arkwright more than redeem the errors of Lord North. The improvements of Watt—the genius and taste of Wedgewood sustained the political heroism of Pitt, and enabled him to be the pilot that weathered the storm." The republic's interest required that Americans overcome their distaste for the former colonizer and emulate the British model of industrialization. [25]

The most famous of all early nineteenth-century cases of industrial espionage laid the foundations for America's most interesting industrial experiment—the textile mills of Lowell, Massachusetts. In 1811 Francis Cabot Lowell, a merchant from Boston who was spending a couple of years in Britain for health reasons, took a tour of the Glasgow factories and the following February he visited factories in Manchester. His British hosts generally guarded their secrets and patents. None, however, suspected that this wealthy and frail American living abroad would emerge as a rival. Lowell had a superb memory and was trained in mathematics. He closely observed his surroundings and each night in his hotel he made sketches of what he had seen. When he came back to the United States he contacted a local mechanical expert, Paul Moody, and together they replicated the machines he had observed in Manchester. Moody and Lowell, however, were not satisfied with mere duplication. They wanted to improve upon British technology and, after some tinkering, succeeded. They developed a new machine for spinning cotton and invented a power loom that allowed all stages of textile production (carding, spinning, weaving, and dressing) to be housed in a single factory. The world's first integrated cotton mill opened its doors in Waltham, Massachusetts, and was an immediate success.

By the mid 1820s English newspapers began to acknowledge that Americans were catching up with British technical innovations. When the American Zachariah Allen visited England in 1825, he was surprised to discover that American textile technology was more advanced than its English counterpart. Patriotism rather than factual comparison of the state of the textile industry in Britain and the United States probably clouded Allen's judgment. All the same, he was not the only one profoundly impressed by the rapid pace at which Americans were catching up with England's textile technologies. Englishmen who traveled to New England in the second quarter of the nineteenth century expressed similar views.[26]

The integrated factory marked a new stage in the development of textile manufacturing in the United States. Before 1814, small family-owned mills that followed by and large the model Slater brought with him to America had dominated textile manufacturing in New England. These mills prospered when American industry was sheltered from British competition from 1805 to 1815, but many collapsed when Anglo-American trade resumed. The Waltham factory, however, competed effectively with the British imports. This success signaled the beginning of a shift away from family-operated to corporation-led mills. To be sure, the transformation was neither sudden nor complete. Many mills, primarily in southern New England, conformed to the Slater model well into the 1840s. Yet, they consistently lost market share to the bigger, more efficient, and more advanced integrated factories of northern New England. However, enterprises like the one Lowell and Moody built were expensive. Lowell was wealthy and had connections. He had little trouble organizing his investors as the "Boston Associates." Such an operation, however, was beyond the financial abilities of the small operators, who were quickly replaced by large companies. Meanwhile, Boston Associates went even bigger. In 1823, the company built an entire town at the junction of the Merrimack and Concord rivers and named it after Lowell, who had died in 1817.[27]

The Lowell model of technology acquisition was replicated in other locations and in other industries. A French traveler noted in 1814 that nearly all the machinery used in American manufacturing had "been borrowed from England." Skilled immigrants were in great demand because they had experience operating and fixing these machines. The "constant migration hither of needy and desperate talent from Europe," complained one British attorney, "helps to swell the aggregate of American ingenuity and invention." He reported that "European discoveries in art and science generally reach the United States within a few months after they first see the light in their own country, and soon become amalgamated with those made by Americans themselves." Americans traveled to Europe, primarily to England, to learn "the latest improvements in mechanical inventions"[28] and, to a large extent, the industrialization of the United States in first half of the nineteenth century was founded upon imported know-how. In textiles, some followed Lowell's path and managed to talk their way into factories, while others circumvented the restrictions on the export of machinery by shipping machine parts to the United States as separate components. As late as 1850 immigrants from the British Isles comprised more than three-fourths of the weavers and skilled workers in the textile industry of Germantown, Pennsylvania. Managers of American cotton mills in the first half of the nineteenth century were, for the most part, English immigrants, because native experienced managers were rare. American glass manufacturers recruited European workers aggressively in the first two decades of the nineteenth century and by the 1820s were world leaders. Paper mills in New England and the Mid-Atlantic states relied on a constant stream of skilled

European immigrants before local industry took off in the second quarter of the century. The ironworker Henry Burden, educated and trained in Scotland, migrated to the United States in 1819 and in 1825 constructed a rolling and slitting mill in Springfield, Massachusetts. Burden went back twice to Britain in order to learn the most up-to-date techniques. Later in the century, the American steel industry was founded upon imported technology. In all these cases European know-how was instrumental in getting industries started and turning the United States into a leading industrial nation.[29]

As these examples illustrate, the statutory requirement of worldwide originality and novelty for American patents did not hinder widespread American appropriation of innovations protected under other nations' patent and intellectual property laws. In fact, once a technology was in the New World, its introducers quickly claimed it as their own, and used the courts to discourage infringements. The Boston Manufacturing Company registered nine patents and obtained the rights to two others. It hired the country's most famous lawyer, Daniel Webster, and sued competitors for patent infringement. Claiming ownership of a pirated innovation was quite easy. Obtaining a patent under the 1793 act involved little more than filing the necessary papers and paying the thirty-dollar registration fee. The poorly staffed Patent Office was in no position to examine the merits of the nearly ten thousand patents it issued from 1793 to 1836.[30] As one critic charged, most American inventions registered with the patent office were at best only slightly different from known and operating existing devices. The mechanics of patent registration not only betrayed the spirit of the original legislation by granting patents to innovations of questionable originality, but also, in effect, it allowed wealthy importers of European technology, such as the Boston Associates, to claim exclusive rights to imported innovations and use the courts to validate their claims and intimidate competitors.[31]

The embrace of European technology by early nineteenth-century Americans signifies a cultural and economic shift in the life of the republic. Within seventy years, from the 1780s to the 1850s, the United States was transformed from an industrial nonentity to the fastest-rising industrial power in the world. No less a figure than the self-proclaimed champion of agrarianism, Thomas Jefferson confessed in 1816 that "experience has taught me that manufactures are now as necessary to our independence as to our comfort." In 1828 Ichabad Lord Skinner, a former Congregational clergyman from Connecticut, published a journal that listed important American innovations in order "to give vigor to the inventive faculties of the nation . . . by placing before the ingenious artist the attempts of others." The "most striking characteristic of our age," echoed Justice Story in 1829, is its "superior attachment of practical science." Republican association of industrialization with poverty and corruption gave way to a climate of opinion that considered the pursuit of industrialization profitable and honorable. George White decided to write Samuel Slater's biography in the 1830s in order to persuade his countrymen that manufacturing promised to liberate the United States from the Old World and thus establish the country's independence. In an obvious repudiation of Jefferson's famous passage from *Notes on Virginia,* White declared that the "day is past and gone, when any of our citizens will think it best to have our workshops in Europe."[32]

The market revolution and the rapid democratization of the political process that accompanied it profoundly changed the personal behavior and cultural expectations of Americans residing north of the Mason-Dixon line. Witnessing the radical transformation of their society and political culture, many Americans associated economic expansion and the enlargement of political rights with the embrace of an industrial market economy. The northern cult of progress drew a line connecting democracy, prosperity, and mechanical improvements. Technology ushered in the prosperity that liberated common folks from the dependency and subservience of poverty and allowed them to claim political, social, and economic equality. As Alexis de Tocqueville described it, American democracy "leads men to adopt one type of work rather than another. It gives them a distaste for agriculture and directs them into trade and industry."[33]

Americans continued trying to learn from European creativity without paying for it. In 1814 a manual for American artisans gave as grounds for its publication the fact that the "time has already arrived, when a general diffusion of the knowledge of Europe on these [industrial] subjects cannot fail of being highly interesting and beneficial amongst us." Abraham Rees's multivolume *Cyclopedia*, with its detailed descriptions of British industrial techniques, initially published in London in the 1780s, was reprinted in Philadelphia from 1810 to 1842. Magazines devoted their pages to reporting on European scientific and technological advancements. The journal of the Franklin Institute, which began publishing in the mid 1820s, printed lists of recently registered English patents.[34] American publishers reprinted copies of English books and magazines and sold them in North America and England without compensating either English authors or publishers.[35]

Even American nationalists like Thomas Jefferson believed in the intellectual superiority of Europe. In planning and implementing his plan for the University of Virginia, Jefferson rejected American intellectual luminaries and dispatched Francis Gilmer to hunt down and convince European intellectuals to come and teach at Charlottesville.[36] American scientists recognized European superiority in research and teaching. A treatise on patents published in 1814 listed a number of European inventions, from textile machinery to the steam engine because, "in almost all this knowledge, and in the application of it, as in a thousand similar instances that might be added to this list, our own country is yet behind and has yet to learn." Spurred on by generous support from public and private institutions, and armed with letters of introduction from the political leaders, the number of American scientists who traveled to Europe increased significantly in the second quarter of the century. These trips abroad and the relationships struck with European scientists launched the careers of many American men of letters and science who established friendships and working relationships that created a scientific community transcending national boundaries.[37]

Forging Ahead

Technology transfer was never indiscriminate, and never a one-way street. Since the early days of the Industrial Revolution some innovations that had profound impact in Europe were of little use in the New World. The Newcomen engine, for example, which was widely used in England to pump out water from deep coal mines, never caught on in America even though it was imported to New Jersey in the 1750s and was briefly put to use to improve New York city's water supply in the 1770s. It simply did not provide an efficient cost-effective solution to the conditions in the New World. On the other hand, from the colonial period on Americans invented original machines and adapted European innovations to the local circumstances. American developments, at the same time, from Franklin's stove to the steamboat, were often integrated into European economies. Rufus King, while serving as minister to Great Britain, complained of the British practice of enticing American whalers to work for British fisheries. Machines invented in the United States for making nails and for carding wool and cotton were imported into France by a traveler who saw them in the United States in the first decade of the nineteenth century. By 1825 over a hundred Whittemore card-making machines were in use at Manchester. Jacob Perkins received five medals from the Royal Society of

Arts for inventing high-pressure steam engines and boilers, a hot water heating system, and a vapor-compression refrigerating system. Some American inventors showed little regard for national borders. Robert Fulton, for example, offered his invention of the torpedo first to France against England, then to England against France, and finally to the United States against both. To be sure, before the nineteenth century, the United States was, for the most part, an importer of technology. The technological developments of the first half of the century combined with the end of Anglo-American hostilities, however, created a new world of technology exchange in which increasingly mechanics in different countries regularly communicated about their methods of production. They formed, in effect, an international fraternity of artisans, indifferent to political boundaries and international disputes, that facilitated the progress of technology through unremitting free exchange of technical know-how.[38]

American industrialization was never an exact replica of the English version. The abundance of raw materials, the shortage of labor and capital, and the very different tastes and demands of American consumers made exact duplication inappropriate. American machines in the first half of the century used more wood and less iron and brass than their British counterparts because wood was cheap in America and iron and brass were not. The shorter life span of wooden machinery meant that technical improvements entered the production process faster than in England. American importation of British organizational and technological innovations was selective. Moreover, local mechanics, such as Oliver Evans, Eli Whitney, and Jacob Perkins increasingly took the lead in developing machinery that broke new ground and was particularly suited to American circumstances. American engineers were responsible for the most important and innovative technological accomplishment of the republic in the first quarter of the nineteenth century—the Erie

Canal. Thus, the sense of American technological inferiority was rapidly dissipating.[39]

The Atlantic world of technological exchange founded on the interdependence of all knowledge emerged in the first half of the nineteenth century. As John Quincy Adams told the House of Representatives in 1832, "Every nation is impelled not only to avail itself of the genius of her own sons, but to adopt and to improve those of her neighbors."[40] By the middle of the nineteenth century, improved communication and transportation quickened the diffusion of innovations between the Old and New Worlds. Ironically, patent registration emerged both as a way to confine knowledge to one locality and as a way of diffusing knowledge. Leading British engineers turned to register patents in both England and France, though the American Patent Act did not allow foreign nationals to be issued patents in the United States. Britain's lifting of travel restrictions in 1824 was followed by a radical revision of the laws prohibiting machine exportation the following year. Parliament replaced complete prohibition with a licensing system, by which export licenses were given to nearly all innovations except spinning and weaving machinery. But the licensing system proved equally ineffective. Economic success in the first half of the nineteenth century originated with putting innovations to productive use, not licensing or assigning a patent. In 1843 Britain lifted all restrictions on the export of industrial machinery.[41]

Europeans could not ignore the growing competitiveness of American manufactures which drew an increasingly greater share of consumer markets. Travelers, who in the previous centuries had written elaborate descriptions of wilderness and agriculture in the New World, increasingly reported on the dramatic industrial transformation of the northeastern states. Tocqueville wrote of his own "daily astonishment" at American industrial productivity. "The Americans," he reported, "make great advances in industry because they are all at the same time engaged in it." Even Charles Dickens, whose *American Notes* are laced with critical comments on the republic, was impressed with American industry. He visited Lowell and found it a "thriving place." He examined woolen, cotton, and carpet factories and found them all to be clean, orderly, and efficient. Drawing a contrast between Lowell and English industrial towns, Dickens concluded, would be similar to comparing "Good and Evil, the living light and the deepest shadow."[42]

It took time for Europeans to realize that the former colonies had become their equal. A British commentator predicted in the 1830s that "it will probably require the lapse of a century before the United States can in this respect [manufactures] rival, or even approach, the parent country."[43] Twenty years later some still refused to recognize that the industrial and technological balance of power had been transformed. As late as the 1850s some English engineers argued that American machines lacked the sophistication and durability of English ones. British complacency aside, the antebellum northeastern United States emerged as the center of mechanical innovation. Contemporaries and historians have argued since whether economic necessity, the environmental make-up of the region, or a culture founded on the spirit of freedom and experimentation brought about this unique phenomenon. Americans, building upon European innovation, mechanized industrial operations in a revolutionary manner. Technology took off and became, as Daniel Boorstin called it, "the leitmotif of American civilization."[44]

The 1851 Great Exhibition at the Crystal Palace in London, could have fueled the European sense of superiority over the New World. The American exhibitors were the only ones whose government did not provide them with financial support. Heads of European states, in contrast, sponsored their nations' displays of the latest mechanical novelties and household gadgets to demonstrate technological and intellectual superiority. None other than Prince Albert paid for the British exhibit. In contrast, the undecorated walls of the American display and the squabble over who would pay for the unloading of the American exhibits could have left the impression that the United States was not in the same league with the European nations. To the rescue came the American banker George Peabody, who subsidized the unloading and decoration to the tune of fifteen thousand dollars. Even with Peabody's largess, however, the American display was aesthetically inferior and some of its walls remained bare.

But what started out as another demonstration of American inferiority was transformed by the practical demonstrations of American mechanical ingenuity into the most famous sign that technological leadership had passed to the United States. American plows and reapers, though initially ridiculed, showed power and exactness that had no match. A British crack lock-picker could not open the American Hobbse's lock, whereas British locks fell open to Hobbse's dexterity. American rifles and canon, with their interchangeable parts, were clearly the best small arms in the world. The Morse telegraph, Hayden's cotton-drawing frame, Jersey locomotives, Goodyear rubber materials, and many more items, from textile machinery to artificial limbs, won high praise. The 534 American exhibitors, out of a total of 15,000, won more prizes than most of the continental nations. Only Great Britain, which had more than two-thirds of the exhibitors, won more prizes, though in relation to their number, the American accomplishments dwarfed even those of the British.[45]

In the years immediately following the signing of Anglo-American peace at Ghent the prewar trend of industrial espionage, recruitment, enticement, and smuggling continued. The British government, in turn, slowly recognized that it could do little to stop the outflow of technology. In the 1820s the movement for easing barriers against technology diffusion gained much ground, primarily because the British machine tool industry, circumscribed by these regulations, exerted pressure on the government to allow it to export technologically advanced machinery. Two decades later Parliament struck the laws from the books. Meanwhile, in the United States, American artisans and inventors developed and improved industrial technology, and adapted it to American circumstances. By the time the Crystal Palace exhibition opened in 1851 European observers recognized that it was the Americans who were now leading the world in technological innovation.

The debate over patents and intellectual property in the first half of the nineteenth century pitted free traders and internationally minded statesmen against innovators, protectionists, and champions of industry. Advocates of the free exchange of ideas and innovations had the better of the argument. The failure to prevent technology piracy and the removal of British restrictions on the immigration of artisans and export of machinery demonstrated the practical impossibility of enforcing a counterdiffusion policy.

In Holland, internationalists succeeded in repealing the patent law temporarily in 1869. The Dutch measure, however, was an aberration. The second half of the nineteenth century saw most Western nations moving in the opposite direction, expanding their commitment to protecting and regulating intellectual property. Within national boundaries authors, inventors, and patentees found official agencies of the state on their side. The coercive bodies of states, however, could do nothing to protect intellectual property beyond their borders. Improved communications allowed for faster and more accurate technology transfer and underscored the need for international cooperation to address the question of the national boundaries of knowledge and technology. The governments of the industrializing world, however, failed to agree on a unified international information policy. Without international cooperation on the validity of patents beyond national borders, each country tried to enforce its own regulations while at the same time covering for its own violations of the intellectual property of other nations. Even the international accord on the protection of industrial property that was signed by the United States in the 1880s, while establishing the validity in all nations of patents registered in one nation, did not allow challenges to patents of importation and improvements by original inventors.[46]

From the American Revolution to the Crystal Palace exhibition, United States technology caught up with and surpassed its European rivals. The industrialization that took place along the northeastern seaboard in the first half of the nineteenth century facilitated a dramatic two-thirds growth in per capita income. The United States economy grew faster and was more productive than that of any nation in Europe.[47] Contemporaries and historians have come up with a wide range of social, political, and cultural explanations for this dramatic development. Some celebrate it as the ultimate manifestation of the virtue of the American spirit of enterprise, and others argue that the blood and sweat of slaves provided the capital for the spectacular economic growth of the first half of the nineteenth century. What is often overlooked is the manner in which smuggled technology made for more efficient and more profitable industrialization. Tens of thousands of artisans crossed the Atlantic and brought with them their skills, methods, and tools. American industrialists, scientists, and intellectuals kept abreast of mechanical developments through trips to Europe and growing scientific exchange. Federal and state authorities were officially committed to respecting the intellectual property of others, yet in fact sanctioned smuggling of protected knowledge on a huge scale. American investors and mechanics adapted imported technology to local circumstances. The infant state of American know-how and the absence of artisanal guilds committed to earning their livelihoods from known and tried techniques allowed New World innovators to reject wholesale adoption of imported machinery and processes and opt for selective adaptation and tinkering. Technology transfer, then, accounts not only for the rapid economic growth of the republic in the first half of the nineteenth century, but also for the experimental and innovative reputation of the "American system of manufactures."

Crystal Palace turned out to be the "coming out party" for United States technology. In the span of seventy years an agricultural republic with some household manufactures that had more in common with the Middle Ages than with the industrial world transformed itself into a world leader of cutting-edge industrial technology. American machines and the "American system of manufacturing," as the British press called it, became models for worldwide imitation. Like modern developing nations, early in its history the United States violated intellectual property laws of rivals in order to catch up technologically. Integration into the international community required that the government of the United States distance itself from such rogue operations. In the process the United States had come full circle. The fledgling republic, once committed to technology piracy, had become the primary technology exporter in the world. The years of piracy upon which the new status was founded, however, were erased from the national memory. The intellectual debt to imported and pirated technology did not turn the United States into the champion of free exchange of mechanical know-how. As the technology began to flow eastward across the Atlantic, the United States emerged as the world's foremost advocate of extending intellectual property to the international sphere.

Notes

Introduction

1. James E. Hillhouse, "Reminiscence of the Late Mr. Whitney, Inventor of the Cotton Gin," *American Journal of Science and Arts* 21, no. 2 (1832), 59n.

2. *http://www.wipo.org/about-wipo/en/gib.html*; *European Commission Green Paper on Counterfeiting and Piracy*, June 1999; *American Information Resource Center Newsletter*, March 2002; "WIPEOUT, the International Intellectual Property Counter-Essay Contest," at *http://www.theregister.co.uk/content/6/25047.html*.

3. One of the most interesting debates in the historiography of technology centers on the relationship between technology, and society and its institutions. The debate is between those who see technology developing, for the most part, as a result of its own internal dynamics and then molding society, and those who emphasize the social construction of technology. For an intellectually stimulating taste of this debate, see Langdon Winner, "Do Artifacts Have Politics?" *Daedalus* 109 (Winter 1980), 121–36; John M. Staudenmaier, "Recent Trends in the History of Technology," *American Historical Review* 85 (June 1990), 715–25; Merritt Roe Smith, "Technological Determinism in American Culture," in Merritt Roe Smith and Leo Marx, eds., *Does Technology Drive History? The Dilemma of Technology Determinism* (Cambridge, Mass., 1994), 1–35; Philip Scranton, "Determinism and Indeterminacy in the History of Technology," ibid., 143–68; Leo Marx, "The Idea of 'Technology' and Postmodern Pessimism," ibid., 237–57.

4. Throughout this book, I use the term "piracy" strictly as "an unauthorized appropriation and reproduction of another's production, invention, or conception, esp. in infringement of copyrights" (*Webster's Third New International Dictionary*).

5. Michel Foucault, "What Is an Author?" in Paul Rabinow, ed., *Essential Works of Michel Foucault*, 3 vols. (New York, 1997), II, 205, 214.

Chapter 1. Knowledge as Property in the International State System

1. In France the process of knowledge production was controlled by privilege, while in England the application of knowledge itself was the key to success. As Voltaire wrote in his *Philosophical Letters* in 1732, a seat in the Academy was worth a small fortune for a French intellectual while in London it cost money to be a member of the Royal Society. Francois Marie Arouet de Voltaire, *Philosophical Letters*, trans. Ernest Dilworth (New York, 1961 [1732]), 114.

2. Pamela O. Long, "Invention, Authorship, 'Intellectual Property,' and the Origins of Patents: Notes toward a Conceptual History," *Technology and Culture*, 32 (October 1991), 846–48; Mark Rose, *Authors and Owners: The Invention of Copyright* (Cambridge, Mass., 1993), 3; Frank D. Prager, "A History of Intellectual Property from 1454 to 1787," *Journal of the Patent Office Society* 26 (November 1944), 721; Akos Paulinyi, "Revolution and Technology," in Roy Porter and Mikulas Teich, eds., *Revolution in History* (Cambridge, Mass., 1986), 266; Carolyn C. Cooper, *Shaping Invention: Thomas Blanchard's Machinery and Patent Management in Nineteenth-Century America* (New York, 1991), 30; Euan Cameron, *The European Reformation* (Oxford, 1991); Derek McKay and H. M. Scott, *The Rise of the Great Powers, 1648–1815* (London, 1983).

3. F. M. Scherer, "Invention and Innovation in the Watt-Boulton Steam-Engine Venture," *Technology and Culture* 6 (Spring 1965), 165–87; Thomas P. Hughes, "Transfer and Style: A Historical Account," in Tagi Sagafi-nejad, Richard W. Moxon, and Howard Perlmutter, eds., *Controlling International Technology Transfer: Issues, Perspectives, and Policy Implications* (New York, 1981), 43; E. Wyndham Hulme, "The History of the Patent System under the Prerogative and at Common Law: A Sequel," *Law Quarterly Review* 16 (1900), 62.

4. John Locke, *Two Treatises of Government*, ed. Peter Laslett (London, 1967 [1690]), 305–6.

5. Edward F. Noyes to William Evarts, April 26, 1878, in *Papers Relating to the Foreign Relations of the United States* (Washington, D.C., 1878), 173; "Convention for the Protection of Industrial Property," signed March 20, 1883, ratified by the Senate on March 29, 1887, and signed by the president on June 11, 1887, in Charles I. Bevans, ed., *Treaties and Other International Agreements of the United States of America 1776–1949*, I (Washington, D.C., 1968), 80–88; Christine MacLeod, *Inventing the Industrial Revolution* (Cambridge, 1988), 199; Edith Tilton Penrose, *The Economics of the International Patent System* (Baltimore, 1951), 22.

6. Eric Robinson, "James Watt and the Law of Patents," *Technology and Culture* 13 (April 1972), 115–39.

7. H.I. Dutton, *The Patent System and Inventive Activity during the Indus-*

trial Revolution, 1750–1852 (Manchester, 1984), 17–22; Christine MacLeod, "The Paradoxes of Patenting: Invention and Its Diffusion in 18th- and 19th-Century Britain, France, and North America," *Technology and Culture* 32 (October 1991), 898–90; Peter Mathias, "Skills and the Diffusion of Innovation from Britain in the Eighteenth Century," *Transactions of the Royal Historical Society* (1975), 111–13.

8. Karl Marx, *Capital: A Critique of Political Economy*, trans. Samuel Moore and Edward Aveling, 3 vols. (New York, 1906 [1887]) I, 530. In another piece Marx wrote that "the mode of production conditions the social, political, and intellectual life process in general. It is not the consciousness of men that determines their being, but, on the contrary, their social being that determines their consciousness." "Preface to the Critique of Political Economy," [1859] in Robert C. Tucker, ed., *The Marx Engels Reader* (New York, 1972), 4. Friedrich Engels was even blunter, declaring: "The automatic machinery of a big factory is much more despotic than the small capitalists who employ workers over time." "On Authority," ibid., 731. He saw machines invading all branches of British industry and eliminating handicraft work. Engels equated factory labor with machine labor and assumed that the labor of women and children was the foundation of the latter.

9. MacLeod, *Inventing the Industrial Revolution*, 15, 31; Dutton, *The Patent System*, 1. Critics of the crown often charged that it used the patent system in a corrupt manner as a form of political patronage. The 1624 parliamentary enactment of the Statute of Monopolies was "an attempt to curtail the crown's abuse of patents." MacLeod, *Inventing the Industrial Revolution*, 1. Ironically, when Sir Robert Mansel applied for a renewal of his glass-making patent in 1623, he claimed to have brought from abroad experts in making Murano crystalline glasses, spectacle glass, and mirror glasses. L. M. Agnus Butterworth, "Glass," in Charles Singer, E. J. Holmyard, A. R. Hall, and Trevor I. Williams, eds., *A History of Technology*, 5 vols. (Oxford 1954–58), IV, 362.

10. John N. Adams and Gwen Averley, "The Patent Specification: The Role of Liardet v. Johnson," *Journal of Legal History* 7 (September 1986), 156–77; Karl B. Lutz, "Are the Courts Carrying Out Constitutional Public Policy on Patents?" *Journal of the Patent Office Society* 34, (October 1952), 768–69; Harold G. Fox, *Monopolies and Patents: A Study of the History and Future of Patent Monopoly* (Toronto, 1947), 229; MacLeod, *Inventing the Industrial Revolution*, 54.

11. John R. Harris, "The Transfer of Technology between Britain and France and the French Revolution," in *The French Revolution and British Culture* (Oxford, 1988), 177; Mathias, "Skills and the Diffusion of Innovation," 98–99; Herbert Heaton, "The Industrial Immigrant in the United States, 1783–1812," *Proceedings of the American Philosophical Society* 95 (October 1951), 524.

12. Ian Inkster, *Science and Technology in History: An Approach to Industrial Development* (New Brunswick, N.J., 1991), 36–50, 66–67; Louise A. Tilly, "Connections," *American Historical Review* 99 (February 1994), 19. As Nathan

Rosenberg & L. E. Birdzell declared, the "wealth of the West springs from its technology." *How the West Grew Rich: The Economic Transformation of the Industrial World* (New York, 1986), 144.

13. Paul Kennedy, *The Rise and the Fall of the Great Powers* (New York, 1987), 120. See also Patrick K. O'Brien, "Inseparable Connections: Trade, Economy, Fiscal State, and the Expansion of Empire, 1688–1815," in William Roger Louis, ed., *The Oxford History of the British Empire*, 5 vols. (New York, 1997–1999), II, *The Eighteenth Century*, ed. P. J. Marshall, 53–59; Patrick K. O'Brien, "Path Dependence or Why Britain Became an Industrialized, Urbanized Economy Long before France," *Economic History Review*, 2d ser., 49 (1996), 213–49; Mathias, "Skills and the Diffusion of Innovation," 95. Popular perception aside, historians have long recognized that the textile industry was the exception and that much of the British industry in the second half of the eighteenth century and the first half of the nineteenth was handicraft workshop production. "Such industries did not have cotton's powerful competitive advantage over continental rivals. . . . Historians have tended to emphasize too generally Britain's competitive advantage, ignoring the fact that British manufactures had developed behind a protective wall and that many of them still felt the need for its maintenance." A. E. Musson, "The 'Manchester School' and Exportation of Machinery," *Business History* 16 (January 1972), 18.

14. "Extracts from a Letter from London," *Pennsylvania Gazette*, May 3, 1786; Adam Smith, *An Inquiry into the Nature and Causes of The Wealth of Nations*, ed. Edwin Cannan, 2 vols. (Chicago, 1976 [1776]), I, 304; A. G. Kenwood and A. L. Lougheed, *Technology Diffusion and Industrialization before 1914* (New York, 1982), 188; David S. Landes, *The Unbound Prometheus: Technological Change and Industrial Development in Western Europe from 1750 to the Present* (Cambridge, Mass., 1969), 61. John R. Harris writes that "whatever the overall British industrial lead may have been, and whatever the effect of the progress of British industry in terms of national wealth, contemporary Europeans believed that certain British technologies had produced advantages to Britain which they desired for their own countries. The remarkable lengths to which they were often prepared to go to get the technologies, by hook or by crook, show the strength of that belief." "Movements of Technology between Britain and Europe," in David J. Jeremy, ed., *International Technology Transfer: Europe, Japan and the USA, 1700–1914* (Brookfield, Vt., 1991), 12–13.

15. David J. Jeremy, "Damming the Flood: British Government Efforts to Check the Outflow of Technicians and Machinery, 1780–1843," *Business History Review* 51 (Spring 1977), 1–34; David J. Jeremy, "British Textile Technology Transmission to the United States: The Philadelphia Region Experience, 1770–1820," ibid., 47 (Spring 1973), 25; Joseph Dorfman, *The Economic Mind in American Civilization*, 3 vols. (New York, 1946), I, 264; Dutton, *The Patent System*, 3; MacLeod, *Inventing the Industrial Revolution*, 33, 94.

16. A lengthy report on such efforts was published in the *Pennsylvania Gazette* as "Extracts from a Letter from London" on May 3, 1786. It read:

> The excellence to which the English have attained in the woolen manufacture, and the immense resources they find in it, have made the French ministry turn their attention more seriously than ever to that important branch of commerce. Formerly, they depended on a precarious supply of unwrought wool from Ireland by a "smuggling" trade, without which they could not carry on their manufacture in that branch with any hope of success; but they have lately offered great encouragements to those who could procure a number of English sheep to be smuggled alive into that kingdom; and several societies of gentlemen, in different provinces, have for a considerable time been employed in drawing up plans to instruct their farmers in the English mode of treating their sheep, and breeding them up. The ministry, in consequence, have had the satisfaction to hear, that there was actually, in the county of Boulonnois, a very numerous stock of sheep, which a gentleman had caused to be smuggled from England; and that he had so far succeeded in treating and feeding them after the English method, as to get fleeces from them as fine as any in England; which has convinced them, that they may meliorate their own wool to such a degree, as to be able to do without getting any from England. They have ordered a generous premium to this gentleman; and have also appointed a board to superintend the treatment of sheep in the English manner, at which the ingenious and able M. de Tolosan presides.

See also Harris, "Movements of Technology between Britain and Europe," 14, 18, 26–27; A. E. Musson, "Continental Influences on the Industrial Revolution," in Barrie M. Ratcliffe, ed., *Great Britain and Her World, 1750–1914* (Manchester, 1975), 72; Inkster, *Science and Technology,* 53–55; John R. Harris, "Industrial Espionage in the Eighteenth Century," *Industrial Archeology Review* 7 (Spring 1985), 127–32; Harris, "The Transfer of Technology between Britain and France," 177–80; Mathias, "Skills and the Diffusion of Innovation," 104.

17. Catherine Jones, *Immigration and Social Policy in Britain* (London, 1977), 45; Musson, "Continental Influences on the Industrial Revolution," 82; Harris, "The Transfer of Technology between Britain and France," 160–61.

18. Leibniz did as he preached, shared his discoveries with others, and even fantasized about inventing a universal language for scientific discussions. See also Joel Mokyr, *Gifts of Athena: Historical Origins of the Knowledge Economy* (Princeton, N.J., 2002).

19. Inkster, *Science and Technology in History,* 39, 49; A. E. Musson and Eric

Robinson, *Science and Technology in the Industrial Revolution* (Manchester, 1969), 85; Eugene S. Ferguson, "The Mind's Eye: Nonverbal Thought in Technology," *Science, no.* 197 (August 26, 1977), 831; Peter Gay, *The Enlightenment: An Interpretation*, 2 vols. (New York, 1966—69), II, *The Science of Freedom*, 26; Richard Drayton, "Knowledge and Empire," *Oxford History of the British Empire*, II, 231—52.

20. Leslie Page Moch, *Moving Europeans: Migration in Western Europe since 1600* (Bloomington, Ind., 1992), 60—101.

21. Mathias, "Skills and the Diffusion of Innovation," 107—8. See also Harris, "Movements of Technology between Britain and Europe"; Harris, "Industrial Espionage in the Eighteenth Century," 130.

Chapter 2. The Battle over Technology within the Empire

1. "First General Letter of the Governor and Deputy of the New England Company for a Plantation in Massachusetts to the Governor and Council for London's Plantation in the Massachusetts Bay in New England," April 17, 1629, in Nathaniel B. Shurtleff, ed., *Records of the Governor and Company of Massachusetts Bay in New England*, 5 vols. (Boston, 1853—54), I, 390—91.

2. Henry Harwell, James Blair, and Edward Chilton, *The Present State of Virginia and the College*, ed. Hunter D. Farish (Williamsburg, 1940), 9, 10; as quoted by Carl Bridenbaugh, *The Colonial Craftsman* (New York, 1950), 136.

3. "Order to Encourage Manufacture of linen, May 13, 1640," *Records of the Governor and Company of Massachusetts*, I, 294; "The Liberties of the Massachusetts Collonie in New England, 1641" in Edwin Powers, ed., *Crime and Punishment in Early Massachusetts: A Documentary History* (Boston, 1966), 534; William Penn, "The Frame of the Government of Pennsylvania in America," May 1682, in Mary Maples Dunn, Richard Dunn et al., eds., *The Papers of William Penn*, 6 vols. (Philadelphia, 1981—87), II, 216. See also Bernard Bailyn, *The New England Merchants in the Seventeenth Century* (Cambridge, Mass, 1955), 62.

4. James K. Hosmer, ed., *Winthrop's Journal*, *"History of New England,"* 1630—1649, 2 vols. (New York, 1959 [1908]), II, 222. Subsequent sessions of the court continued to bestow special favors on the company. Historian Edward N. Hartley wrote: "it is doubtful if any single private enterprise in New England, in the whole colonial period, was so well favored by government." *Ironworks on the Saugus: The Lynn and Braintree Ventures of the Company of Undertakers of the Ironworks in New England* (Norman, Okla., 1957), 96.

5. Christine MacLeod, "The Paradoxes of Patenting: Invention and Its Diffusion in 18th- and 19th-Century Britain, France, and North America," *Technology and Culture* 32 (October 1991), 892; Autumn Stanley, *Mothers and Daughters of Invention: Notes for a Revised History of Technology* (Metuchen, N.J., 1993), 30; Bruce W. Bugbee, *Genesis of American Patent and Copyright Law*

(Washington, D.C., 1967), 58–64, 72; P. J. Federico, "Outline of the History of the United States Patent Office," *Journal of the Patent Office Society* 18 (July 1936), 37–39.

6. Thomas Bray, *An Essay Towards Promoting all Necessary and Useful Knowledge both Divine and Human, In all Parts of His Majesty's Dominions, Both at Home and Abroad* (London, 1697).

7. Leo Francis Stock, ed., *Proceedings and Debates of the British Parliament Respecting North America*, 4 vols. (Washington, D.C., 1924–37), II, 278; E. Burke Inlow, *The Patent Grant* (Baltimore, 1950), 37–38.

8. As quoted by Jerome R. Reich, *Colonial America* (Englewood Cliffs, N.J., 1989), 163.

9. Robin Blackburn, *The Making of New World Slavery: From the Baroque to the Modern, 1492–1800* (London, 1997), 515; Commissioners of Trade at the Plantations report to Parliament, May 1701, *Proceedings and Debates of the British Parliament*, II, 386.

10. Brooke Hindle, *The Pursuit of Science in Revolutionary America* (Chapel Hill, N.C., 1965), 209; Bridenbaugh, *The Colonial Craftsman*, 105.

11. See Inlow, *The Patent Grant*, 37. I am not claiming that the restrictions were the most important factor in retarding the growth of American manufactures. Even though they existed on the books, they were not enforced effectively. As John J. McCusker and Russell R. Menard write, the mercantilist regulations were less significant in inhibiting industrial development than "factor prices, market size, and alternative prospects." *The Economy of British America* (Chapel Hill, N.C., 1985), 309.

12. Laurel Thatcher Ulrich, "Wheels, Looms, and the Gender Division of Labor in Eighteenth-Century New England," *William and Mary Quarterly*, 3d ser., 55 (January 1998), 21; Ruth Schwartz Cowan, *A Social History of American Technology* (New York, 1997), 25. See also Thomas C. Cochran, *Frontiers of Change: Early Industrialization in America* (New York, 1981), 6; Bridenbaugh, *The Colonial Craftsman*, 35–37; Stuart Bruchey, *The Roots of American Economic Growth, 1607–1861: An Essay in Social Causation* (New York, 1965), 71.

13. Adolph B. Benson, ed., *Peter Kalm's Travels in North America [1753–61]: The English Version of 1770*, 2 vols. (New York, 1937), I, 307. See also William Cronon, *Changes in the Land: Indians, Colonists and the Ecology of New England* (New York, 1983).

14. Steam power began to outweigh waterpower only in the second half of the nineteenth century. Before then, the numerous waterfalls provided "an expanding and progressive industrial base." The census of 1870 which was the first to ask questions regarding types of power used in industry found "steam horsepower in manufacturing leading water horsepower in the ratio of 52 to 48, a margin which widened progressively in succeeding decades." Louis C. Hunter, "Waterpower in the Century of Steam Engines," in Brooke Hindle, ed., *America's Wooden Age: Aspect of Its Early Technology* (Tarrytown, N.Y., 1975), 170. See

also Dolores Greenberg, "Reassessing the Power Patterns of the Industrial Revolution: An Anglo-American Comparison," *American Historical Review* 87 (December 1982), 1237–61; McCusker and Menard, *The Economy of British America*, 354; Brooke Hindle, *Emulation and Invention* (New York, 1981), 9–10.

15. Alice Hanson Jones, "Wealth Estimates for the American Middle Colonies, 1774," *Economic Development and Cultural Change* 18 (1970), 130; McCusker and Menard, *The Economy of British America*, 283–85. Some historians have gone so far as to reverse the order of the Industrial Revolution. Before any significant technological development was introduced, writes Cary Carson, "people up and down the social order had discovered and were indulging in the most extraordinary passion for consumer goods in quantities and varieties that were unknown, even unimaginable, to their fathers and grandfathers. It was indeed a revolution, but a consumer revolution in the beginning. The better known Industrial Revolution followed in response." "The Consumer Revolution in Colonial America: Why Demand?" in Cary Carson, Ronald Hoffman, and Peter J. Albert, eds., *Of Consuming Interests: The Style of Life in the Eighteenth Century* (Charlottesville, Va., 1994), 486.

16. Whitfield J. Bell Jr., "Philadelphia Medical Students in Europe, 1750–1800," *Pennsylvania Magazine of History and Biography* 67 (January 1943), 1–29; Hindle, *The Pursuit of Science*, 36–38. Benjamin Franklin, for one, whose faith in the intellectual equality of his countrymen with Europeans was never in doubt, greatly appreciated the value of this education to the development of American medicine, and predicted that the men educated in London and Edinburgh would be of great value to the colonies. See Franklin to Alexander Dick, June 2, 1765, *Franklin Papers*, XII, 157–58.

17. See, for example, *Virginia Gazette*, June 6, 1751, and November 18, 1775, and *Pennsylvania Gazette*, October 6, 1768, November 15, 1770, and March 16, 1769.

18. Peter Hasenclever, *The Remarkable Case of Peter Hasenclever, Merchant* (London, 1773), 9.

19. It was far more difficult to export prohibited machinery than to smuggle goods into Britain because ships leaving for the New World had to depart from established ports in front of the watchful eyes of customs officials. The crown's efforts to stop smuggling in the eighteenth century were mostly ineffective. The British Isles, with their six thousand miles of coastline in close proximity to Europe and at the edge of the Atlantic Ocean, were particularly vulnerable. Goods were not the only items smuggled. The smuggling of people across national borders, and of unfree and free immigrants into other nations' colonies, was equally lucrative. The efforts of the Board of Customs, the English Excise Board, and the Royal Navy failed to stem the tide. Smuggling steadily increased and even grew bolder throughout the century. Geoffrey Morley, *The Smuggling War: The Government's Fight Against Smuggling in the 18th and 19th Centuries* (Stroud, 1994); Harvey Benham, *The Smugglers' Century: The Story of*

Smuggling on the Essex Coast, 1730–1830 (Chelmsford, 1986); Kenneth M. Clark, *Many a Bloody Affair: The Story of Smuggling in the Port of Rye and District* (Rye, 1968); Duncan Fraser, *The Smugglers* (Montrose, 1971); Cyril Noall, *Smuggling in Cornwall* (Truro, 1971); David Phillipson, *Smuggling: A History 1700–1970* (Newton Abbot, 1973).

20. *American Apollo* 1 (1792), 68–69.

21. *New York Journal,* October 8, 1767; Mildred Campbell, "English Emigration on the Eve of the American Revolution," *American Historical Review* 61 (October 1955), 16; Arlene Palmer Schwind, "The Glassmakers of Early America," in Ian M. G. Quimby, ed., *The Craftsman in Early America* (New York, 1984), 162; Bridenbaugh, *The Colonial Craftsman,* 6–7. Bridenbaugh emphasizes the voluntary nature of immigration—that individuals who heard of opportunities in America decided to cross the Atlantic for their own reasons. Ibid., 67–69. While most English workers chose North America, many migrated to France. As John R. Harris writes, they were "highly bribable, adventurous, and footloose." "The Transfer of Technology between Britain and France and the French Revolution," in C. Crossley and I. Small, eds., *The French Revolution and British Culture* (Oxford, 1998), 176.

22. Thomas Barnard, "A Sermon Preached in Boston New England before the Society for Encouraging Industry and Employing the Poor" (Boston, 1758), 13, 19. Many of the arguments for manufacturing at the time were couched in terms of assisting the urban poor to find means of supporting themselves.

23. James H. Trumbull and Charles J. Hoadley, eds., *Public Records of the Colony of Connecticut,* 14 vols. (Hartford 1850–90), VII, 174–75, X, 231; Schwind, "The Glassmakers of Early America," 162; Richard B. Morris, *Government and Labor in Early America* (New York, 1946), 33; Federico, "Outline of the History of the United States Patent Office," 36, 42; Edith Tilton Penrose, *The Economics of the International Patent System* (Baltimore, 1951), 11; Victor S. Clark, *History of Manufactures in the United States,* 2 vols. (New York, 1929), I, 50; Bridenbaugh, *The Colonial Craftsman,* 112–13; Bugbee, *Genesis of America Patent and Copyright Law,* 68–69.

24. As quoted by Bridenbaugh, *The Colonial Craftsman,* 136; Moch, *Moving Europeans,* 64; Richard Hofstadter, *America at 1750: A Social Portrait* (New York, 1971), 3–4; Cowan, *A Social History of American Technology,* 47–49. As Bernard Bailyn has pointed out, many eighteenth-century Englishmen moved mostly from the countryside to the cities. Migration to North America "was a spill-over—an outgrowth, an extension—of these established patterns of mobility in England. It tapped into these existing flows without basically altering them or modifying their magnitude." *The Peopling of British North America: An Introduction* (New York, 1986), 25.

25. Governor Moore to the Board of Trade, January 12, 1767, in H. B. O'Callaghan, ed., *Documents Relative to the Colonial History of the State of New York,* 15 vols. (Albany, N.Y., 1856–87), VII, 888–89; Thomas Gage to Lord

Barrington, August 5, 1772, in Clarence E. Carter, ed., *The Correspondence of General Thomas Gage with the Secretaries of State,* 2 vols. (New Haven, Conn., 1931–33), II, 616.

26. Adam Smith, *An Inquiry into the Nature and Causes of the Wealth of Nations,* ed. Edwin Cannan, 2 vols. (Chicago, 1976 [1776]), II, 95; Daniel Dulany, *Considerations on the Propriety of Imposing Taxes in the British Colonies* (Annapolis, Md., 1765), 43, 45.

27. As cited by Brooke Hindle, "The Underside of the Learned Society in New York, 1754–1854," in Alexandra Olson and Sanborn C. Brown, eds., *The Pursuit of Knowledge in the Early American Republic* (Baltimore, 1976), 89; Governor Moore to the Board of Trade, January 12, 1767, in O'Callaghan, *Documents Relative to the Colonial History of the State of New York,* VII, 888; "A North American," *Pennsylvania Gazette,* June 27, 1765.

28. *Pennsylvania Gazette,* January 30, 1772; Hindle, *The Pursuit of Science,* 205; Clark, *History of Manufactures in the United States,* I, 215; William R. Bagnall, *The Textile Industry of the United States* (Cambridge, Mass., 1893), 63–72; Jeremy, "British Textile Technology Transmission," 28.

29. Carrol W. Pursell Jr., "Thomas Digges and William Pearce: An Example of the Transit of Technology," *William and Mary Quarterly,* 3d ser., 21 (October 1964), 551; Hindle, *Emulation and Invention,* 1; Samuel Rezneck, "The Rise of Industrial Consciousness in the United States," *Journal of Economic and Business History* 4 (August 1932), 785. As John Kasson writes, American independence "began not one revolution, but two." *Civilizing the Machine* (New York, 1976), 3.

30. Thomas Jefferson, "A Summary View of the Rights of British America" (1774), in Merrill D. Peterson, ed., *The Portable Thomas Jefferson* (New York, 1975), 4; "Declaration of the Massachusetts Provincial Congress, December 8, 1774" in Merrill Jensen, ed., *English Historical Documents: American Colonial Documents to 1776* (New York 1955), 823–25; David Rittenhouse, *An Oration* (Philadelphia, 1775), 20. The *Massachusetts Gazette,* for example, reported on October 29, 1767, that a gathering chaired by James Otis the previous day in Boston's Faneuil Hall voted to "take all prudent and legal measures to encourage the produce of manufactures of this Province and to lessen the use of superfluities . . . from abroad." See also Hindle, *The Pursuit of Science,* 367.

31. Rush to Thomas Bradford, April 15, 1768; Rush to ——, January 26, 1769, *Letters of Benjamin Rush,* I, 54, 74–75; "Plan of an American Manufactory," *Pennsylvania Magazine* 1 (March 1775), 140–41; Jeremy, "British Textile Technology Transmission," 24–52; Benjamin Rush, "A Speech delivered in Carpenter's Hall, March 16th, before the Subscribers towards a Fund for establishing Manufactories of Woolen, Cotton, and Linen, in the City of Philadelphia, Published at the Request of the Company," *Pennsylvania Evening Post,* April 11 and 13, 1775, 1775.

32. David Ramsay, "An Oration on the Advantages of American Independence," *United States Magazine* 1 (January 1779), 25; A Plain but Real Friend to

America, "Three Letters on Manufactures," *American Museum* 1 (January–March, 1787), 119; Timothy Matlack, *An Oration* (Philadelphia, 1780), 17; Sylvius [Hugh Williamson], "Letter III," *American Museum* 2 (August 1787), 117.

33. Robert Styrettel Jones (March 1777), *American Museum* 5 (March 1789), 266; Thomas Paine, *Rights of Man, Common Sense, and Other Political Writing*, ed. Mark Philip (New York, 1994 [1776]), 41; Hector St. John de Crèvecoeur, *Letters from an American Farmer*, ed. Susan Manning (New York, 1997 [1782]), 55, 56.

34. James H. Henretta, "The War for Independence and American Economic Development," in Ronald Hoffman, John T. McCusker, Russell R. Menard, and Peter J. Albert, eds., *The Economy of Early America* (Charlottesville, Va., 1988); Bagnall, *The Textile Industries of the United States*, 111; Ulrich, "Wheels, Looms, and the Gender Division of Labor," 3–38. English artisan Henry Wansey, who visited New England in the 1790s, commented that wool carding was "a trade well encouraged here, for every housewife keeps a quantity of these cards by her, to employ her family in the evening, when they have nothing to do out of doors." David John Jeremy, ed., *Henry Wansey and His American Journal, 1794* (Philadelphia, 1970), 61.

35. John Jay to Colonel McDougall, December 23, 1775, April 27, 1776, Henry P. Johnston, ed., *The Correspondence and Public Papers of John Jay*, 4 vols. (New York, 1890–93), I, 40, 57; Continental Congress resolution, November 10, 1777, in W. C. Ford, ed., *Journals of the Continental Congress*, 34 vols. (Washington, D.C., 1904–37), IX, 884; Benjamin Rush, *Essays upon the Making of Salt-Petre and Gun Powder* (New York, 1776); Neil Longley York, *Mechanical Metamorphosis: Technological Change in Revolutionary America* (New York, 1985), 63–86. John Adams suggested attacking the British colony of Antigua to find the necessary supplies. Adams to James Warren, October 12, 1775, in Robert J. Taylor, ed., *The Papers of John Adams*, 11 vols. to date (Cambridge, Mass., 1977–), III, 197–98. As Elizabeth Miles Nuxoll demonstrates, Congress and the states recognized that local arms manufacture was inferior. It attacked the problem in two ways: by encouraging the development of home manufactures and by purchasing arms from foreign sources. *Congress and the Munitions Merchants: The Secret Committee of Trade during the American Revolution, 1775–1777* (New York, 1985). These shortages, however, taught some industries, "particularly iron and steel . . . more advanced, efficient technologies and organizational forms." McCusker and Menard, *The Economy of British America*, 363. As John R. Harris points out, as soon as the War of American Independence ended the French government sent an espionage party to spy on English munitions production. They reported finding "that there was nothing difficult in getting a good view of English Manufacturers, one needs to know the language with facility, not show any curiosity, and wait till the hour when punch is served to instruct oneself and acquire the confidence of the manufacturers and their foremen, one must avoid recommendations from Ministers and Lords which

226 NOTES TO PAGES 45–50

will do little good and make contacts with some of the principal industrialists who can open every door." "Industrial Espionage in the Eighteenth Century," *Industrial Archeology Review* 7 (Spring 1985), 133.

Chapter 3. Benjamin Franklin and America's Technology Deficit

1. Benjamin Franklin, "Information to Those Who Would Remove to America" (Passy, France, 1784), *American Museum* 2 (September 1787), 213–14.

2. Benjamin Franklin, "Observations Concerning the Increase of Mankind, Peopling of Countries, &c." (1751), Leonard W. Labaree et al., eds., *The Papers of Benjamin Franklin*, 36 vols. to date (New Haven, Conn., 1959–), IV, 233–34. For an excellent discussion of the problematic passage and its context see Edmund S. Morgan, *Benjamin Franklin* (New Haven, 2002), 73–80.

3. Benjamin Franklin, *The Autobiography of Benjamin Franklin*, ed. Leonard W. Labaree, Ralph L. Ketcham, Helen C. Boatfield, and Helene H. Fineman (New Haven, Conn., 1964), 58; W. J. Rorabaugh, *The Craft Apprentice: From Franklin to the Machine Age in America* (New York, 1986), 7.

4. *Complete Magazine* (London), August 1764, cited in William R. Bagnall, *The Textile Industry of the United States* (Cambridge, Mass., 1893), 51; Franklin to printer of the *London Chronicle*, May 9, 1759, to William Franklin, March 13, 1768, *Franklin Papers*, VIII, 342, XV, 77.

5. Franklin, "Observations Concerning the Increase of Mankind," *Franklin Papers*, IV, 228; Franklin to Peter Collinson, April 30, 1764, ibid., XI, 182–83. I thank Gavin Lewis and Carolyn Cooper for their help in deciphering the humorous tone of Franklin's letter. Brooke Hindle writes that Collinson "gave coherence and direction" to the American scientific effort. Moreover, Collinson was "Franklin's most important" supporter and that it was "Collinson who introduced Franklin to the world." Brook Hindle, *The Pursuit of Science in Revolutionary America* (Chapel Hill, N.C., 1965), 18, 77.

6. Franklin, *The Interest of Great Britain With Regard to Her Colonies* (1760), *Franklin Papers*, IX, 79; Brook Hindle, *Emulation and Invention* (New York, 1981), 13.

7. "The Printer to the Reader" (October 2, 1729), *Franklin Papers*, I, 158; Franklin, "A Proposal for Promoting Useful Knowledge among the British Plantations in America" (May 14, 1743), ibid., II, 381. I wish to thank the members of the McNeil Center for Early American Culture Seminar in Philadelphia, and Susan Klepp in particular, for helping me to develop this idea when I presented this chapter in February 1999.

8. Franklin, *Autobiography*, 192; emphasis in the original. On Franklin the gentleman, see Gordon S. Wood, *The Radicalism of the American Revolution* (New York, 1992), 85–86.

9. Franklin to Joseph Priestley, February 8, 1780, *Franklin Papers*, XXXII, 455–56. See also I. Bernard Cohen, *Benjamin Franklin's Science* (Cambridge,

Mass., 1990), 31–39, 199. Henry Butler Allen wrote that Franklin was committed to finding "ways to increase human happiness," and "giving his inventions to the world." Henry Butler Allen, *Benjamin Franklin, Philosophical Engineer* (Princeton, N.J., 1943), 11, 12. See also Douglas McKie, "Scientific Societies at the End of the Eighteenth Century," *Philosophical Magazine* (July 1948), 136–137. Franklin's position was consistent with the eighteenth-century approach to authorship. Many authors freely borrowed from the books of others without acknowledging the original authors. See, for example, Elaine Forman Crane's study of the rhetoric of Abigail Adams in "Political Discourses and the Spring of Abigail's Discontent" (essay presented at Columbia University Early American Seminar, September 8, 1998).

10. Franklin to Lebegue de Presle, October 4, 1777; to John Lining, March 18, 1755; to William Shipley, November 27, 1755; *Franklin Papers,* XXV, 25; V, 526–27; VI, 276.

11. Gottlieb Mittelberg, *Journey to Pennsylvania in the year 1750 and Return to Germany in the year 1754,* trans. Carl Theo Been (Philadelphia 1898), 31; Stephen Hopkins, *The Rights of the Colonies Examined* (1765), in Bernard Bailyn, ed., *Pamphlets of the American Revolution* (Cambridge, Mass., 1965), 511; William Moraley, *The Infortunate: or the Voyage of William Moraley,* ed. Susan E. Klapp and Billy C. King (University Park, Pa., 1992 [1743]); Aaron Spencer Fogleman, *Hopeful Journeys: German Immigration, Settlement, and Political Culture in Colonial America,* (Philadelphia, 1996), 36–39; Leslie Page Moch, *Moving Europeans: Migration in Western Europe since 1650* (Bloomington, Ind., 1992), 64; R. J. Dickson, *Ulster Emigration to Colonial America, 1718–1775* (London, 1966), 181; Emberson E. Proper, "Colonial Immigration Laws: A Study of the Regulation of Immigration by the English Colonies in America," *Studies in History, Economics and Public Law* 12 (January, 1900), 200.

12. David J. Jeremy, "British Textile Technology Transmission to the United States: The Philadelphia Region Experience, 1770–1820," *Business History Review* 47 (Spring 1973), 24–52, 26; Darwin H. Stapleton, *The Transfer of Early Industrial Technologies to America* (Philadelphia, 1987), 6, 13; Floyd L. Vaughan, *The United States Patent System: Legal and Economic Conflicts in American Patent History* (Norman, Okla., 1956), 15–16.

13. David S. Landes, *The Unbound Prometheus: Technological Change and Industrial Development in Western Europe from 1750 to the Present* (New York, 1969), 85. Textiles led the way because, as Landes explains, "it was the first to convert to modern techniques of production," ibid., 40. See also James Kasson, *Civilizing the Machine: Technology and Republican Values in America, 1776–1900* (New York, 1976), 21.

14. Robert Wallace, *A View of the Internal Policy of Great Britain* (London, 1764), 70; Andrew Burnaby, *Travels through the Middle Settlements in North-America In the Years 1759 and 1760* (London, 1775), 89. Other publications

continued to encourage prospective immigrants. In 1774, for example, an instruction book for Scottish emigrants headed for America was published in recognition of the dimensions of the migration. It simply stated that in spite of all governmental efforts to halt the flow of men across the Atlantic to the "sole hope and refuge of the oppressed," the movement would continue. Dominick Cornyn, *A Present for an Emigrant* (Edinburgh, 1774), 1. E. A. Wrigely and R. S. Schofield estimated that 20 percent of England's natural population growth from 1695 to 1801 ended in North America. *The Population History of England* (Cambridge, Mass., 1981), 175. The debate over emigration and the need to take account of the real demographic trends in English society gave rise to the Population Bill of 1800 and to the first of the periodic British censuses. Eugene S. Ferguson, "Technology as Knowledge," in Edwin T. Layton Jr., ed., *Technology and Social Change in America* (New York, 1973), 11.

15. Ray Nicholas, *The Importance of the Colonies of North America* (London, 1766), 8, 13; Bernard Bailyn, *Voyagers to the West: A Passage in the Peopling of America on the Eve of the Revolution* (New York, 1986), 29–33, 42.

16. H. B. O'Callaghan, ed., *Documents Relating to the Colonial History of New York,* 15 vols. (Albany, N.Y., 1856–87), VII, 474; Bernard Bailyn, *The Peopling of British North America: An Introduction* (New York, 1986), 39; Bailyn, *Voyagers to the West,* 55; E. R. R. Green, "Queensborough Township: Scotch-Irish Emigration and the Expansion of Georgia, 1763–1776," *William and Mary Quarterly,* 3d ser., 17 (April 1960), 185–86; Mildred Campbell, "English Emigration on the Eve of the American Revolution," *American Historical Review* 61 (October 1955), 1–20.

17. Josiah Child, *A New Discourse of Trade* (London 1775), 135. Official anti-immigration sentiment was not "sufficiently strong to incline the government to consider the imposition of restrictions" on Irish immigration to America. Dickson, *Ulster Emigration,* 198, 200.

18. Franklin, "Observations Concerning the Increase of Mankind," *Franklin Papers,* IV, 233; Franklin to Samuel Cooper, February 5, 1771; to William Franklin, January 30, 1772, August 19, 1772, July 14, 1773, *Franklin Papers,* XVIII, 24; XIX, 47–49, 258; XX, 310; Franklin, "A Method of Humbling Rebellious American Vassals," *Public Advertiser* (London), May 21, 1774, *Franklin Papers,* XXI, 221–22.

19. Franklin, "On a Proposed Act to Prevent Emigration," December 1773, *Franklin Papers,* XX, 522–28. Franklin never published the essay since Parliament opted to study the problem before taking further steps and the issue lost much of its immediate relevance as the crisis between the metropolis and the colonies worsened.

20. Franklin to Thomas Gilpin, March 18 1770, to Samuel Rhodes, June 26, 1770; to Robert Towers and Joseph Leacock, August 22, 1772; to Richard Bache, January 17, 1774, *Franklin Papers,* XVII, 103–8, 181–83; XIX, 282, XXI, 102. See also Stapleton, *Transfer of Early Industrial Technologies,* 42–43.

21. *Pennsylvania Gazette,* January 30, 1772, July 20, 1774; Harold E. Gillingham, "Calico and Linen Printing in Philadelphia," *Pennsylvania Magazine of History and Biography* 52 (April 1928), 99; Bagnall, *The Textile Industry of the United States,* 111. In 1788 Hewson was granted a patent monopoly by Pennsylvania. P. J. Federico, "Outline of the History of the United States Patent Office," *Journal of the Patent Office Society* 18 (July 1936), 45.

22. Michael Warner, *Letters of the Republic: Publication and the Public Sphere in Eighteenth-Century America* (Cambridge, Mass., 1990), 1. Franklin's standing as the preeminent American man of letters was validated by his election to the presidency of the American Philosophical Society in November 1768, even though he was in London at the time. In our time, as Gordon S. Wood put it, Franklin "has come to stand for America in all its many-sidedness." "Not So Poor Richard," *New York Review of Books,* 6 June, 1996, 47. See also Gerald Stourzh, *Benjamin Franklin and American Foreign Policy* (Chicago, 1954), 249.

23. Franklin's first successful flirtation with imperial policy occurred on behalf of British nationalism as he assembled an armed militia in 1747 in hitherto pacifist Pennsylvania to defend Philadelphia against French and Spanish attacks. Esmond Wright, *Franklin of Philadelphia* (Cambridge, Mass., 1986), 77–81. As Linda Colley has brilliantly shown, eighteenth-century English nationalist tradition was intensely exclusive, emphasizing religious, ethnic, and linguistic purity. Linda Colley, *Britons: Forging the Nation, 1707–1837* (New Haven, Conn., 1992). Richard Helgerson's *Forms of Nationhood: The Elizabethan Writing of England* (Chicago, 1992) shows how English intellectuals invented a distinct and exclusionary definition of English identity in the late sixteenth and early seventeenth centuries. For the transfer of this spirit to America see, for example, Avihu Zakai, *Exile and Kingdom: History and the Apocalypse in the Puritan Migration to America* (Cambridge, 1992); Kathleen Wilson, "Empire, Trade, and Popular Politics in Mid-Hanoverian Britain: The Case of Admiral Vernon," *Past and Present,* no. 121 (November 1988), 74–109: Margot Finn, "An Elect Nation? Nation, State, and Class in Modern British History," *Journal of British Studies* 28 (April 1989), 181–91. For an opposing view of English nationalism that sees the constitutional evolution of the sixteenth and seventeenth centuries as the foundation of "England's peculiarity," see Liah Greenfeld, *Nationalism: Five Roads to Modernity* (Cambridge, Mass., 1992), 77. For a theoretical discussion of the importance of exclusion to the formation of national loyalties see Russel Hardin, *One For All: The Logic of Group Conflict* (Princeton, N.J., 1995). For brilliant critical analysis of the limits of speech-modeled imagined nationalism, see Jed Rubenfeld, *Freedom and Time: A Theory of Constitutional Self-Government* (New Haven, Conn., 2001), 145–59.

24. Benjamin Franklin, "Observations Concerning the Increase of Mankind," *Franklin Papers,* IV, 234. Walter LaFeber has argued that this piece was the "central document" of Franklin's "imperial philosophy." "Foreign Policies of a New Nation: Franklin, Madison, and the 'Dream of a New Land to Fulfill with

People in Self-Control,'" in William Appleman Williams, ed., *From Colony to Empire: Essays in the History of American Foreign Relations* (New York, 1972), 12. I take issue with this categorization. Franklin's views, as this chapter demonstrates, underwent profound changes. Franklin did not allow publication of the pamphlet until 1754 and he edited it before publication, deleting a number of statements, including the controversial racist passage. On the other hand, Franklin continued to use ethnic stereotypes. In 1763, for example, he associated idleness and the propensity to extravagance with Spanishness. Franklin to Richard Jackson, March 8, 1763, *Franklin Papers*, X, 208-9.

25. Fogleman, *Hopeful Journeys*, 127-30, 202; John P. Roche, "Immigration and Nationality: A Historical Overview of United States Policy," in Uri Raanan, ed., *Ethnic Resurgence in Modern Democratic States: A Multidisciplinary Approach to Human Resources* (New York, 1980), 34-35; James H. Hutson, "The Campaign to Make Pennsylvania a Royal Province, 1764-1770," *Pennsylvania Magazine of History and Biography* 44 (October 1970), 427-63, and *Pennsylvania Politics, 1746-1770: The Movement for Royal Government and Its Consequences* (Princeton, N.J., 1972); J. Philip Gleason, "A Scurrilous Colonial Election and Franklin's Reputation," *William and Mary Quarterly* 18 (January 1961), 68-84. Franklin's stand regarding immigration in 1764 is related to the "Paxton Boys Massacre" of the previous December in which a mob composed primarily of Scots-Irish settlers brutally murdered some twenty-two Moravian Indians who lived around Lancaster, Pennsylvania. The mob then marched toward Philadelphia with the intention to kill 140 Indians who had fled there for protection, only to be turned back by a strong show of military might organized by the colony's elite. Brooke Hindle, "The March of the Paxton Boys," ibid., 3 (October 1946), 461-86; James Kirby Martin, "The Return of the Paxton Boys and the Historical State of the Pennsylvania Frontier," *Pennsylvania History* 38 (April 1971), 117-33; Alden T. Vaughan, "Frontier Banditti and the Indians: The Paxton Boys' Legacy," ibid., 51 (January 1984), 1-29. Franklin was outraged by the brutality and the threat to public order, and published a scathing critique of the rioters as *Narrative of the Late Massacres in Lancaster County* . . . (Philadelphia, 1764), *Franklin Papers*, XI, 42-69. Franklin's manifest hostility to immigrants in the 1764 election could be seen as inclusive toward Indians. Yet, I believe his outrage at the massacre was firmly within the exclusive British identity. The protection of indigenous tribes was an integral part of patronizing ethnocentric nationalism. Wilson, "Empire, Trade and Popular Politics," 149-50.

26. Franklin to *Gazetteer and New Daily Advertiser*, 28 December 1765, *Franklin Papers*, XII, 414; Esmond Wright, "Benjamin Franklin: 'The Old England Man,'" in Randolph Shipley Klein, ed., *Science and Society in Early America: Essays in Honor of Whitfield J. Bell, Jr.* (Philadelphia, 1986), 49; Jack P. Greene, "The Alienation of Benjamin Franklin—British American," *Journal of the Royal Society of Arts* 124 (January 1976), 52-73. On Franklin's emergence as America's spokesman in London, see Jonathan R. Dull, "Franklin the Diplomat:

The French Mission," *Transactions of the American Philosophical Society* 72 (1982), 3. Ironically, as Franklin was coming to terms with the dissolution of a common national identity, English writers, such as Arthur Young, assumed that Britain's dominions worldwide cannot be considered "in any other light than as part of one whole." *Political Essays Concerning the Present State of the British Empire* (London, 1772), 1.

27. Franklin in *The Gentleman's Magazine,* January 1768, *Franklin Papers,* XV, 37; Richard R. Johnson, " 'Parliamentary Egotism': The Clash of Legislatures in the Making of the American Revolution," *Journal of American History* 74 (September 1987), 347; Christine Gerrard, *The Patriot Opposition to Walpole: Politics, Poetry, and National Myth, 1725–1742* (Oxford, 1994), 185–227; John Sainsbury, "John Wilkes, Debt, and Patriotism," *Journal of British Studies* 34 (April 1995), 165–95. In revolutionary culture "George III became the soul of Britain itself, reconstituted as the enemy." David Waldstreicher, "Rites of Rebellion, Rites of Assent: Celebrations, Print Culture, and Origins of American Nationalism," *Journal of American History* 82 (June 1995), 47.

28. Franklin to Robert R. Livingston, 15 April 1783, and to William Strahan, 19 August 1784, in Albert Henry Smyth, ed., *The Writings of Benjamin Franklin,* 10 vols. (New York, 1907) IX, 34, 264. Upon his return Franklin became the president of the Pennsylvania Abolitionist Society and in 1789 published a manifesto that not only called slavery "an atrocious debasement of human nature" but went on to urge that assistance to "emancipated black people . . . will become a branch of our national policy." Franklin, *An Address to the Public: from the Pennsylvania Society for Promoting the Abolition of Slavery and the Relief of Free Negroes Unlawfully Held in Bondage* (1789), ibid., X, 67.

29. John Hancock, "Declaration of Causes of Taking Up Arms" (6 July 1775), in Samuel Eliot Morrison, ed., *Sources and Documents Illustrating the American Revolution 1764–1788,* 2d ed. (New York, 1929), 144; Franklin, "The Interests of Great Britain Considered" (1760), *Franklin Papers,* IX, 90. See also David Bell, "Recent Works on Early Modern French National Identity," *Journal of Modern History* 68 (March 1996), 90–91.

30. This position was in line with that of the emerging British neomercantilists of the late eighteenth-century who "combined economic liberalism with economic nationalism." John E. Crowley, *The Privileges of Independence: Neomercantilism and the American Revolution* (Baltimore, 1993), 77. See also Cathy D. Matson and Peter S. Onuf, *A Union of Interests: Political and Economic Thought in Revolutionary America* (Lawrence, Kansas, 1990), 29.

31. Cadwalader Evans to Franklin, January 25, 1768, *Franklin Papers,* XV, 260 n. 8. On the importance of this sentiment to the Revolution, see Timothy Breen, " 'Baubles of Britain': The American and Consumer Revolutions of the Eighteenth Century," in Gary Carson, Ronald Hoffman, and Peter J. Albert, eds., *Of Consuming Interests: The Style of Life in the Eighteenth Century* (Charlottesville, Va., 1994), 444–82.

32. *A Verse*, (Boston, 1769).

33. Cadwalader Evans to Franklin, November 20, 1767, *Franklin Papers*, XIV, 313–14.

34. Franklin to Polly Stevenson, March 25, 1763; to Thomas Cushing, June 10, 1771; to Humphrey Marshall, April 22, 1771, *Franklin Papers*, X, 232–33; XVIII, 126, 82.

35. Franklin to Cadwalader Evans, February 20, 1768; to Thomas Cushing, 13 January 1772, *Franklin Papers*, XV, 52; XIX, 23; Franklin, "Information to Those who Would Remove," 215. Franklin replied to Evans shortly after returning from a trip to France where he had come under the influence of Physiocrats. Industrialization was but another element in Franklin's complicated love-hate relationship with the mother country. See also Esmond Wright, "Benjamin Franklin: 'The Old England Man,'" in Randolph Shipley Klein, ed., *Science and Society in Early America: Essays in Honor of Whitfield J. Bell, Jr.* (Philadelphia, 1986), 39–55. For a superb analysis of Franklin's hostility to manufactures see Stourzh, *Benjamin Franklin*, 56–60, 104–05. The years of the colonial struggle with England made Franklin, according to historian Drew R. McCoy, an anti-industrialist who "barely stopped short of wholesale indictment of advanced civilization and an endorsement of primitive simplicity." Drew R. McCoy, *The Elusive Republic: Political Economy in Jeffersonian America* (Chapel Hill, N.C., 1980), 57. Similarly, LaFeber has argued that Franklin's vision for the new nation depended on "continued landed expansion" in order to prevent the moral corruption associated with the market economy. "Foreign Policies of a New Nation," 13–14. I discuss the association of the American Revolution in the minds of many revolutionaries with the preservation of civic virtue and agricultural political economy in the New World, in contrast to the social polarization and political tyranny of Europe, in Doron Ben-Atar, "Republicanism, Liberalism and Radicalism in the American Founding," *Intellectual History Newsletter* 14 (Fall 1992), 47–59.

36. "Examination before the Committee of the Whole of the House of Commons," February 13, 1766, *Franklin Papers*, XIII, 140; Franklin to Benjamin Vaughn, July 26, 1784, Smyth, *Writings*, IX, 243; Franklin, "Consolation for America, or remarks on her real situation, interests, and policy," *American Museum* 1 (January 1787), 15–16. Unlike many of his compatriots, Franklin could not even pretend to be working the land. He made his fortune as a businessman and worked hard to cultivate a reputation as an urbane scientist-inventor. When he came back from Paris he did not reinvent himself as a landed aristocrat, but settled in the largest urban center in North America. He did send his grandson to live on a farm in New Jersey. He saw the bucolic life as an educational institution, a preferred way to mold the citizens of the future republic. For himself, however, Franklin chose Philadelphia, London, and Paris. For an imaginative account of Franklin's relationship with William Temple Franklin and the reasons the statesman was so keen to have his grandson live on

a farm see Claude-Anne Lopez, *My Life with Benjamin Franklin* (New Haven, Conn., 2000), 242, and Lopez and Eugenia W. Herbert. *The Private Franklin: The Man and His Family* (New York, 1975), 287. See also Charles M. Andrews, *The Colonial Background of the American Revolution* (1924; rev. ed., New Haven, Conn., 1931), 149.

37. In the midst of the optimistic fervor of the revolutionary moment Americans predicted that their industrial path would be free of the atrocities of the English one just as their politics was to be free of British corruption and tyranny. For example, Benjamin Rush, first president of the United Company of Philadelphia for Promoting American Manufactures, declared that the misery of England's industrial workers was caused by "unwholesome diet, damp houses, and other bad accommodations," and not by the nature of their occupation. Benjamin Rush, "A Speech delivered in Carpenter's Hall, March 16th [1775] . . . ," *Pennsylvania Evening Post,* April 11 and 13, 1775. See also Leo Marx, *The Machine in the Garden: Technology and the Pastoral Ideal in America* (New York, 1964), 146–50; Michael Lienesch, *New Orders of the Ages: Time, the Constitution and the Making of Modern American Political Thought* (Princeton, N.J., 1988), 92; Charles S. Olton, *Artisans for Independence: Philadelphia Mechanics and the American Revolution* (Syracuse, N.Y., 1975).

38. Alexander Deconde, "The French Alliance in Historical Speculation," in Ronald Hoffman and Peter J. Albert, eds., *Diplomacy and Revolution: The Franco-American Alliance of 1778* (Charlottesville, Va., 1981), 5–25; I. Bernard Cohen, "Science and the Revolution," *Technology Review* 47 (April 1945), 374. Congress had instructed the Committee of Correspondence to recruit French engineers. Yet, little progress was made before Franklin arrived in France in December 1776. Even during his brief stay in America between his London and Paris missions Franklin continued to receive letters from artisans looking for him to help them migrate to America. Charles Edwards, for example, asked him to support the establishment of a "Paper-hanging Manufactory in America." Charles Edwards to Franklin, January 27, 1775, *Franklin Papers,* XXI, 456.

39. Robert Styrettel Jones, "Oration" (March 1777), *American Museum* 5 (March 1789), 265.

40. Charles Carroll to Franklin, August 12, 1777; Franklin to Charles Carroll, January 12, 1779, *Franklin Papers,* XXIV, 420; XXIX, 603. Emigrants often had both personal and economic motives. E. Cayrol, for example, wrote to Mr. Couder March 13, 1777, that he planned to go to America and build a factory for cloth. He asked Couder not to disclose his plan to Franklin lest his debtors and wife realize that he planed to skip France. Benjamin Franklin Papers, American Philosophical Society, Philadelphia (hereafter APS).

41. Franklin's journal, December 13, 1778, *Franklin Papers,* XXVIII, 224. Evidence of such appeals abounds. For example, the Franklin Papers at the American Philosophical Society include a 1779 list of Irish tenants from towns in northern Ireland from Castlebaney to Newtownhamilton. It is probably a list of

prospective immigrants. Thirty out of the seventy-eight heads of households counted were weavers, and most of the others were other professionals like tailors and carpenters. "List of Irish Immigrants" (1779), APS.

42. Richard White to Franklin, November 11, 1779, January 6, 1780; letter to Franklin, undated 1783; Joseph Martineau to Franklin, August 22, 1783; all APS.

43. Fleury le Jeune to Franklin, November 21, 1780; Aubry to Franklin, March 6, 1779; Richard White to Franklin, November 11, 1779, January 6, 1780; all APS. Quemizet to Franklin, January 1778, *Franklin Papers*, XXV, 555; editorial note, ibid., XXVI, 45–46; Hieronymus Gradelmüller to Franklin, November 11, 1779, APS.

44. Franklin to John Huske, September 6, 1772, *Franklin Papers*, XIX, 295. See also Franklin to Charles Carroll, January 12, 1779, ibid., XXIX, 603.

45. Newenham to Franklin, November 6, 1780; Franklin to Edward Newenham, May 27, 1779, *Franklin Papers*, XXIX, 565. See also Dixon Wecter, "Benjamin Franklin and an Irish 'Enthusiast,'" *Huntington Library Quarterly* 4 (January 1941), 205–33. Newenham apparently also wrote to George Washington: See Washington to David Humphreys, June 4, 1784, John C. Fitzpatrick ed., *The Writings of George Washington*, 39 vols. (Washington, D.C., 1931–44), XXVII, 414–15.

46. Jesse Taylor to Franklin, November 21, 1778; Franklin to Jesse Taylor, March 18, 1779; Jesse Taylor to Franklin, April 10, 1779; Franklin to Edward Bancroft, May 31, 1779, *Franklin Papers*, XXVIII, 147–48; XXIX, 158, 306, 580.

47. Henry Royle, Joseph Heathcote, John Rowbotham, and John Schofield to Franklin, November 23, 1781, APS. See also Robert Glen, "Industrial Wayfarers: Benjamin Franklin and a Case of Machine Smuggling in the 1780s," *Business History* 23 (November 1981), 309–26; Robert Glen, "The Milnes of Stockport and the Export of English Technology during the Early Industrial Revolution," *Cheshire History* 3 (1979), 15–21.

48. Henry Wyld to Franklin, January 2 1782, APS; Franklin's journal, January 2, 1782, Benjamin Franklin Papers, Library of Congress, Washington, D.C. (hereafter LC).

49. Franklin to Henry Royle, Joseph Heathcote, John Rowbotham, and John Schofield, January 4, 1782, LC. Franklin's suggestion to the Wyld group that they go via Ulster reflected a popular immigration trend. Within a month of the signing of the Treaty of Paris, ships full of emigrants sailed from Ulster to the New World. By the end of the year emigrants already numbered over 5,000. In fact, from 1783 to 1812, over 150,000 Ulster emigrants settled in the United States; many of them settled in the urban seaboard where they worked in the newly established industries. Matthew Ridley to Thomas Digges, February 16, 1782, Robert H. Elias and Eugene D. Finch, eds. *Letters of Thomas Attwood Digges (1742–1821)* (Chapel Hill, N.C., 1982), 392–93; Carlton Jackson, *A Social History of the Scotch-Irish* (New York, 1993), 137–38; David J. Jeremy, "Damming the

Flood: British Government Efforts to Check the Outflow of Technicians and Machinery, 1780–1843," *Business History Review* 51 (Spring 1977), 4.

50. Franklin to William Hodgson, January 7, 1782, LC; William T. Franklin's list of passes given by Franklin in 1782; Henry Wyld to Franklin, February 12 and March 18, 1782; all APS. Ironically, the man who used to write down the tips he paid to his gardener failed to record the loan to Wyld in his account book.

51. William Hodgson to Franklin, February 22, 1782, APS; Franklin to Henry Wyld, March 31, 1782, William L. Clements Library, Ann Arbor, Mich. Edmond Clegg to Franklin, April 4 and April 24, 1782; Henry Wyld to Franklin, April 9 and 21 1782, all APS.

52. Thomas Digges to Thomas Jefferson, May 12, 1788, Julian Boyd et al., eds., *The Papers of Thomas Jefferson*, 30 vols. to date (Princeton, N.J., 1950–), XIII, 153. The development of Irish manufacturing that could compete in price and quality with English industrial goods was a prominent issue in the Anglo-Irish adjustment of the late eighteenth century. George Chalmers, *A Short View of the Proposals lately made for the Final Adjustment of the Commercial System between Great Britain and Ireland* (London, 1785), 11–12. The 1770s and 1780s witnessed severe unemployment in Dublin, and the generally distressed Irish economy gave rise to the idea of erecting manufacturing towns in Ireland. Ironically, the would-be innovators in America were lured to participate in the erection of the manufacturing town of Prosperous—Ireland's most "famous industrial venture of the eighteenth century." The setback did not discourage the three leaders of the group. Edmund Clegg arrived in the United States in 1784, approached William Livingston, governor of New Jersey, with Franklin's letters and asked for assistance. Wyld made contacts with Digges in the late 1780s and together they appealed to Jefferson for similar assistance. Royle arrived in the New World in 1784 and two years later made contact with Franklin. His New World patriotism was short-lived. The following year, in 1787, he was involved in buying pirated machinery and shipping it back to England with the assistance of Phineas Bond. Suddenly he was shocked by the existence of industrial spying in America. Edmund Clegg to William Livingston, April 21, 1784, Willimam Livingston Papers; Massachusetts Historical Society, Thomas Digges to Thomas Jefferson, May 12, 1788 and Henry Wyld to Thomas Jefferson, May 20, 1788, *Jefferson Papers*, XIII, 183–84, 260–61; Henry Royle to Franklin, September 23, 1786, APS. For Bond's account, see Phineas Bond to Lord Carmarthen, 29 November 1787, Franklin J. Jameson ed., "Letters of Phineas Bond, British Consul at Philadelphia . . . 1787, 1788, 1789," *American Historical Association Annual Report for 1896*, 2 vols. (Washington, D.C., 1897), I, 553–55. See also Gillingham, "Calico and Linen Printing in Philadelphia," 97–110; Doron Ben-Atar, "Alexander Hamilton's Alternative: Technology Piracy and the Reports on Manufactures," *William and Mary Quarterly* 52 (July 1995), 407. See also Robert Glen, "The Milnes of Stockport and the Export of English Technology during

the Early Industrial Revolution," *Cheshire History* 3 (1979), 15–21; and A. K. Longfield, "Prosperous, 1776–1798," *Journal of the County Kildare Archeological Society* 14 (1964–70), 212–31.

53. John Swindell to Thomas Townshend, August 3, 1782, Public Record Office, H.O. 42/1/222–23. See also John M. Norris, "The Struggle for Carron," *Scottish Historical Review* 37 (October 1958), 140–41.

54. Stanley Elkins and Eric McKittrick, *The Age of Federalism* (New York, 1993), 69; Harvey Nathaniel Davis, *Benjamin Franklin: A Bridge between Science and the Mechanic Arts* (New York, 1949), 11.

55. Richard Bache to Franklin, September 8, 1783; Thomas Pownall to Franklin, July 5, 1782; Earl of Buchan to Franklin, February 18, 1783 all APS. Franklin to the Earl of Buchan, March 17, 1783, LC.

56. Two Frenchmen from Bordeaux wrote to him in 1783 for aid, promising in return to make wine in Philadelphia. Another Frenchman offered to send one hundred qualified workers to America to introduce the United States to the continental technologies of glass and iron manufacture without pollution and without producing luxury. A group of glass makers from Normandy offered technology in exchange for emigration assistance, and even specified their projected expenses. Undated and unidentified letters to Franklin presumed to have been written in 1783, APS.

57. John Vaughn to Franklin, December 13, 1781; Lacour to Franklin, November 8, 1783; both APS. Lacour wanted to open a factory for making and painting dishes in Philadelphia. He offered to bring all the necessary workers and asked Franklin what kind of help he could expect from the American state and federal governments.

58. Washington to Jefferson, February 13, 1789, *Jefferson Papers*, XIV, 546; Milne to Franklin, May 19, 1780, *Franklin Papers*, XXXII, 396; James Milne to Franklin, 1783, APS. See also Glen, "The Milnes of Stockport," 17. In September 1789, just before Jefferson left Paris, he went together with Gouverneur Morris to see Milne machinery at la Muette, forwarded to William Bingham, a member of the Philadelphia Society for the Encouragement of Useful Manufactures who was coming to Paris with his family, Milne's memo on his machines, and recommended that Bingham purchase them. Anne Cary Morris, ed., *The Diary and Letters of Gouverneur Morris*, 2 vols. (New York, 1970), I, 51; Jefferson to William Bingham, September 25, 1789, *Jefferson Papers*, XV, 476. Note that William Bingham was involved in the American diplomatic efforts in Europe, and was a candidate for the Hague position.

59. Du Radier to Franklin, March 1783; Charles Crossett to Franklin, January 17, 1784; both APS.

60. Franklin to Charles Thomson, March 9, 1784, Papers of the Continental Congress, National Archives; Charles Thomson to Franklin, January 14, 1784, APS. The *American Museum*, which printed the pamphlet in 1787, published a letter in 1790 that sought to sooth the discouraging tone of Franklin's "Informa-

tion to Those Who Would Remove to America." A Philadelphia resident, under the guise of expanding on Franklin's thesis, wrote that "mechanics and manufactures of every description, will find certain encouragement in the United States. . . . our country abounds with resources for manufactures of all kinds; and . . . most of them may be conducted with great advantage in all states." *American Museum* 7 (May 1790), 236.

61. Joseph Guillotin to Franklin, June 18, 1787; James Hughes to Franklin, September 25, 1786; Franklin to William Strahan, August 19, 1784; Miers Fisher to Franklin, August 5, 1788; all APS. Strahan defended the restrictions, explaining: "the Loss of useful Hands must by hurtful to any state." Strahan to Franklin, November 21, 1784, APS.

62. Jonathan R. Dull, "Benjamin Franklin and the Nature of American Diplomacy," *International History Review* 3 (August 1983), 351.

63. Franklin "to All Captains and Commanders of Armed Ships," March 10, 1779, *Franklin Papers*, XXIX, 186–87; Franklin to Benjamin Vaughan, August 22, 1783, APS; Franklin's letter of introduction to Benjamin Vaughan explained that Rumsey was the only true inventor of the steamboat. Franklin to Benjamin Vaughan, May 14, 1788, APS. Thomas Paine, another revolutionary internationalist, developed a plan for constructing a bridge of iron bars. Americans, however, were not enthusiastic about the plan. Paine took it to France where it received much praise, and then to London where it was actually implemented. Philip Foner, ed., *The Complete Writings of Thomas Paine*, 2 vols. (New York, 1945), II, 1026–47, 1266–68, 1411–12.

Chapter 4. After the Revolution

1. For Bond's accounts of the affair, see his letters to Lord Carmarthen, November 20, 1787, and March 30, 1788, in J. Franklin Jameson, ed., "Letters of Phineas Bond, British Consul at Philadelphia, to the Foreign Office . . . 1787, 1788, 1789," *American Historical Association Annual Report for the Year 1896*, 2 vols. (Washington, D.C., 1897), I, 552–55, 564. See also Joanne Loewe Neel, *Phineas Bond: A Study in Anglo-American Relations, 1786–1812* (Philadelphia, 1968), 55–60. I thank Greg Flynn, a graduate student at Yale, for alerting me to this incident and for describing it to me in a manner that inspired me to write this book.

2. *The Statutes at Large of Pennsylvania from 1682 to 1801*, 16 vols. (Harrisburg, 1896–1911), XIII, 138–39; Minutes of the Manufacturing Committee, I, January 19, 22, and March 12, 1788, Papers of Tench Coxe, Historical Society of Pennsylvania, Philadelphia.

3. Jack P. Greene, "Social and Political Capital in Colonization and State-Building in the Early Modern Era: Colonial British America as a Case Study" (essay presented at the Columbia University Seminar on Early American History and Culture, October 13, 1998).

4. Jack N. Rakove, *The Beginnings of National Politics: An Interpretive History of the Continental Congress* (Baltimore, 1979), 273–96; E. James Ferguson, *The Power of the Purse: A History of American Public Finance, 1776–1790* (Chapel Hill, N.C., 1961), 57–69.

5. Eugene S. Ferguson, "The American-ness of American Technology," *Technology and Culture* 20 (January 1979), 3–24; Thomas C. Cochran, *Frontiers of Change: Early Industrialization in America* (New York, 1981); Richard Stott, "Artisans and Capitalist Development," *Journal of the Early Republic* 16 (Summer 1996), 257–71. David J. Jeremy and Darwin Stapleton have pointed out that, with a few notable exceptions, most of the emigrant workers who came to the United States from England in the early national period were "carriers of obsolete skills." "Transfers between Culturally-Related Nations: The Movement of Textile and Railroad Technologies between Britain and the United States, 1780–1840," in David J. Jeremy, ed., *International Technology Transfer: Europe, Japan and the USA, 1700–1914* (Brookfield, Vt., 1991), 35.

6. "Letter Reflecting on the State of American Manufactures &c. From a Gentleman in Philadelphia to his Friend at Montego Bay," *American Museum* 6 (September 1789), 237–38; *The New Haven Gazette and the Connecticut Magazine,* July 19, 1787; Thomas C. Cochran, *Frontiers of Change: Early Industrialization in America* (New York, 1981), 72; Eugene S. Ferguson, *Early Engineering Reminiscences (1815–40) of George Escol Sellers* (Washington, D.C., 1965), 94. Such sentiments are in line with the recent fashionable trend in studies of the Industrial Revolution to minimize the centrality, leadership, and uniqueness of Great Britain. Some historians have argued that British industrialization was gradual rather than sudden, and that the industrialization of other European countries, most notably France, was more balanced and humane, though not technologically inferior. Rondo Cameron, "A New View of European Industrialization," *Economic History Review* 38 (February 1985), 1–23; Robert Aldrich, "Late-Comer or Early Starter? New Views on French Economic History," *Journal of European Economic History* 16 (Spring 1987), 89–100; David S. Landes, *The Wealth and Poverty of Nations: Why Some Are So Rich and Some So Poor* (New York, 1998), 222.

7. Silas Deane to Robert Morris, June 10, 1781, E. James Ferguson et al., eds., *The Papers of Robert Morris, 1781–1784,* 9 vols. to date (Pittsburgh, 1979–), I, 131, 130; Neil Longley York, *Mechanical Metamorphosis: Technological Change in Revolutionary America* (New York, 1985), 40; John R. Harris, "Industrial Espionage in the Eighteenth Century," *Industrial Archeology Review* 7 (Spring 1985), 136. Landes writes: "In the European world of competition for power and wealth, then, Britain became the principal target of emulation from the beginning of the eighteenth century. Other countries sent emissaries and spies to learn what they could of British techniques. Merchants and industrialists visited the island to see what they could." *The Wealth and Poverty of Nations,* 235.

8. David Rittenhouse, *An Oration* (Philadelphia, 1775), 20; Norman and

Coles, *Subscription Address* (Boston, 1785), as cited by York, *Mechanical Metamorphosis*, 158; Owen Biddle, *An Oration* (Philadelphia, 1781), 2, 22, 30. On the importance of clockmakers to the innovative process of the Industrial Revolution, see David S. Landes, *Revolution in Time: Clocks and the Making of the Modern World* (Cambridge, Mass., 1983).

9. Jones, "Oration," *American Museum* 5 (March 1789), 265; "Homespun," "Plain Thoughts on Home Manufacturing," *Columbian Magazine* 1 (February 1787), 281; Hugh Williamson, *Letters from Sylvius to the freemen inhabitants of the United States* (New York, 1787)," 114; *Boston Gazette,* January 31, 1785; "American," "Letter II," *American Museum* 2 (October 1787), 332; A Plain but Real Friend to America, "Three Letters on Manufactures," *American Museum* 1 (January 1787), 16–17," 16–17.

10. Rush, "A Speech delivered. . . .'"; Robert Bell, *Select Essays: Collected from the Dictionary of Arts and Sciences, and from various modern Authors* (Philadelphia, 1778); *American Museum* 2 (October 1787), 394; *Pennsylvania Gazette,* April 30, 1788. See also *New Haven Gazette,* May 24, 1787.

11. Eric Robinson, "James Watt and the Law of Patents," *Technology and Culture* 13 (April 1972), 125–31; F. M. Scherer, "Invention and Innovation in the Watt-Boulton Steam-Engine Venture," ibid., 6 (Spring 1965), 182–86; Samuel Rezneck, "The Rise of Industrial Consciousness in the United States," *Journal of Economic and Business History* 4 (August 1932), 793; As Carroll W. Pursell Jr., explains, "Had he [Fitch] been able, like Robert Fulton, to buy a Watt engine in England and merely attach it to a boat, he might have been more successful. As it turned out, he wasted his substance and that of the company on fruitless attempts to build what might better have been purchased abroad." *Early Stationary Steam Engines in America* (Washington, D.C, 1969), 22.

12. John R. Harris, "Movements of Technology between Britain and Europe in the Eighteenth Century," in Jeremy, *International Technology Transfer,* 12–13; H. I. Dutton, *The Patent System and Inventive Activity during the Industrial Revolution* (Manchester, 1984), 21. For an opposing view on the value of drawings to technology diffusion, see Eugene S. Ferguson, "The Mind's Eye: Nonverbal Thought in Technology," *Science* 197 (August 26, 1977), 827–36. Ferguson, however, agrees that drawings played a minimal role in the diffusion of knowledge in the early republic. "Technology as Knowledge," in Edwin T. Layton Jr., ed., *Technology and Social Change in America* (New York, 1973), 14.

13. Robert B. Gordon and Patrick M. Malone, *The Texture of Industry: An Archaeological View of the Industrialization of North America* (New York, 1994), 14, 20; Christine MacLeod, *Inventing the Industrial Revolution* (Cambridge, 1988), 108; Peter Mathias, "Skills and the Diffusion of Innovation from Britain in the Eighteenth Century," *Transactions of the Royal Historical Society* (1975), 93–113; Cochran, *Frontiers of Change,* 14; David J. Jeremy, *Transatlantic Industrial Revolution: The Diffusion of Textile Technologies between Britain and America* (Cambridge, Mass., 1981), 43–49; A. E. Musson and Eric Robinson, *Science*

and Technology in the Industrial Revolution (Manchester, 1969), 85; Victor S. Clark, *History of Manufactures in the United States*, 3 vols. (New York, 1929), I, 220. "Industrial espionage on site or the defection of workmen was much more likely to spring the secret than was anyone searching for the specification in Whitehall." Christine MacLeod, "The Paradoxes of Patenting: Invention and Its Diffusion in Eighteenth- and Nineteenth-Century Britain, France, and North America," *Technology and Culture* 32 (October 1991), 898. Because registering a patent in England included no objective examination and "involved purely clerical acts," most of the patents registered were of dubious utility. Adams and Averley, "The Patent Specification . . . ," 159–60. On the other hand, many developments were not registered because of the cost involved in registration and protection of patents. See, for example, Allan A. Gomme, "Patent Practice in the 18th Century: The Diary of Samuel Taylor, Thread Maker and Inventor, 1722–1723," *Journal of the Patent Office Society* 19 (April, 1937), 256–72.

14. Samuel Wetherill, "Report of the Committee for Manufactures to the Managers of the Pennsylvania Society for Promoting Manufactures and Useful Arts," *Columbia Magazine* 2 (December 1788), 737; *The New Haven Gazette and the Connecticut Magazine*, August 9, 1787; William Barton, *The True Interest of the United States, and Particularly of Pennsylvania, Considered* (Philadelphia, 1785), 27; "A Plain but Real Friend," 117.

15. *American Museum* 2 (June 1787), 437.

16. James Hughes to Franklin, September 25, 1786, Franklin Papers, American Philosophical Society, Philadelphia, hereafter APS; "A Plain but Real Friend," 116–19; Rush, "A Speech delivered . . . ."; "A Plain but Real Friend," 19.

17. "Homespun," "Plain Thoughts," 282.

18. John Dickinson, *Letters from a Farmer in Pennsylvania to the Inhabitants of the British Colonies* (London, 1768), 15; John Morgan, "Whether it be most beneficial to the united states to promote agriculture, or to encourage the mechanic arts and manufactures," *American Museum* 6 (July 1789), 73–74. Morgan himself, like many other colonial physicians, learned to practice his trade abroad. He received his medical degree from the University of Edinburgh.

19. See J. E. Crowley, *This Sheba, Self: The Conceptualization of Economic Life in Eighteenth-Century America* (Baltimore, 1974), 140–41. As Brook Hindle writes, "After the Revolution, agriculture received more attention than any other economic activity." *The Pursuit of Science in Revolutionary America* (Chapel Hill, N.C., 1965), 355.

20. "American," "Letter II," *American Museum* 2 (October 1787), 331. Ultimately, the new industrial technology came to rely on the cheap labor of women and children, though in the 1780s Americans had hoped to avoid the exploitive industrial circumstances that plagued the British Isles. See also *The New Haven Gazette and the Connecticut Magazine*, August 30, 1787.

21. *Pennsylvania Gazette*, April 30, 1788; Rush, "A Speech delivered . . . ." Worrying that British reviewers would criticize his work harshly because of the

tensions between the two countries, Rush wrote that "In science of every kind men should consider themselves as citizens of the whole world." Rush to Richard Price, April 22, 1786; L. H. Butterfield, ed., *Letters of Benjamin Rush*, 2 vols. (Princeton, N.J., 1951), I, 386. For Rush, scientific internationalism could coexist with cultural nationalism and the competitive pursuit of superior technology.

22. Continental Congress resolution, March 21, 1776, in Worthington C. Ford, ed., *Journals of the Continental Congress*, 34 vols. (Washington, D.C., 1904–37), IV, 224. The duck and sail cloth Adams referred to were probably made of flax. For other early exhortations by John Adams, see "Autobiography of John Adams," in L. H. Butterfield, ed., *The Adams Papers: Diary and Auto-biography of John Adams*, 4 vols. (New York, 1964), III, 372. Adams's motion to establish a permanent commission in Congress whose responsibility would be to assist and correspond with societies for the improvement of agriculture, manufacturing, the arts, and commerce, was defeated. See Joseph Smith diary, in Paul H. Smith, ed., *Letters of Delegates to Congress*, 26 vols. (Washington, D.C., 1976–98), I, 402.

23. John F. Amelung, *Remarks on Manufactures* (Boston, 1787), 3.

24. George C. Groce, Jr., "Benjamin Gale," *New England Quarterly* 10 (December 1937), 708; Hindle, *Pursuit of Science*, 124–25, 191.

25. *Pennsylvania Chronicle*, March 7, 1768.

26. Richard Henry Lee, *The Life of Arthur Lee*, 2 vols. (Boston, 1829), I, 17; *American Museum* 5 (February 1789), 174–75.

27. Joseph Stancliffe Davis, *Essays in the History of American Corporations*, 2 vols. (Cambridge, Mass., 1917), I, 258; Lawrence A. Peskin, "From Protection to Encouragement: Manufacturing and Mercantilism in New York City's Public Sphere, 1783–1795," *Journal of the Early Republic* 18 (Winter 1998), 602, 606–7.

28. *The Plan of the Pennsylvania Society For the Encouragement of manufactures and the Useful Arts* (Philadelphia 1787), 2; Wetherill, "Report of the Committee for Manufactures," 738; Samuel Miles, "Address of the Managers of the Pennsylvania Society for the Promotion of Manufactures and the Useful Arts," *American Museum* 2 (October 1787), 360.

29. Wetherill, "Report of the Committee for Manufactures," 737; David J. Jeremy, "British Textile Technology Transmission to the United States: The Philadelphia Region Experience, 1770–1820," *Business History Review* 47 (Spring 1973), 29.

30. Similarly, the New York Manufacturing Society, after receiving a one-thousand-pound grant from the state legislature, had established a factory for producing flax and linen yarn and hired over 130 spinners to work the carding and spinning machines. Samuel Slater was briefly employed by the company. Yet Slater found the machinery worthless and left to open a more modern facility in Rhode Island. Peskin, "From Protection to Encouragement," 611.

31. "Report of a Committee of the Board of Managers of the Pennsylvania Society for Promoting Manufactures and Useful Arts," *Columbian Magazine* 2

(December 1788), 739. The report was written by George Clymer, Samuel Miles, and Tench Coxe. Clymer and Miles were vice presidents of the society. Jacob Cox Parsons, *Extracts from the Diary of Jacob Hiltzheimer of Philadelphia, 1765–1798* (Philadelphia, 1893), 143.

32. Wetherill, "Report of the Committee for Manufactures," 738; *American Museum* 6 (September 1789), 237–38.

33. Jacob E. Cooke, *Tench Coxe and the Early Republic* (Chapel Hill, N.C., 1978), 183; Davis, *Essays in the Earlier History of American Corporations*, I, 354–57; Leo Marx, *The Machine in the Garden: Technology and the Pastoral Ideal in America* (New York, 1964), 151–66; Philip Scranton, *Proprietary Capitalism: The Textile Manufacture at Philadelphia, 1800–1885* (New York, 1983), 95.

34. Tench Coxe, *An Address to an Assembly of the Friends of American Manufactures. Convened for the Purpose of Establishing a Society for the Encouragement of Manufactures and the Useful Arts* (Philadelphia, 1787), 10.

35. Tench Coxe, *An Enquiry into the Principles on which a Commercial System for the United States Should be Founded* (Philadelphia, 1787), 19. A month later, while the convention was still in session, Coxe explained that "there is another grand source from which supplies of manufacturers may be obtained—Emigration from foreign countries," and implored Franklin to persuade his convention colleagues to include immigration-inducing clauses in the plan for the new government. Tench Coxe to Benjamin Franklin, June 22, 1786, APS.

36. Coxe, *An Address*, 13, 22; *American Museum* 1 (January 1787), 19.

37. Coxe, *An Address*, 21–22, 11.

38. Tench Coxe, "Address to the Friends of American Manufactures" (October 20, 1788), *American Museum* 4 (October, 1788), 342. Coxe and George Clymer, wrote in their "Report to the Managers of the Pennsylvania Society for Promoting Manufactures and Useful Arts" that since the high cost of labor had hitherto delayed the development of American manufactures, the acquisition of machines must receive top priority. *American Museum* 4 (November, 1788), 407.

39. Coxe, *Observations on the Agriculture, Manufactures, and Commerce of the United States* (New York, 1789), 15; Tench Coxe to Franklin, June 22, 1786, APS; Coxe, "Address to the Friends of American Manufactures," 346.

40. Coxe, "Address to the Friends of American Manufactures," 343–44, 346.

41. Coxe, "Address to the Friends of American Manufactures," 343. Pennsylvania prohibited exporting machines and enticing artisans to emigrate in recognition of their importance to its industrial development.

42. Tench Coxe to Andrew Mitchell, August 9, 1787, and October 21, 1787, Tench Coxe Papers, Historical Society of Pennsylvania; Anthony F. C. Wallace and David J. Jeremy, "William Pollard and the Arkwright Patents," *William and Mary Quarterly*, 3d ser., 34 (July 1977), 409–10; Cooke, *Tench Coxe*, 107; George S. White, *Memoir of Samuel Slater, the Father of American Manufactures Connected with a History of the Rise and Progress of the Cotton Manufacture in England and America with Remarks on the Moral Influence of Manufactures in the*

United States (Philadelphia, 1836), 71; William R. Bagnall, *The Textile Industry of the United States* (Cambridge, Mass. 1893), 75.

43. *Pennsylvania Gazette*, May 27, 1785; "Extracts from the minutes of the board of managers of the Pennsylvania Society of Arts and Manufactures," *American Museum* 5 (January, 1789), 51, 52.

Chapter 5. Official Orchestration of Technology Smuggling

1. "Loan to John F. Amelung," June 2, 1790, *American State Papers: Finance*, IX, 62; *Annals of the Congress of the United States, 1789–1842*, 42 vols. (Washington, D.C., 1834–56), I, 1686–1688. Neil Longley York, who examined the numerous petitions for Congressional assistance in the first two sessions, found many who pleaded for transportation subsidies. Yet Congress consistently turned them all away. *Mechanical Metamorphosis: Technological Change in Revolutionary America* (Westport, Conn., 1985), 174.

2. John F. Amelung, *Remarks on Manufactures, Principally on the New Established Glass-House, near Frederick-Town . . .* (Boston, 1787), 10, 11. See also Arlene Palmer Schwind, "The Glass Makers of Early America," in *The Craftsman in Early America*, ed. Ian M. G. Quimby (New York, 1984), 162–63.

3. Herman Heyman to Franklin, January 19, 1784, Franklin Papers, American Philosophical Society, Philadelphia; hereafter APS. Heyman claimed that this was his second letter, though no other letter from Hyman to Franklin survives. Heyman's plan to travel to North America was mentioned to Franklin in another context in a letter from a prominent Bremen merchant. Arnold Delius to Franklin, February 7, 1783, APS.

4. While I have found no record of a correspondence with Amelung in the Adams and Franklin papers, Amelung was probably telling the truth. Both Adams and Franklin were alive when he published *Remarks on Manufactures*, and could have easily disputed his story, which they didn't. I thank Kate Ono of the Franklin Papers and Greg Lint of the Adams Papers for their help in this matter.

5. Amelung, *Remarks on Manufactures*, 10–12; *Laws of the Maryland Assembly*, May session, 1788, ch. VII; statement of J. F. M. Amelung, Chancery cases, MS 1767, Hall of Records, Annapolis, Land Office; petitions of J. F. Amelung, May 26 and June 29, 1790, Records of U.S. Senate, 1st Congress, 2d session, National Archives, Washington, D.C.; George Washington to Thomas Jefferson, February 13, 1789, John C. Fitzpatrick, ed., *George Washington: Writings*, 39 vols. (Washington, D.C., 1931–1944), XXX, 198–99; *Annals*, 1st Congress, 2d session, May 26, 1790, June 3, 1790, 1616, 1629–32, 1687.

6. John Baker Holroyd, first earl of Sheffield, *Observations on the Commerce of the American States with Europe and the West Indies; Including the several Articles of Import and Export; and on the Tendency of a Bill now depending in Parliament* (London 1783), 65, 66. On the impact of Sheffield's report see

Stanley Elkins and Eric McKitrick, *The Age of Federalism: The Early American Republic, 1788–1800* (New York, 1993), 70; Charles Ritcheson, *Aftermath of Revolution: British Policy toward the United States 1783–1795* (New York, 1971), 6.

7. James Huges to Franklin, September 25, 1786, APS; J. F. D. Smyth, *A Tour in the United States of America*, 2 vols. (London, 1784), II, 448; Sheffield, *Observations on the Commerce of the American States*, 67.

8. Rush to Jon C. Lettsom, November 15, 1783, L. H. Butterfield, ed., *Letters of Benjamin Rush*, 2. vols. (Princeton, N.J., 1951), I, 312.

9. William Bingham, *A Letter from an American, now resident at London* (Philadelphia, 1784), 13, 23.

10. Tench Coxe, *A Brief Examination of Lord Sheffield's Observations on the Commerce of the United States* (Philadelphia, 1791), 39–42.

11. Robert Owen, *The Life: Robert Owen* (London, 1857), 31.

12. The episode and Arkwright's threat are recalled by Anthony F. C. Wallace and David J. Jeremy, "William Pollard and the Arkwright Patents," *William and Mary Quarterly*, 3d. ser., 34 (July 1977), 404.

13. As quoted by Maldwyn A. Jones, "Ulster Emigration, 1783–1815," in E. R. R. Green, ed., *Essays in Scotch-Irish History* (London, 1969), 51.

14. William Smith, *A Caveat against Emigration to America* (London, 1803), 15, 26, 31; Jones, "Ulster Emigration," 54.

15. Charles J. Hoadley, ed., *Public Records of the Colony of Connecticut*, 16 vols. to date (Hartford, 1894–) XII, 527; Robert H. Elias and Eugene D. Finch, eds., *Letters of Thomas Attwood Digges (1742–1821)* (Chapel Hill, N.C., 1982), 401n.; David John Jeremy, ed., *Henry Wansey and His American Journal, 1794* (Philadelphia, 1970), 73 n. 58; Digges to Jefferson, May 12, 1788, Julian P. Boyd et al., eds., *Papers of Thomas Jefferson*, 30 vols. to date (Princeton, N.J., 1950–), XIII, 153, 154.

16. The information in this section on the British restrictions on the movement of machinery and migrants is drawn from David J. Jeremy, "Damming the Flood: British Government Efforts to Check the Outflow of Technicians and Machinery, 1780–1843," *Business History Review* 51 (Spring 1979), 1–34; John R. Harris, "Industrial Espionage in the Eighteenth Century," *Industrial Archeology Review* 7 (Spring 1985), 128–29; A. E. Musson, "The 'Manchester School' and Exportation of Machinery," *Business History* 14 (January 1972), 20–21; Jones, "Ulster Emigration," 54; Carroll W. Pursell Jr., *Early Stationary Steam Engines in America* (Washington, D.C, 1969), 13; Emberson E. Proper, "Colonial Immigration Laws: A Study of the regulation of Immigration by the English Colonies in America," *Studies in History, Economics and Public Law* 12 (January 1900), 201–2.

17. Robert Holditch, *The Emigrant's Guide to the United States of America* (London, 1818), 40.

18. Darwin H. Stapleton, *Accounts of European Science, Technology, and Medicine by American Travelers Abroad, 1735–1860, in the Collection of the American Philosophical Society* (Philadelphia, 1985), 12; see also David J. Jeremy, *Trans-*

atlantic Industrial Revolution: The Diffusion of Textile Technologies between Britain and America (Cambridge, Mass., 1981), 40.

19. As Gilbert Chinard wrote long ago, "The only men who had constantly to think of the United States as one nation were the American ministers abroad." *Thomas Jefferson: The Apostle of Americanism*, 2d rev. ed. (Boston, 1939), 202. I have discussed the international origins of American identity in "Nationalism, Neo-Mercantilism, and Diplomacy: Rethinking the Franklin Mission," *Diplomatic History* 22 (Winter 1998), 101–6. See also Peter and Nicholas Onuf, *Federal Union, Modern World: The Law of Nations in an Age of Revolutions, 1776–1814* (Madison, Wis., 1993), which demonstrates that the model for Americanism was the eighteenth-century European international state system celebrated by Emmerich de Vattel. Peter Onuf further develops the importance of the transnational federation to the formation of American identity in "American Revolution and National Identity," an essay presented at the Johns Hopkins Seminar on National Cultures and the Construction of the Modern World, April 20, 1998. The Constitution is usually held to be the body and soul of American unity and identity. Yet "the cult of the Constitution," as Michael Kammen observed, "did not arise as early, nor so pervasively, as scholars have believed." *A Machine That Would Go of Itself: The Constitution in American Culture* (New York, 1994), 46. As Bernard Bailyn explains in his 1992 "Postscript" to *The Ideological Origins of the American Revolution*, the task of the constitutional movement was "the creation . . . of national power," not national identity (Cambridge, Mass., 1992), 325.

20. Robert R. Livingston to John Jay, September 12, 1782, in Henry P. Johnston, ed., *The Correspondence and Public Papers of John Jay*, 4 vols. (New York, 1890–93), II, 340–41; John Adams, *Observations on the Commerce of the American States* (Philadelphia, 1783), 38–39.

21. Jefferson, *Notes on the State of Virginia*, in Merrill D. Peterson, ed., *The Portable Thomas Jefferson* (New York, 1975), 217.

22. Jefferson to Jeudy de l'Hommande, August 9, 1787, *Jefferson Papers*, XII, 11; Jefferson to Thomas Digges, June 19, 1788, ibid., XIII, 260. I have elaborated on this subject and on Jefferson's own conflicting sentiments in Doron S. Ben-Atar, *The Origins of Jeffersonian Commercial Policy and Diplomacy* (New York, 1993).

23. Adams to Franklin, August 17, 1780, Leonard W. Labaree et al., eds., *The Papers of Benjamin Franklin*, 36 vols. to date (New Haven, Conn., 1959–), XXIII, 201–2; Adams, *Defense of the Constitutions of the United States of America*, 3 vols. (London, 1787), I, 2; "Discourse on Davila," in Charles Francis Adams, ed., *The Works of John Adams*, 10 vols. (Freeport, N.Y., 1977 [1850]), VI, 246, 279.

24. Henry Wyld to Jefferson, May 20, 1788, *Jefferson Papers*, XIII, 184.

25. Joseph Fielding to Jefferson, October 28, 1789, *Jefferson Papers*, XV, 528.

26. Proceedings of the Continental Congress, March 28, 1785, Worthington C. Ford et al., eds., *Journals of the Continental Congress, 34 vols.*,

(Washington. D.C., 1904–37) (hereafter JCC*),* XXVIII, 221; February 7, 1786, ibid., XXX, 53. See also York, *Mechanical Metamorphosis,* 162.

27. Charles Thomson to Franklin, January 14, 1784, APS; Jefferson to Thomas Digges, June 19, 1788, *Jefferson Papers,* XIII, 261.

28. Silas Deane to Simeon Dean, May 20, 1785, in *The Deane Papers: Correspondence between Silas Deane and His Brothers and Their Business and Political Associates, 1771–1795,* in *Collections of the Connecticut Historical Society,* 36 vols., (Hartford, Conn., 1930), XXIII, 211; Thomas Digges to William Carmichael, April 3, 1783, *Letters of Digges,* 389–90; Samuel Rezneck, "The Rise of Industrial Consciousness in the United States," *Journal of Economic and Business History* 4 (August 1932), 793.

29. James Warren to Mathew Carey, April 19, 1787, *American Museum* 2 (September 1787), 261. Adams was referring to an invention by Henry Cort, a procurement agent in the Royal Navy, who patented in 1784 a puddling and rolling process.

30. John Leander Bishop, *A History of American Manufactures from 1608 to 1860,* 3 vols. (Philadelphia, 1866), I, 498–99. William Bingham to Jefferson, April 16, 1789; Jefferson to Bingham, September 25, 1789.

31. Jefferson, "Hints on European Travel" (1788). Jefferson to Rev. James Madison, October 2, 1785; to Charles Thomson, April 22, 1786; to John Page, May 4, 1786, *Jefferson Papers,* XIII, 269; VIII, 574; IX, 400–401, 445. Jefferson saw no contradiction between his embrace of technology and his hostility to large-scale manufacturing. Jefferson believed that America's unique political economy, primarily the abundance of land, assured that technology would benefit production without the negative social consequences of English industrial towns. Further, as Leo Marx explains, Jefferson believed that knowledge and improvement were always for the good, and could not "imagine that a genuine advance in science or the arts, such as the new steam engine, could entail consequences as deplorable as factory cities." Leo Marx, *The Machine in the Garden: Technology and the Pastoral Ideal in America* (New York, 1964), 150.

32. Proceedings of the Continental Congress, May 11, 1785, JCC, XXVIII, 349–50; Bruce W. Bugbee, *Genesis of American Patent and Copyright Law* (Washington, D.C., 1967), 95–99, 128; P. J. Federico, "Outline of the History of the United States Patent Office," *Journal of the Patent Office Society* 18 (July 1936), 47–50; York, *Mechanical Metamorphosis,* 192.

33. Connecticut, Act for Encouraging Literary Genius, *Acts and Laws of the States of Connecticut,* January 1783, 133; Oliver Wolcott to Oliver Wolcott Jr., January 29, 1783; Elias Boudinot to the States, May 6, 1783, Paul H. Smith, ed., *Letters of Delegates to Congress, 1774–1789,* 26 vols. (Washington, D.C., 1976–98), IXX, 646–47; XX, 227–28; Proceedings of the Continental Congress, March 10, March 26, May 2, 1783, JCC, XXIV, 180, 211, 326–27.

34. North Carolina, An Act of Securing Literary Property (November 19,

1785), in *Copyright Enactments of the United States*, ed. Thorvald Solberg (Washington, D.C., 1906), 25.

35. E. Burke Inlow, *The Patent Grant* (Baltimore, 1950), 44; Jeremy, *Transatlantic Industrial Revolution*, 17; Brook Hindle, *Emulation and Invention* (New York, 1981), 17; Federico, "Outline," 45.

36. David J. Jeremy, "British Textile Technology Transmission to the United States: The Philadelphia Region Experience, 1770–1820," *Business History Review 47 (Spring 1973)*, 32, 33; York, *Mechanical Metamorphosis*, 158; Inlow, *Patent Grant*, 43. See also the discussion of the Bond incident, above, pp. 78–80.

37. *An Act to Incorporate and Establish a Society for Cultivation and Promotion of Arts and Sciences* (Boston, 1780); James Bowdoin, *A Philosophical Discourse Addressed to the American Academy of Arts and Science* (Boston, 1780), 7; S. P. Griffiths, "National Arithmetic, or 'Observations on the Finances of the Commonwealth of Massachusetts," *American Museum* 5 (June 1789), 547; *Memoirs of the American Academy of Arts and Sciences, vol. I* (Boston, 1785), iv.

38. William R. Bagnall, *The Textile Industry of the United States* (Cambridge, Mass., 1893), 89–94; Joseph Stancliffe Davis, *Essays in the History of American Corporations*, 2 vols. (Cambridge, Mass., 1917), I, 271–72. President Washington visited the Beverly factory during his tour of New England and wrote in his diary on October 30, 1789, that the manufacturing processes there "seemed perfect" and the product was "excellent." John C. Fitzpatrick, ed., *The Diaries of George Washington*, 4 vols. (New York, 1925), IV, 41.

39. *Acts and Laws of the State of Connecticut in America* (New London, 1788, 1789), 361, 375; Hoadley, *Public Records of the State of Connecticut*, VII, 241; petition of the Hartford Woolen Manufactory, October 16, 1790, ibid., 204–5; Bagnall, *Textile Industry*, 85–86; Jeremy, *Transatlantic Industrial Revolution*, 17; Jeremy, *Henry Wansey*, 73 n. 58.

40. Silas Deane to Simeon Deane, April 3, 1784, *Deane Papers*, XXIII, 198; Bowdoin, *Philosophical Discourse*, 20; *Pennsylvania Gazette*, April 30, 1788.

41. Silas Deane to Simeon Deane, April 3, 1784; Jacob Sebor to Silas Deane, November 10, 1784; Silas Deane to Simeon Deane, May 20, 1785, *Deane Papers*, XXIII, 197, 204–05, 211.

42. Frederick William Geyer to Silas Deane, May 1, 1787, *Deane Papers*, XXIII, 244. See also Bugbee, *Genesis*, 86–87; Federico, "Outline of the History of the United States Patent Office," 46.

43. William Grayson to William Short, June 15, 1785, Edmund C. Burnett, ed., *Letters of Members of the Continental Congress*, VIII vols. (Washington, D.C., 1921–36), VIII, 141. Authority over naturalization and immigration resided in the states. Under the Articles of Confederation United States citizenship was derived from state citizenship. John P. Roche, "Immigration and Nationality: A Historical Overview of United States Policy," in Uri Ra'anan, ed., *Ethnic Resurgence in Modern Democratic States* (New York, 1980), 36.

44. Tench Coxe, "An Enquiry into the Principles, on which a commercial system for the United States of America should be reordered," *American Museum* 1 (May 1787), 443, 445; Joel Barlow, *An Oration* (Hartford, Conn., 1787), 20.

45. Dr. Kilham to Rufus King, October 1785, in Charles R. King, ed., *The Life and Correspondence of Rufus King*, 5 vols. (New York, 1894) II, 608; William Barton, *The True Interests of the United States, and particularly of Pennsylvania Considered* (Philadelphia, 1786), 28.

46. Frederick William Geyer to Silas Deane, May 1, 1787, *Deane Papers*, XXIII, 244.

47. James Madison, "Act Securing Copyright for Authors" (November 16, 1785), William T. Hutchinson et al., eds., *The Papers of James Madison*, 17 vols. (Chicago, 1962–91), VIII, 418–19. The rights applied only to those "being a citizen of any of the United States." The bill also specified that should a foreign reprint be imported, "the person or persons offending herein, shall forfeit to the party injured, double the value of all copies so printed, reprinted, or imported." George Mason's remarks, September 13, 1787, in Max Farrand, ed., *The Records of the Federal Convention of 1787*, 3 vols. (New Haven, Conn., 1911), II, 606.

48. Gillard Hunt and James Brown Scott, eds., *The Debates in the Federal Convention of 1787 which Framed the Constitution of the United States of America (as reported by James Madison)* (New York, 1920), 420, 573; Jonathan Elliot, ed., *The Debates in the several State Conventions on the Adoption of the Federal Constitution*, 5 vols., (Washington, D.C, 1987 [1836]), V, 510–12; Morgan Sherwood, "The Origins and Development of the American Patent System," *American Scientist* 71 (September–October 1983), 501. For the debate over authorship see Karl Fenning, "The Origins of the Patent and Copyright Clause of the Constitution," *Journal of the Patent Office Society* 11 (October 1929), 438–45. The most important legal analysis of the origins of the clause is Kenneth J. Burchfiel, "Revising the 'Original' Patent Clause: Pseudo-History in Constitutional Construction," *Harvard Journal of Law and Technology* 2 (Spring 1989), 155–218.

49. Donald W. Banner, "An Unanticipated, Nonobvious, Enabling Portion of the Constitution: The Patent Provision—The Best Mode," *Journal of the Patent Office Society* 69 (November 1987), 637.

50. Tench Coxe, *A Memoir* (Philadelphia, 1817), 1; Coxe to Franklin, June 22, 1787, APS; Coxe, "An Address," *American Museum* 2 (September 1787), 248–55; Benjamin Rush, "Address to the People of the United States," ibid., 1 (January 1787), 10.

51. Inlow, *Patent Grant*, 44; York, *Mechanical Metamorphosis*, 194–95; Frank D. Prager, "A History of Intellectual Property from 1454 to 1787," *Journal of the Patent Office Society* 26 (November 1944), 739. New York continued to issue state patents into the nineteenth century. Placing the intellectual property clause in this context is in line with Donald S. Lutz's argument that the origins of American constitutionalism rested on the experiences of Americans both as colonials

and as citizens of the Confederation. *The Origins of American Constitutionalism* (Baton Rouge, La., 1988).

52. Thomas McKean, speech at the Pennsylvania ratifying convention, November 28, 1787, in Merrill Jensen et al., eds., *The Documentary History of the Ratification of the Constitution*, 14 vols. to date(Madison, Wis., 1976–), II, 415.

53. Samuel Chase speech notes, Maryland ratifying convention, in Herbert J. Storing, ed., *The Complete Anti-Federalist*, 7 vols. (Chicago, 1981), V, 88–89; James Iredell, *Answers to Mr. Mason's objections to the new Constitution* (Newbern, N.C., 1788), in Paul Leicester Ford, ed., *Pamphlets on the Constitution of the United States* (Brooklyn, N.Y, 1888), 357.

54. Jefferson to Madison, July 31, 1788; Madison to Jefferson, October 17, 1788; Jefferson to Madison, August 28, 1789, *Jefferson Papers*, XIII, 433; XIV, 21; XV, 368. See also Silvio Bedini, *Thomas Jefferson: Statesman of Science* (New York, 1990), 177–79; Doron Ben-Atar, "Private Friendship and Political Harmony," *Reviews in American History* 24 (March 1996), 11–12; York, *Mechanical Metamorphosis*, 200.

55. Karl B. Lutz, "Are the Courts Carrying Out Constitutional Public Policy on Patents," *Journal of the Patent Office Society* 34 (October 1952), 773; Arthur H. Seidel, "The Constitution and the Standard of Patentability," ibid., 48 (January 1966), 17–23.

56. Jeremy, *Transatlantic Industrial Revolution*, 17; Harrold E. Gillingham, "Calico and Linen Printing in Philadelphia," *Pennsylvania Magazine of History and Biography* 52 (January 1928), 104; *Pennsylvania Gazette*, April 30, 1788. On the importance of celebrations to the formation of American nationalism in general, and on the July 4, 1788, processions in particular, see David Waldstreicher, *In the Midst of Perpetual Fetes: the Making of American Nationalism, 1776–1820* (Chapel Hill, N.C., 1997), esp. 104–6.

Chapter 6. Constructing the American Understanding of Intellectual Property

1. Franklin to William Hodgson, April 1, 1781, Leonard W. Labaree et al., eds., *The Papers of Benjamin Franklin*, 36 vols. to date (New Haven, Conn., 1959–), XXXIV, 507–08.

2. Digges to Washington, July 1, 1791, and November 12, 1791, in Robert H. Elias and Eugene D. Finch, eds., *Letters of Thomas Attwood Digges (1742–1821)* (Chapel Hill, N.C., 1982), 428–34, 435. Digges to Jefferson, April 28, 1791, Julian Boyd et al., eds., *Papers of Thomas Jefferson*, 30 vols. to date (Princeton, N.J., 1950–), XX, 313–15.

3. Hamilton, *Report On Manufactures*, in Harold C. Syrett et al., eds., *The Papers of Alexander Hamilton*, 27 vols. (New York, 1961–87), X, 296–97.

4. Thomas Digges to Hamilton, April 6, 1792; Samuel Paterson to Hamilton, Feb. 16, 1793, *Hamilton Papers*, XI, 242, 244–45; XIV, 87. Paterson repeated a

suggestion he made two years earlier "to give Some Encouragement to Ships bringing over Passengers of Certain Descriptions."

5. W. Row, *Look Before You Leap; seriously addressed to Artizans, Farmers, husbandmen and Others, Who are desirous of emigrating to America* (London, 1795), xii.

6. Washington to John Fitzgerald, April 27, 1794, in John C. Fitzpatrick, ed., *The Writings of George Washington*, XXXIII, 340–41.

7. Row, *Look Before You Leap*, v, xiii, xii, vii, viii, 43. The extent of Digges's activities can be learned from his letters to Washington, July 1, 1791 and November 12, 1791; to Jefferson, April 28, 1791, March 10, 1793; to Hamilton, April 6, 1792; and to Thomas Pinckney, March 12, 1793, March 21, 1793, in *Letters of Thomas Attwood Digges*, 428–49, and *Jefferson Papers*, XX, 313–15; XXV, 347–48.

8. Thomas Digges to Jefferson, March 10, 1793, *Jefferson Papers*, XXV, 348. See also Kenneth R. Bowling, *Pierre Charles L'Enfant: Vision, Honor and Male Friendship in the Early American Republic* (Washington, D.C., forthcoming); Robert H. Elias and Eugene D. Finch, introduction to the *Letters of Thomas Attwood Digges*, xii–lxxvii; Lynn Hudson Parsons, "The Mysterious Mr. Digges," *William and Mary Quarterly*, 3d ser., 22 (July 1965), 486–92; Carrol W. Pursell, Jr., "William Digges and William Pearce: An Example of The Transit of Technology, ibid., 21 (October 1964), 551–60; William Bell Clark, "In Defense of Thomas Digges," *Pennsylvania Magazine of History and Biography* 77 (October 1953), 381–438; David J. Jeremy, *Transatlantic Industrial Revolution: The Diffusion of Textile Technologies between Britain and America* (Cambridge, Mass., 1981), 78–82. I thank Ken Bowling for sharing his manuscript with me prior to publication.

9. Washington to Sir Edward Newenham, March 2, 1789, *Writings of George Washington*, XXX, 218; Washington to the Delaware Society for Promoting Domestic Manufactures, April 19–20, 1789 in W. W. Abbot, Dorothy Twohig et al., eds., *The Papers of George Washington, Presidential Series*, 8 vols. (Charlottesville, Va., 1987–), II, 78.

10. "To the President and Congress of the United States, the petition of the tradesmen, mechanics, and others, of the town of Baltimore," April 11, 1789, *American State Papers: Finances*, IX, 2; "Essay on Manufactures," *American Museum* 7 (January 1790), 24; "A Friend to American Manufactures," "Observations on American Porter and Cheese," ibid., 10 (July 1791), 8; Tench Coxe, *Observations on the Agriculture, Manufactures and Commerce of the United States* (New York, 1789), 25.

11. William Barton, "Remarks on the State of American Manufactures and Commerce," *American Museum* 6 (June 1790), 288; John Keil, *Thoughts on Emigration* (London, 1791), 25–27; "Information to Europeans who are disposed to migrate to the United States," *American Museum* 7 (May 1790), 237; *Constitution of the Germantown Society for Promoting Domestic Manufactures* (Phila-

delphia, 1790), 6; *Philadelphia Monthly Magazine* 1 (January 1794), 41–44. See also ibid. (March 1798), 166.

12. Memorandum submitted to Daniel Stevens by Charleston manufacturers, September 1, 1791; O. Burr & Co. to John Chester, September 12, 1791; Samuel Beck to Hamilton, September 3, 1791; George Cabot to Hamilton, September 6, 1791; all in Arthur H. Cole, ed., *Industrial and Commercial Correspondence of Alexander Hamilton Anticipating His Report on Manufactures* (Chicago, 1928), 90, 22, 61, 62. Hamilton was also familiar with the technological difficulties that led to the downfall of the Pennsylvania Society for the Encouragement of Manufactures and the Useful Arts. The society's inferior machinery and untrained laborers produced coarse cloth that was no match for the superior and cheaper British imports. Despite legislative and financial support from the Pennsylvania legislature the factory closed its doors following a fire early in 1790. William R. Bagnall, *The Textile Industries of the United States*, 2 vols. (Cambridge, Mass., 1893), I, 77–79, 84–86.

13. Unknown writer from Connecticut, *American Museum* 7 (January 1790), 24. See also W. O. Henderson, *Britain and Industrial Europe, 1750–1870: Studies in British Influence in the Industrial Revolution in Western Europe* (Liverpool, 1954), 23.

14. "American Manufactures," *Universal Asylum and Columbian Magazine* 6 (July 1790), 61; John Mix to John Chester, October 5, 1791; Elisha Colt to John Chester, August 20, 1791, Cole, *Industrial and Commercial Correspondence of Alexander Hamilton*, 51–52, 7–9; Bagnall, *Textile Industries*, 167. As Ian Inkster has explained, "technology could be organizational rather than mechanical, procedural rather than chemical." *Science and Technology in History: An Approach to Industrial Development* (New Brunswick, N.J., 1991), 2.

15. W. Winterbotham, *An Historical and Philosophical View of the American United States and the European Settlements in American and the West-Indies*, 4 vols. (London, 1799), III, 309, 328. See also Darwin H. Stapleton, *The Transfer of Early Industrial Technologies to America* (Philadelphia, 1987), 103, 119; Sidney M. Edelstein, "Papermaker Joshua Gilpin Introduces the Chemical Approach to Papermaking in the United States," *The Paper Maker* 28 (September 1961), 8.

16. Rowland T. Berthoff, *British Immigrants in Industrial America* (Cambridge, Mass., 1953), 137; David John Jeremy, ed., *Henry Wansey and His American Journal, 1794 (Philadelphia, 1970)*, 68 n. 34.

17. "Pastor Americanus," *The Shepard's Contemplation* (Philadelphia, 1794), 5–6; Jeremy, *Henry Wansey and His American Journal*, 73–74, 62 n. 32. See also Jeremy, *Transatlantic Industrial Revolution*, 118–19; Stapleton, *The Transfer of Early Industrial Technologies*, 15.

18. *Pennsylvania Gazette*, March 24, 1791; George Parkinson to Benjamin Franklin, December 22, 1789, Franklin Papers, American Philosophical Society, Philadelphia; Coxe to George Clymer, January 17, 1790, Tench Coxe Papers, Historical Society of Pennsylvania, Philadelphia. See also Jacob E. Cooke,

"Tench Coxe, Alexander Hamilton, and the Encouragement of American Manufactures," *William and Mary Quarterly*, 3d ser., 32 (1975), 381. John Kendrew and Thomas Porthouse patented machines for spinning yarn from cotton, flax, and wool in 1787, that were further developments rather than replicas of Arkwright's invention. Arkwright's machines proved useful only for cotton because they could not handle the long fibers of flax, hemp, or combed wool, even though in his patents of 1769 and 1775 Arkwright claimed his machines were suitable for all these functions. Kendrew and Porthouse added many additional heavy feed rollers and a damp band of material for the flax input to pass through before reaching the very traditional Arkwright spindles. The rollers and damp band were differences significant enough for Kendrew and Porthouse to get a patent. Whether these machines were significantly different than Arkwright's or not is less important than the fact that contemporaries like Coxe and Parkinson thought they were and patented them on that basis. Intellectual property, as I maintain throughout this book, is a legal, cultural, and social construct, not a physical and historical fact. I thank Carolyn Cooper helping me sort out this complex issue. For a discussion and illustrations of the different innovations in textiles see Julia de L. Mann, "The Textile Industry: Machinery for Cotton, Flax, Wool, 1760–1850," in Charles Singer et al., eds., *A History of Technology*, 5 vols. (Oxford, 1954–58), IV, 277–327.

19. *Gazette of the United States,* June 9, 1792; William Pollard to Thomas Jefferson, Henry Knox, and Edmund Randolph, June 26, 1792, *Jefferson Papers*, XXIV, 126.

20. Jeremy, *Henry Wansey and His American Journal*, 83, 127.

21. Washington to Jefferson, February 13, 1789, *Jefferson Papers*, XIV, 546; Washington to the United States Senate and House of Representatives, January 8, 1790, *Washington Papers, Presidential Series*, IV, 545.

22. Joseph Barnes, *As John Fitch has procured a number of handbills* (Philadelphia, 1789).

23. Washington to Lafayette, January 29, 1789, *Writings of George Washington*, XXX, 187.

24. *Connecticut Courant,* October 26, 1789.

25. James Madison to Jefferson, June 30, 1789; Madison in Congress, May 17, 1790, in William T. Hutchinson et al., eds., *The Papers of James Madison*, 17 vols. (Chicago, 1962–91), XII, 270; XIII, 218.

26. Coxe to Madison, March 21, 1790; Madison to Coxe, March 28, 1790, ibid., XIII, 113, 128.

27. European nations should not consider immigration a loss because citizens who migrated to the New World would be inclined to purchase products from their home. Madison, Population and Emigration, *National Gazette,* November 19, 1791, in *Madison Papers,* XIV, 117–22.

28. Coxe, *Observations on the Agriculture*, 20, 34, 32.

29. Coxe's draft of the *Report on Manufactures*, and undated paper "A," *Hamilton Papers*, XXVI, 636, 638–39, 639, 646–47; X, 18–19.

30. As Hamilton's best modern biographer has put it, "during the torrid summer of 1791, Hamilton stuck to his desk, turning out draft after draft," revising the original Coxe plan, and taking on the philosophy of laissez-faire. Jacob Ernest Cooke, *Alexander Hamilton,* (New York, 1982), 99. So different was the final product that Cooke and Nelson, the two authorities on the *Report on Manufactures*, conclude that Hamilton added many theoretical arguments but eliminated Coxe's practical suggestions. The reason, they suggest, was that Coxe's program, fully carried out, would have cut down significantly the need for British imports and thus undermined Hamilton's financial plans: it would reduce the government revenues Hamilton counted on to finance the public debt and check the economic power of merchants trading with England, the very group whose allegiance to the national government Hamilton deemed crucial to its survival. Cooke and Nelson exonerate Coxe of any international partiality and place the responsibility for the plan's supposed Anglophile short-comings at Hamilton's door. Cooke concludes that Hamilton saw nothing wrong with the nation's continuing dependence on English manufactured imports. Nelson even questions Hamilton's "commitment to the economic development of the United States," charging that he "acted in a manner unquestionably hostile to domestic manufacturers" and that he abandoned "domestic manufacturers to their British competitors." Jacob Ernest Cooke, *Tench Coxe and the Early Republic* (Chapel Hill, N.C., 1978), 183; John R. Nelson, Jr., *Liberty and Property: Political Economy and Policymaking in the New Nation, 1789–1812* (Baltimore, 1987), 53, 52, 37. See also Marx, *The Machine in the Garden*, 167–68; Douglass Adair, *Fame and the Founding Fathers* (New York, 1974), 81. Nelson's contention that the *Report on Manufactures* was actually an attempt to stall the development of American manufactures would have come as a surprise to contemporaries like Madison, who feared it planned to sacrifice the interests of the entire nation for the sake of developing manufactures. James Madison to Henry Lee, January 21, 1792, *Madison Papers*, XIV, 193–94.

31. *Report on Manufactures, Hamilton Papers* , X, 271, 340, 82, 270–71. For further elaboration on the report and its place in Hamilton's political economy, see Doron Ben-Atar, "Alexander Hamilton's Alternative: Technology Piracy and the Reports on Manufactures," *William and Mary Quarterly*, 3d ser., 52 (July 1995), 389–414.

32. *Report on Manufactures, Hamilton Papers*, X, 308; Hamilton, "Prospectus of the Society for Establishing Useful Manufactures" (August, 1791), *Hamilton Papers*, IX, 146, 147.

33. Hamilton to Benjamin Walker, July 11, 1792; Roger Newberry to Hamilton, undated; Hamilton to the directors of the Society for Establishing Useful Manufactures, December 7, 1791, *Hamilton Papers*, XII, 26; XXVI, 828; X, 346,

347. See also Hamilton to Benjamin Walker, July 11, 1792, *Hamilton Papers*, XII, 26. Hamilton also signed with John Campbell, another smuggler of British machinery to America, to go to Scotland to acquire men and machinery for the Society for Establishing Useful Manufactures. Agreement with John Campbell and Receipt from John Campbell, November 9, 1792, *Hamilton Papers*, XIII, 31–32. See also Joseph Stancliffe Davis, *Essays in the History of American Corporations*, 2 vols. (Cambridge, Mass., 1917), I, 398–99, 485; Anthony F. C. Wallace and David J. Jeremy, "William Pollard and the Arkwright Patents," *William and Mary Quarterly*, 3d ser., 34 (July 1977), 407, 413.

34. Joyce Appleby, *Capitalism and a New Social Order: The Republican Vision of the 1790s* (New York, 1984), 49. Similarly, Michel Foucault writes: "the pressure exerted by the biological on the historical had remained very strong for thousand of years; epidemic and famines were to two dramatic forms of this relationship that was always dominated by the menace of death. But through a circular process, the economic—and primarily agricultural—development of the eighteenth century . . . the period of great ravages from starvation and plague had come to a close before the French Revolution; death was ceasing to torment life so directly." *The History of Sexuality: An Introduction*, Robert Hurley trans., 3 vols. (New York, 1978), I, 142.

35. George S. White, *Memoir of Samuel Slater, The Father of American Manufactures, Connected with a History of the Rise and Progress of the Cotton Manufacture in England and America with Remarks on the Moral Influence of Manufactures in the United States* (Philadelphia, 1836), 37; Henry Howe, *Memoirs of the Most Eminent American Mechanics: Also Lives of Distinguished European Mechanics* (New York, 1841), 87.

36. John Melish, *Travels through the United States of America* (Belfast, 1818), 73. See also Jonathan Prude, *The Coming of Industrial Order: Town and Factory Life in Rural Massachusetts, 1810–1860* (New York, 1983), 34–49; Barbara M. Tucker, *Samuel Slater and the Origins of the American Textile Industry* (Ithaca, N.Y., 1984), 50; Howe, *Memoirs of the Most Eminent American Mechanics*, 91; White, *Memoir of Samuel Slater*, 96–97; Herbert Heaton, "The Spread of the Industrial Revolution," in Melvin Kranzberg and Caroll W. Pursell, Jr., eds., *Technology in Western Civilization*, 2 vols. (New York, 1967), 506; Thomas C. Cochran, *Frontiers of Change: Early Industrialization in America* (New York, 1981), 63; David J. Jeremy, "British and American Entrepreneurial Values in the Early Nineteenth Century: A Parting of the Ways?" in Robert A. Burchell, ed., *The End of Anglo-America: Historical Essays in the Study of Cultural Divergence* (Manchester, 1991), 34–42.

37. Bagnall, *Textile Industries*, I, 77–79, 84–86.

38. John Fitch, "Application of Steam to Navigation," June 22, 1790, in *American State Papers: Miscellaneous*, XXXVII, 12–13.

39. Washington to Congress, January 8, 1790, *American State Papers: Foreign Relations*, I, 12.

40. Linda G. De Pauw et al., eds., *Documentary History of the First Federal Congress of the United States of America*, vol. I: *Senate Legislative Journal* (Baltimore, 1972), 271 n. 91; ibid., vol. VI: *Legislative Histories* (Baltimore, 1986) 1632–33. The best recent work on the origins of the first Patent Act is Edward C. Walterscheid, *To Promote the Progress of Useful Arts: American Patent Law and Administration, 1787–1836* (Littleton, Colo., 1998), 81–143. There is little record of public debate on or opposition to the House version that may have led to the revision. Philadelphia ironmaker Richard Wells had petitioned against giving introducers patent monopolies. In his previous work Walterscheid argued that a petition from Philadelphian Richard Wells dissuaded Congress from allowing patents of importation. "Novelty in Historical Perspective (Part II)," *Journal of the Patent and Trademark Office Society* 77 (1993), 781–82. Yet it is unlikely that Congress followed the perspective of an unknown artisan over that of the president and the secretary of the Treasury. "Richard Wells Petition," March 2, 1790, and Wells to Henry Wynkoop, March 3, 1790, Records of the U.S. House of Representatives, HR 1A-E1, National Archives, Washington, D.C. In his more recent book Walterscheid acknowledges the unlikelihood that a petition from an individual with no particular political clout carried more weight in Congress than the specific recommendation of a president as powerful and popular as Washington. Constitutional considerations, he now believes, moved members of Congress to reject the president's instructions and establish strict patenting criteria in America. See also Steven Lubar, "The Transformation of Antebellum Patent Law," *Technology and Culture* 32 (1991), 935; Pamela O. Long, "Invention, Authorship, 'Intellectual Property,' and the Origins of Patents: Notes toward a Conceptual History," *Technology and Culture* 32 (October 1991), 877.

41. Jefferson to Hugh Williamson, April 1, 1792, *Jefferson Papers*, XXIII, 363; editorial note, *Jefferson Papers*, XX, 733–34. Jefferson prepared an alternative draft as early as December 1791. "A Bill to Promote the Progress of the Useful Arts," ibid., XXII, 359–61. See also Dumas Malone, *Thomas Jefferson and the Rights of Man* (Boston, 1951), 283; Floyd L. Vaughan, *The United States Patent System: Legal and Economic Conflicts in American Patent History* (Norman, Okla. 1956), 18–19; Silvio A. Bedini, *Thomas Jefferson: Statesman of Science* (New York, 1990), 177–79, 206–10.

42. The number of patents issued from 1790 to 1814 roughly doubled in each five-year period. Under these circumstances it was not humanly possible for the secretary of state to personally inspect each and every application. John M. Murrin, "The Great Inversion or Court versus Country: A Comparison of the Revolution Settlements in England (1688–1721) and America (1776–1816)," in J. G. A. Pocock, ed., *Three British Revolutions: 1641, 1688, 1776* (Princeton, N.J., 1980), 409.

43. Stephen D Law, *Digest of American Cases Relating to Patents for Inventions and Copyright from 1789 to 1862*, 5th rev. ed. (New York, 1877), 42; Daniel Preston, "The Administration and Reform of the U.S. Patent Office, 1790–1836," *Journal of the Early Republic* 5 (Fall 1985), 332–34.

44. Coxe to Madison, March 21, 1790, *Madison Papers,* XIII, 112–13; Hamilton, *Report on Manufactures, Hamilton Papers,* X, 296. Coxe admitted that his own self-interest was at stake. Granting imported technologies the privileges of inventions would "prove advantageous to me from the several objects I possess some of wch. are not inventions but importations."

45. *Annals of the Congress of the United States, 1789–1842,* 42 vols. (Washington, D.C., 1834–56), March 1, 1792, II, 432; P. J. Federico, "Outline of the History of the United States Patent Office," 79; Bruce Bugbee, *The Genesis of American Patent and Copyright Law* (Washington, D.C., 1967), 150. When a new patent law was adopted early in 1793, however, it did not include such a program. It voided patents if "the thing thus declared was not originally discovered by the patentee." Richard Peters, ed., *The Public Statues at Large of the United States of America . . . 1789–1873,* 17 vols. (Boston, 1850–73), I, 318–23. For a discussion of the mounting criticism of the 1790 act that led to the 1793 reform see York, *Mechanical Metamorphosis,* 202. Jefferson's ally Joseph Barnes attacked the proposal's effort to reintroduce protection only for American inventions. *Treatise on the Justice Policy and Utility of Establishing an Effectual System for Promoting the Progress of Useful Arts, by Assuring Property in the Products of Genius* (Philadelphia, 1792), 24–25.

46. Cooke, *Alexander Hamilton,* 104. See also Davis, *Essays,* I, 370–75, 410–26; Forrest McDonald, *Alexander Hamilton: A Biography* (New York, 1979), 232; Stanley Elkins and Eric McKitrick, *The Age of Federalism: The Early American Republic, 1788–1800* (New York, 1993), 262–63. The *Report on Manufactures* was according to Nelson but a "jingle" for the Society for the Establishment of Useful Manufactures. It was created only to "convince investors of the Society for Establishing Useful Manufactures' viability" and once the company's stock began its climb, Hamilton lost interest in American industrialization. *Liberty and Property,* 48.

47. Thomas Howell to Washington, July 14, 1789, *Washington Papers, Presidential Series,* III, 192–94.

48. Washington to Beverly Randolph, November 22, 1789, *Writings of George Washington,* XXX, 462–63.

49. "Jefferson Opinion on Proposal for Manufacture of Woolen Textiles in Virginia," December 3, 1790, *Jefferson Papers,* XVIII, 121. Julian Boyd skillfully traces the evolution of Jefferson's view, concluding that "the Secretary of State was responsible for the closing of the door and on this ground of national dignity." *Editorial note, ibid.,* 123–24.

50. Washington to Beverly Randolph, January 13, 1791, *Writings of George Washington,,* XXXI, 193–94.

51. Quoted in *Jefferson Papers,* XVII, 387. The correspondence is Beckwith to Lord Dorchester, July 27, 1790; to Grenville, August 10, 1790; and to Dorchester a year later.

52. Phineas Bond to Lord Grenville, September 10, 1791, in J. Franklin Jameson, ed., "Letters of Phineas Bond, British Consul at Philadelphia . . . , 1790–1794," *American Historical Association Annual Report for 1897* (Washington, D.C., 1898), 487; George Hammond to Lord Grenville, October 3, 1792, as cited by Herbert Heaton, "The Industrial Immigrant in the United States, 1783–1812," *Proceedings of the American Philosophical Society* 95 (October 1951), 523; Hammond to Lord Grenville, December 6, 1791, in Bernard Mayo, ed., "Instructions to the British Ministers to the United States, 1791–1812," *Annual Report of the American Historical Association for the Year 1936*, 3 vols. (Washington, D.C., 1936), III, 81. Darwin H. Stapleton has pointed out that for all the British efforts to hide their technology, Americans "seldom had difficulty obtaining the information they sought. Occasional obstinacy was often overcome by more-or-less deliberate industrial espionage." *Accounts of European Science, Technology, and Medicine by American Travelers Abroad, 1735–1860, in the Collection of the American Philosophical Society* (Philadelphia, 1985), 12.

53. Paterson to Hamilton, February 10, 1791; Thomas Marshall to Hamilton, July 19, 1791, Cole, *Industrial and Commercial Correspondence of Alexander Hamilton*, 111, 185; Digges to Jefferson, April 28, 1791, *Jefferson Papers*, XX, 314; Digges to Washington, November 12, 1791, *Letters of Thomas Attwood Digges*, 435.

54. Quoted in the *Columbian Gazette* (New York), March 3, 1794; *Emigration to America candidly considered, in a series of letters, from a gentleman, resident there, to his friend in England* (London, 1798), iii–iv.

55. H. I. Dutton, *The Patent System and Inventive Activity during the Industrial Revolution, 1750–1852* (Manchester, 1984), 21 n. 27; David J. Jeremy, "Damming the Flood: British Government Efforts to Check the Outflow of Technicians and Machinery, 1780–1843," 3–4, 6, 15; Jeremy, *Transatlantic Industrial Revolution*, 40–41. Prohibitions were enforced only in those industries that directly competed with British industries. The Board of Trade allowed and even encouraged the export of machines that assisted in the processing of raw materials that were going to end up in British manufactures.

56. Hamilton, *Report on Manufactures, Hamilton Papers*, X, 296, 60, 296–97; "Prospectus of the Society for Establishing Useful Manufactures" (August 1791), ibid., IX, 147.

57. Thomas Marshall to Hamilton, September–October 1791, *Hamilton Papers*, IX, 251, 252; Davis, *Essays*, I, 490; Benjamin Davies and Thomas Stephens, *One Thousand Valuable Secrets in Elegant and Useful Arts* (Philadelphia, 1795), iv.

58. *Hymns performed at the Anniversary Election of the Officers of the Providence Association of Mechanics and Manufactures* (April 14, 1794); *Hymns performed at the Anniversary Election of the Offices of the Providence Association of Mechanics and Manufactures on Monday, April 13, 1795* (Providence, R.I., 1795); Tristan Burges, *The Spirit of Independence: an Oration Delivered before the*

Providence Association of Mechanics and Manufacturers at the Annual Election (April 14, 1800), (Providence, R.I., 1800), 22.

59. Howe, *Memoirs of the Most Eminent American Mechanics*, 151–52; Caroline C. Cooper, "The Portsmouth System of Manufactures," *Technology and Culture* 25 (April 1984), 192–206; Carroll W. Pursell, Jr., *Early Stationary Steam Engines in America* (Washington, D.C., 1969), 33. Whittemore did not share Howe's assessment of the success of his invention for he was disappointed with the English reception and quickly returned to the United States.

60. Z. Y., "Some Accounts of the Cotton and Wool Card Manufactories in the Commonwealth of Massachusetts," *Massachusetts Magazine* (May 1791), III, 268; James Currie to Hamilton, July 1793, *Hamilton Papers*, XV, 153.; Heaton,, "The Industrial Immigrant," 527.

61. Thomas Cooper, *Some Information Respecting America* (London 1794), 235–36; Davis, *Essays*, I, 277; Berthoff, *British Immigrants in Industrial America*, 37; Jeremy, *Transatlantic Industrial Revolution*, 78.

62. Tench Coxe, *A View of the United States of America* (London, 1795), 95, 99, 43.

63. *Constitution of the Lancaster County Society for promoting Agriculture, Manufactures and the Arts* (Lancaster, Pa., 1800), 16; "Facts, showing the progress of Family Manufactures in the United States," *Universal Asylum and Columbian Magazine* 7 (November 1791), 328–32; Burges, *The Spirit of Independence*, 17; George Logan, *Address delivered before the Tammany Society* (New York, 1798). Logan, who challenged Coxe's view of industrialization in the pages of the *American Museum* in 1792, came out later in the decade in favor of an aggressive industrialization policy. See Brian Greenberg, "Tench Coxe, George Logan and Political Economies of Early America," essay presented at the Library Company of Philadelphia Inaugural Conference on The Past and Future of Early American Economic History: Needs and Opportunities, April 2001.

64. Albert Gallatin, *A Sketch of the Finances of the United States* (New York, 1796), 25, 154, 26.

65. *Constitution of the Lancaster County Society for promoting Agriculture, Manufactures and the Arts*, 17.

Chapter 7. The Path to Crystal Palace

1. Tench Coxe, *A Report on the State of Manufactures in the United States* . . . (Philadelphia, 1804), 20, 21, 23, 26.

2. George W. Custis, *An Address to the People of the United States on the Importance of Encouraging Agriculture and Domestic Manufactures* (Alexandria, Va., 1808).

3. Albert Gallatin, *Report on American Manufactures* (April 17, 1810), *American State Papers: Finance*, II, 430.

4. Petition to Congress by the Subscribers, Mechanics and Manufacturers of New York City (February 2, 1801), *American State Papers: Finance,* IX, 694; Robert Fulton to Albert Gallatin, December 8, 1807, *American State Papers: Miscellaneous,* I, 917–21.

5. Madison to William Pinckney, October 23, 1809, in Robert A. Rutland, et al., eds., *The Papers of James Madison, Presidential Series,* 4 vols. to date (Charlottesville, Va., 1984–), II, 28–29. Madison repeated this claim to his domestic audience in his annual message to Congress of November 29, 1809, ibid., 94; *http://www.myoutbox.net/poinvtrs.htm;* Chevalier Felix de Beaujour, *Sketch of the United States of America,* trans. William Walton (London, 1814), 89–90; James Mease, "To the Cultivators, The Capitalists, and Manufacturers of the United States," *Archives of Useful Knowledge* 1 (January 1811), 230. See also Anthony F. C. Wallace, *Rockdale: The Growth of an American Village in the Early Industrial Revolution* (New York, 1972), 74.

6. "On Foreigners," *Niles Weekly Register,* May 22, 1813; Herbert Heaton, "The Industrial Immigrant in the United States, 1783–1812," *Proceedings of the American Philosophical Society* 95 (October 1951), 520–526; Heaton, "The Spread of the Industrial Revolution," in Melvin Kranzberg and Carol W. Pursell Jr., eds., *Technology in Western Civilization,* 2 vols. (New York, 1967), I, 506–07; David J. Jeremy, "Damming the Flood: British Government Efforts to Check the Outflow of Technicians and Machinery, 1780–1843," 4–5, 12–13. Jeremy has estimated that even in the years 1809–13, during the height of Anglo-American tensions, 806 skilled workers in the textile industry alone successfully made the illegal crossing. David J. Jeremy, *Transatlantic Industrial Revolution: The Diffusion of Textile Technologies between Britain and America* (Cambridge, Mass., 1981), 149. Thomas M. Doerflinger reports a similar pattern in his study of iron manufacturing in New Jersey, "Rural Capitalism in Iron Country: Staffing a Forest Factory, 1808–1815," *William and Mary Quarterly,* 3d ser., 59 (January 2002), 7. The Anglo-American scenario was not unusual. Eighteenth-century artisans emigrated frequently during wartime to enemy countries. Peter Mathias, "Skills and the Diffusion of Innovation from Britain in the Eighteenth Century," *Transactions of the Royal Historical Society* (1975), 104.

7. Thomas Cooper, "Prospectus," *Emporium of Arts and Sciences* n.s., 1 (June 1813), 8; Henry Clay, "Speech on Domestic Manufactures" (March 26, 1810), in James F. Hopkins et al., eds., *The Papers of Henry Clay,* 11 vols. to date (Lexington, Ky., 1959–), I, 462.

8. Thomas Fessenden, *An Essay on the Law of Patents for New Inventions* (Boston, 1810), 213–14; *Annals of the Congress of the United States, 1789–1842,* 42 vols. (Washington, D.C., 1834–56), February 1811, XXII, 967, 969. The same petition that asked for federal sponsorship of the violation of the intellectual property rights of Europeans advocated intellectual protectionism at home. It complained about the "many valuable American discoveries [that] have thus

been pirated, sent to Europe, and there patented and published as European inventions, to the manifest injury of the true inventor, and derogatory to the honor and interests of the United States."

9. *A Bill to Promote the Progress of Sciences and Useful Arts* (Washington, D.C., 1812), (9–10), *Annals,* January 22, 1812, XXIII, 104; *Annals,* February 4, 1812, XXIII, 1018, 1021; *National Intelligencer,* February 6, 1812; *Annals,* March 9, 1812, XXIII, 1161; "Inquiry into the State of the Patent Office—Proposition to Establish a 'Home Department,' " June 12, 1812, *American State Papers: Miscellaneous,* II, 188–89.

10. The merino sheep was to turn the American woolen industry into the world leader. For a fascinating account of the venture see Steven Stoll, *Larding the Lean Earth: Soil and Society in the Early Republic and the Origins of Conservation* (New York, 2003).

11. William Thornton, "Patents" (March 5, 1811), *Journal of the Patent Office Society* 6 (November 1923), 98. The old patent system could not handle the number of legal challenges and applications. In 1836 Congress enacted a new patent law that provided for examiners who passed judgment whether a machine for which protection was sought was truly original and worthy of federally sanctioned monopoly. See also Edward C. Walterscheid's insightful discussion of administration of the 1793 Patent Act in *To Promote the Progress of Useful Arts: American Patent Law and Administration, 1787–1836* (Littleton, Colo., 1998), 243–304.

12. Peter A. Browne, "Mechanical Jurisprudence—No. 7," *The Franklin Journal and American Mechanic Magazine* 2 (July 1826), 21.

13. My discussion of nineteenth-century law and its relationship with the market economy is shaped by Steven Lubar, "The Transformation of Antebellum Patent Law," *Technology and Culture* 32 (October 1991), 932–59; J. Willard Hurst, *Law and the Conditions of Freedom in the Nineteenth-Century United States* (Madison, Wis., 1956); Leonard W. Levy, *The Law and the Commonwealth and Chief Justice Shaw* (New York, 1957); Morton J. Horowitz, *The Transformation of American Law, 1780–1860* (Cambridge, Mass., 1977); Peter Karsten, *Head versus Heart: Judge-Made Law in Nineteenth-Century America* (Chapel Hill, N.C., 1997); Charles Sellers, *The Market Revolution: Jacksonian America, 1815–1860* (New York, 1991); Robert H. Weibe, *The Opening of American Society: From the Adoption of the Constitution to the Eve of Disunion* (New York, 1984).

14. Joseph Story, *Commentaries on the Constitution of the United States*, 3 vols. (Boston, 1832), III, 49, 50. Chief Justice John Marshall, who did not render an opinion on the subject, nevertheless held a general philosophy that was in line with Story's point of view. Frances Howell Rudko, *John Marshall and International Law: Statesman and Chief Justice* (New York, 1991). For a fuller discussion of the legal reasoning see Walterscheid, *To Promote the Progress of Useful Arts,* 378–97.

15. *Address of the Connecticut Society for Encouragement of American Manufactures* (Middletown, Conn., 1817), 13.

16. *Raleigh Star,* December 22, 1815; A. E. Musson, "The 'Manchester School' and Exportation of Machinery," *Business History* 16 (January 1972), 19.

17. *Emigration; or, England and Paris* (London, 1816), iii–iv; Richard Parkinson, *A Tour in America . . .* , 2 vols. (London, 1805), I, dedication; II, 585, 572. Some English mechanics came via third countries. Timothy Claxton, for example, went as part of a group of English mechanics to St. Petersburg to build a gas lighting system for the Russian army. Unhappy with the working conditions and the wages, he bargained his way out of his contract and in 1823, instead of returning to England, sailed for America where he quickly found his skills in great demand. George Washington Light, *Life of Timothy Claxton* (Boston, 1839), 38, 41, 55.

18. Robert Holditch, *The Emigrant's Guide to the United States of America* (London, 1818), 21. See also Jeremy, "Damming the Flood," 6–33; Jeremy, "British Textile Technology Transmission to the United States: The Philadelphia Region Experience, 1770–1820," *Business History Review* 47 (Spring 1973), 27–37; Jeremy, *Transatlantic Industrial Revolution,* 138. As David J. Jeremy and Darwin H. Stapleton write, "the laws proved impossible to apply effectually." "Transfers between Culturally Related Nations: The Movement of Textile and Railroad Technologies between Britain and the United States, 1780–1840," in Jeremy, ed., *International Technology Transfer: Europe, Japan, and the USA 1700–1914* (Brookfield, Vt., 1991), 33. The restrictions also failed to stem similar immigration to France. As John Harris writes, "whatever the legal position, a large number of British workers went to France in the eighteenth century." "Movements of Technology between Britain and Europe," ibid., 22.

19. "An Englishwoman," *Views of Society and Manners in America . . .* (London, 1821), 389, 40; S. H. Collins, *Emigrant's Guide to and Description of the United States of America* (London, 1830), 17, 75; Charlotte Erickson, *Invisible Immigrants: The Adaptation of English and Scottish Immigrants in Nineteenth-Century America* (Ithaca, N.Y., 1972), 230.

20. Holditch, *The Emigrant's Guide,* 41. See also Thomas Young, *A Course of Lectures on Natural Philosophy and the Mechanical Arts,* 2 vols. (London, 1807), I, 2; Lucy Brown, *The Board of Trade and the Free Trade Movement* (Oxford, 1958), 161–65; Jeremy, "Damming the Flood," 14–21.

21. John Adams to Wiliam E. Richmond, December 14, 1819, in Charles Francis Adams ed., *The Works of John Adams, Second President of the United States,* 10 vols. (Boston, 1850–56), X, 384.

22. Mathew Carey, *National Interests & Domestic Manufactures* (Boston, 1819), 84.

23. Samuel Ogden, *Thoughts, What Probable Effect the Peace with Great Britain Will Have on the Cotton Manufactures* (Providence, R.I., 1815), 8, 9–10, 15, 12. As Nathan Rosenberg writes, "When the United States began to

industrialize in the nineteenth century, she was following a path which had been blazed earlier by Great Britain. Much of the technology which was introduced into America during this period was in fact borrowed from that country, with varying degrees of modification." *Technology and American Economic Growth* (New York, 1972), 59.

24. *Report from the Committee on Manufactures*, May 23, 1832, 22d Cong., 1st sess., H. Doc. 481, 9, 16.

25. Shamrock Society of New York, *Hints to Emigrants from Europe . . .* (New York, 1816), 8, 3; Pamphlet of the Pennsylvania Society for the Encouragement of American Manufactures (March 22, 1825), Pamphlet Collection of the American Philosophical Society, Philadelphia; William Hunter, *Annual Address Delivered Before the Rhode Island Society for the Encouragement of Domestic Industry* (October 20, 1824), (Providence, R.I., 1826), 40–41. See also Thomas C. Cochran, *Frontiers of Change: Early Industrialization in America* (New York, 1981), 76. Just as they did in the eighteenth century, manufacturing societies promised to improve the lot of the poor. The New York–based Society for the Encouragement of Manufactures, for example, celebrated the "American aptitude for mechanical inventions" and promised that the industrialization would provide employment and income to the poor. *Address to the People of the United States by the American Society for the Encouragement of Manufactures* (New York, 1817).

26. Zachariah Allen, *The Science of Mechanics, as Applied to the Present Improvements in the Useful Arts in Europe, and the United States of America* (Providence, R.I., 1829); H. J. Habakkuk, *American and British Technology in the Nineteenth Century: The Search for Labour-Saving Inventions* (Cambridge, 1962), 4. For all the improvements made by the American textile industry, recruiting of English textile workers continued well into the second half of the nineteenth century. See Daniel Creamer, "Recruiting Contract Laborers for the Amoskeag Mills," *Journal of Economic History* 1 (May 1941), 42–56.

27. Robert F. Dalzell, *Enterprising Elite: The Boston Associates and the World They Made* (Cambridge, Mass., 1987); Thomas Dublin, *Women at Work: The Transformation of Work and Community in Lowell Massachusetts 1826–1860* (New York, 1975); Jonathan Prude, *The Coming of Industrial Order: Town and Factory Life in Rural Massachusetts, 1810–1860* (New York, 1983).

28. Beaujour, *Sketch of the United States of America*, 97; John Bristed, *America and Her Resources . . .* (London, 1818), 58; Allen, *The Science of Mechanics*, iv.

29. Darwin H. Stapleton, *The Transfer of Early Industrial Technologies to America* (Philadelphia, 1987), 20, 23, 70; David J. Jeremy, "Immigrant Textile Machine Makers along the Brandywine, 1810–1820," *Textile History* 13 (1982), 225–48; Jeremy, *Transatlantic Industrial Revolution*, 38–39, 43; Wallace, *Rockdale*, 117–18; Philip Scranton, *Proprietary Capitalism: The Textile Manufacture at Philadelphia, 1800–1885* (New York, 1983), 87, 237, 239; Arlene Palmer Schwind, "The Glassmakers of Early America," in Ian M. G. Quimby, ed., *The Craftsman*

in Early America (New York, 1984), 165–66; Judith A. McGaw, *Most Wonderful Machine: Mechanization and Social Change in Berkshire Paper Making 1801–1885* (Princeton, N.J., 1987), 35–36, 74; Sidney M. Edelstein, "Papermaker Joshua Gilpin Introduces the Chemical Approach to Papermaking in the United States," *The Paper Maker* 28 (September 1961), 3–12; Geoffrey Tweedale, *Sheffield Steel and America: A Century of Commercial and Technological Interdependence 1830–1930* (New York, 1987). As Charlotte Erickson wrote, "nearly every new industry begun in American before 1840 was fertilized with British skills." *American Industry and the European Immigrant* (New York, 1957), 4–5. Thomas C. Cochran, on the other hand, has argued that historians overestimate the importance of imported technology to the growth of American industry in the first half of the nineteenth century, and that "highly specialized British machinists were more skilled at their particular tasks than their counterparts in the United States." *Frontiers of Change*, 73.

30. Carl E. Prince and Seth Taylor, "Daniel Webster, the Boston Associates, and the U.S. Government's Role in the Industrialization Process, 1815–1830," *Journal of the Early Republic* 2 (Fall 1982), 291. The patent registration fee did not represent the entire cost of registering a patent. There were drawing fees, copying costs, legal fees, and other expenditures. Walterscheid estimates that the average cost of obtaining a patent under the 1793 act was "on the order of $100 or roughly five times less than the cost of obtaining a comparable English patent." *To Promote the Progress of Useful Arts*, 248–49. For a study of the internal workings of the Patent Office see Daniel Preston, "The Administration and Reform of the U.S. Patent Office, 1790–1836," *Journal of the Early Republic* 5 (Fall 1985), 331–53.

31. Ogden, *Thoughts*, 38–39. As Carolyn C. Cooper has argued, skillful management of the patent through "interaction with businessmen, lawyers, patent officials and so on . . . not only determined how quickly or widely an invention was adopted but also sometimes had the surprising effect of reshaping the invention." "A Patent Transformation: Woodworking Mechanization in Philadelphia, 1830–1856," in Judith A. McGaw, ed., *Early American Technology: Making and Doing Things from the Colonial Era to 1850* (Chapel Hill, N.C., 1994), 279. This view of the patent system was not shared by all. Naturally, there were many who defended the system. William Alexander Duer, for example, rhetorically asked: "Do you, as a Lawyer after 'five and twenty years of the most unremitted application to your profession' seriously maintain, that where a person in perfect good faith obtains a Patent for an invention, which he believes to be original, but afterwards, appears to have been known for a century, he could enforce or defend his rights as a Patentee, even though he might be enabled to demonstrate his entire ignorance of the previous discovery, and vindicate his claim to the essential merit of an inventor?" William Alexander Duer, *A Reply to Mr. Golden's Vindication of the Steam-Boat Monopoly* (Albany, N.Y., 1819), 29.

32. Jefferson to Benjamin Austin, January 9, 1816, in Paul Leicester Ford, ed. *The Works of Thomas Jefferson*, 12 vols. (New York, 1904–5), XI, 504–5; I. L. Skinner, *The American Journal of Improvements in the Useful Arts, and Mirror of the Patent Office in the United States* 1 (January 1828), 11; Joseph Story, "A Discourse delivered before the Boston Mechanics' Institution, at the Opening of their Annual Course of Lectures, November 1829," *The American Library of Useful Knowledge* 1 (1831), 7, 16; George S. White, *Memoir of Samuel Slater, The Father of American Manufactures, Connected with a History of the Rise and Progress of the Cotton Manufacture in England and America with Remarks on the Moral Influence of Manufactures in the United States* (Philadelphia, 1836), 14.

33. Alexis de Tocqueville, *Democracy in America*, trans. George Lawrence, ed. J. P. Mayer, 2 vols. (New York, 1969) II, 552. See also Hugo A. Meier, "Technology and Democracy, 1800–1860," *Mississippi Valley Historical Review* 43 (March 1957), 618–40; John F. Kasson, *Civilizing the Machine: Technology and Republican Values in America* (New York, 1977); Eugene S. Ferguson, "The Critical Period of American Technology, 1788–1853" (Hagley Museum paper, Wilmington, Del., 1965) ; Eugene S. Ferguson, "The American-ness of American Technology," *Technology and Culture* 20 (January 1979), 3–24. For a concise and balanced account of the northern cult of progress see James. M. McPherson, *Battle Cry of Freedom: The Civil War Era* (New York, 1988), 6–21.

34. James Cutbush, *The American Artist's Manual*, 2 vols. (Philadelphia, 1814), I, iii; Abraham Rees, *The Cyclopedia; or, Universal Dictionary of Arts, Sciences, and Literature*, 47 vols. (Philadelphia, 1810–42). Peter Browne, a prominent Philadelphia lawyer, published an essay entitled "Mechanical Jurisprudence—No. 7," on American and British patent law in the second volume of the *Franklin Journal* (see above, note 12), so that readers could find ways to circumvent restrictions on the diffusion of technical knowledge. The *Franklin Journal*, however, was not the only magazine devoted to this subject. See also John Redman Coxe, "Prospectus," *The Emporium of Arts and Sciences* (Philadelphia), 1st ser., 1 (May 1812), v–viii. The desire to import knowledge from Europe was not confined to champions of industry. Proponents of American agriculture shared these sentiments. See Hunter, *Annual Address*, 17, 20–21.

35. The American copyright law, which was passed by Congress in 1831, avoided the issue of international literary piracy. Infuriated British authors like Harriet Martineau, Thomas Moore, Charles Dickens, and other, lesser-known literary figures repeatedly tried to put an end to the piracy of works. In 1836 they petitioned Congress to have the United States recognize international copyright law. Their petition was presented to the Senate by no less a figure than Henry Clay and was supported by American authors. For a while it seemed as if Congress would take action, but then the economy collapsed in 1837 and the issue lost its urgency. England tried to minimize the loss for its authors by banning the entry of all reprints of books, but the prohibition could not be enforced. The English then turned to lobbying Congress in the 1850s and the

groundswell of petitions that were presented to Congress persuaded some, like secretaries of state Daniel Webster, Edward Everett, and William Marcy, that the United States should sign onto the international agreement. In February 1853 the lame duck administration of President Millard Fillmore signed an Anglo-American copyright agreement and forwarded it to the Senate for ratification. Alas, the United States Congress was in no mood for cooperative action in the 1850s and the copyright of foreign authors and publishers had to wait for calmer times. Ironically, although the United States allowed international copyright piracy until 1890, some English authors earned more from payments made by American publishers than they did from royalties paid by their original publishers. James J. Barnes, *Authors, Publishers, and Politicians: The Quest for an Anglo-American Copyright Agreement* (Columbus, Ohio, 1974).

36. Jefferson considered Francis Walker Gilmer, the son of his close friend Dr. George Gilmer, the best-educated man in Virginia. Gilmer went to Europe and returned with five little-known European academics. Jefferson assumed they were renowned and was thus satisfied. For the exchanges between Jefferson and Gilmer regarding the recruitment of European intellectuals see Richard Beale Davis, ed., *Correspondence of Thomas Jefferson and Francis Walker Gilmer, 1814–1826* (Columbia, S.C., 1946), 81–109. For secondary discussion of this controversial stand see Merrill D. Peterson, *Thomas Jefferson and the New Nation* (New York, 1970), 977; Dumas Malone, *Jefferson and His Time*, 6 vols. (Boston, 1948–81), VI, 397–402.

37. Thomas Cooper, "On Patents," *The Emporium of Arts and Sciences*, n.s., 2 (May 1813), 3. On the emergence of an international community of scientists see Bruce Sinclair, "Americans Abroad: Science and Cultural Nationalism in the Early Nineteenth Century," in Nathan Reingold, ed., *The Sciences in the American Context: New Perspectives* (Washington, D.C., 1979), 41; John C. Greene, "American Science Comes of Age, 1780–1820," *Journal of American History* 55 (June 1968), 22–41.

38. Brooke Hindle, *Emulation and Invention* (New York, 1981), 10; Rufus King to Nicholas Vansittart Esq., January 3, 1803, in Charles R, King, *The Life and Correspondence of Rufus King*, 6 vols. (New York, 1894–1900), IV, 204–5; Beaujour, *Sketch of the United States of America*, 94; Ferguson, "The Americanness of American Technology," 18; Eugene S. Ferguson, "Technology as Knowledge," in Edwin T, Layton, Jr., ed., *Technology and Social Change in America* (New York, 1973), 17; Wallace, *Rockdale*, 218.

39. As Brooke Hindle wrote, "We took the ball and ran with it on our own 8turf, playing a somewhat different game." "The American Industrial Revolution through Its Survivors," in Randolph Shipley Klein, ed., *Science and Society in Early America: Essays in Honor of Whitfield J. Bell* (Philadelphia, 1986), 272. The best work on these issues is Habakkuk, *American and British Technology*, chap. 4. See also Carol Sheriff, *The Artificial River: The Erie Canal and the Paradox of Progress* (New York, 1996), 35.

40. "Report from the Committee on Manufactures," 16.

41. Mathias, "Skills and the Diffusion of Innovation," 101; Jeremy, "Damming the Flood," 28–33; Habakkuk, *American and British Technology,* 97. British courts' responsiveness to challenges of licensing monopolies reduced their economic value.

42. Tocqueville, *Democracy in America,* II, 554; Charles Dickens, *American Notes for General Circulation,* ed. John S. Whitley and Arnold Goldman (New York, 1972 [1842]), 114, 118. Similarly, George Wallis, who toured the northeast in the early 1850s, was surprised to discover "very few Englishmen compared with what I expected to find . . . engaged in the industrial establishments of the United States." Nathan Rosenberg, ed., *The American System of Manufactures* (Edinburgh, 1969), 207.

43. Collins, *Emigrant's Guide,* 17.

44. Daniel J. Boorstin, *The Republic of Technology: Reflections on Our Future Community* (New York, 1978), 60. For an example of this association of machines with American culture and civilization see Edward Everett, *An Address delivered before the Massachusetts Charitable Mechanic Association* (September 20, 1837) (Boston, 1837). The inventive mind in the United States was inclined to apply itself to practical rather than theoretical improvements. Some historians, like H. J. Habakkuk and Eugene S. Ferguson, have argued that the shortage of labor in the United States pointed mechanical innovation in the direction of labor-saving machines. Habakkuk, *American and British Technology,* 118; Ferguson, "The American-ness of American Technology," 7; Arnold Pacey, *Technology in World Civilization: A Thousand-Year History* (Oxford, 1990), 113. I do not find this explanation satisfactory. There are many cases in which necessity has not yielded significant innovation. Focusing on impersonal forces overlooks human agency in the creation of innovation. In the American case, a cultural inclination to reject the old for the new and a spirit of experimentation are necessary for invention to be born out of necessity. See also Cochran, *Frontiers of Change,* 76.

45. Historians of technology tell the familiar story of how the quest for interchangeable parts, fueled partly by government demand for weapons, brought about the development of machine tools that gradually transformed the other industries using metal parts, from sewing machines to automobiles. The best work on this process is David A. Hounshell, *From the American System to Mass Production, 1800–1932: The Development of Manufacturing Technology in the United States* (Baltimore, 1984). Within a few years after Crystal Palace, the British government acknowledged the superiority of American manufactures when it decided to adopt American rifle production methods for the British Army. D. C. Coleman and Christine MacLeod, "Attitudes to New Technology: British Businessmen, 1800–1850," *Economic History Review,* 2d ser., 39 (November 1986), 591.

46. "Convention for the Protection of Industrial Property," in Charles I. Bevans, ed., *Treaties and Other International Agreements of the United States of America, 1776–1849*, 13 vols. (Washington, D.C., *1968–76*), I, 86.

47. Paul A. David, "New Lights on a Statistical Dark Age: Real Product Growth before 1840," *American Economic Review* 47 (May 1967), 294–306; Stuart Weems Bruchey, *The Roots of American Economic Growth, 1607–1861* (London, 1965), 87–94; Thomas C. Cochran, "The Business Revolution," *American Historical Review* 79 (December 1974), *1449–67*.

Index